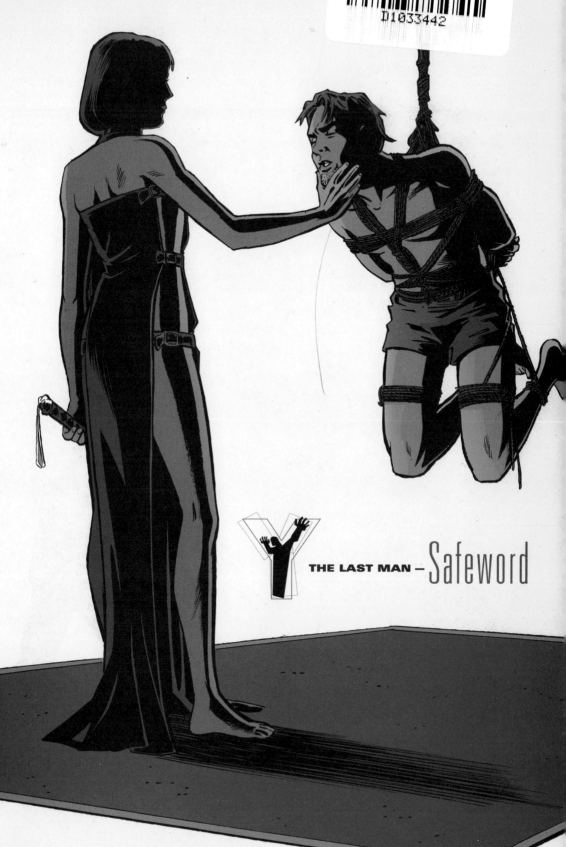

THE LAST MAN — Safeword

THE LAST MAN — Safeword

Brian K. Vaughan
Writer

Pia Guerra
Penciller — "Safeword"

Goran Parlov
Penciller — "Widow's Pass"

José Marzán, Jr.
Inker

Zylonol
Colorist

Clem Robins
Letterer

Aron Wiesenfeld
Massimo Carnevale
Original series covers

Y: THE LAST MAN created by Brian K. Vaughan and Pia Guerra

FICTION
VAUGHAN
SAF
04/06

Y: THE LAST MAN — SAFEWORD
Published by DC Comics. Cover and compilation
copyright © 2004 DC Comics. All Rights Reserved.

Originally published in single magazine form as Y: THE LAST MAN 18-23.
Copyright © 2004 Brian K. Vaughan and Pia Guerra. All Rights Reserved.
All characters, the distinctive likenesses and related elements featured
in this publication are trademarks of Brian K. Vaughan and Pia Guerra.
VERTIGO is a trademark of DC Comics. The stories, characters and
incidents featured in this publication are entirely fictional. DC Comics
does not read or accept unsolicited submissions of ideas, stories or artwork.

DC Comics, 1700 Broadway, New York, NY 10019
A Warner Bros. Entertainment Company.
Printed in Canada. Second Printing.
ISBN: 1-4012-0232-2
Cover illustration by Aron Wiesenfeld.
Logo design by Terry Marks.

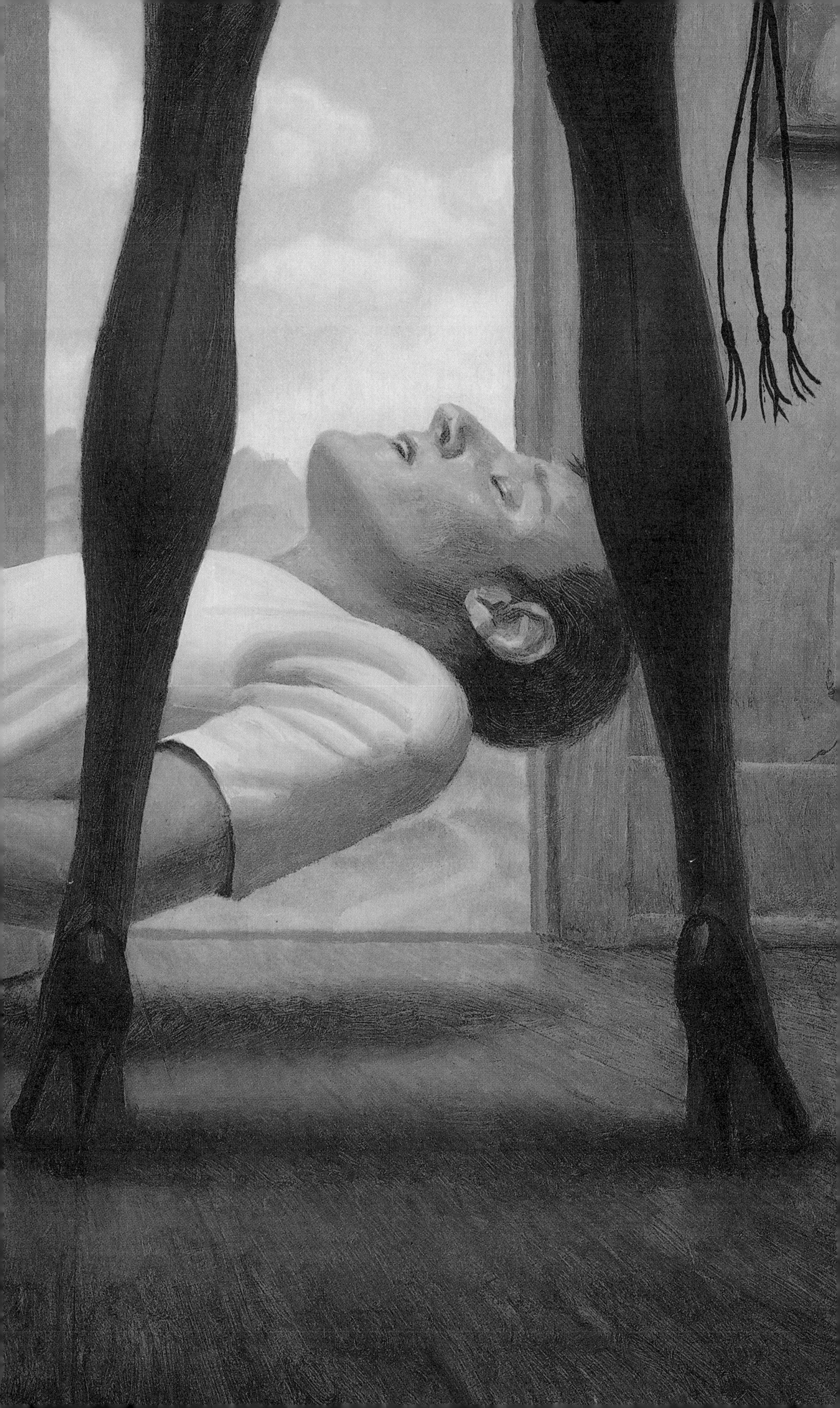

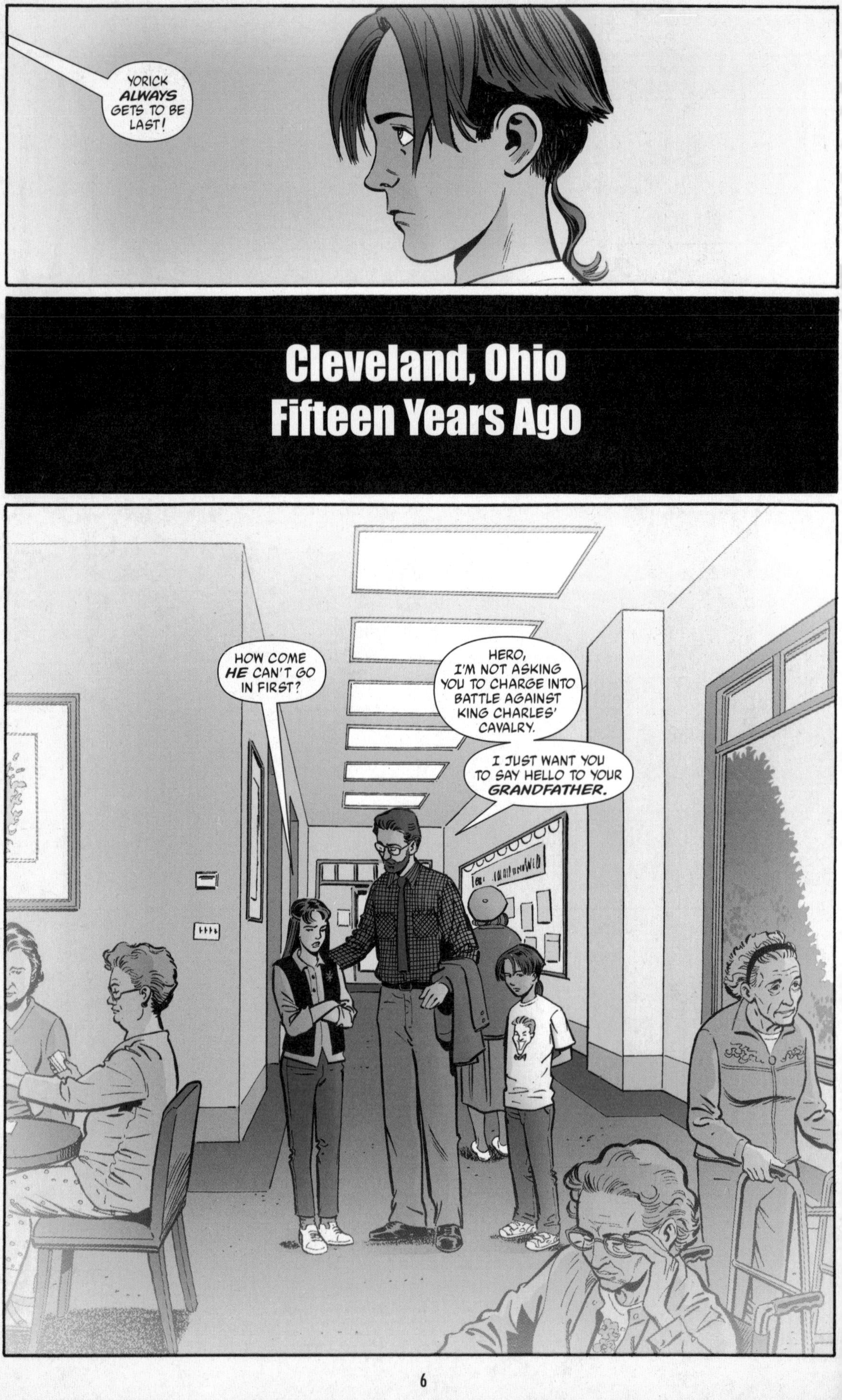

YORICK ALWAYS GETS TO BE LAST!
Cleveland, Ohio
Fifteen Years Ago
HOW COME HE CAN'T GO IN FIRST?
HERO, I'M NOT ASKING YOU TO CHARGE INTO BATTLE AGAINST KING CHARLES' CAVALRY.
I JUST WANT YOU TO SAY HELLO TO YOUR GRANDFATHER.

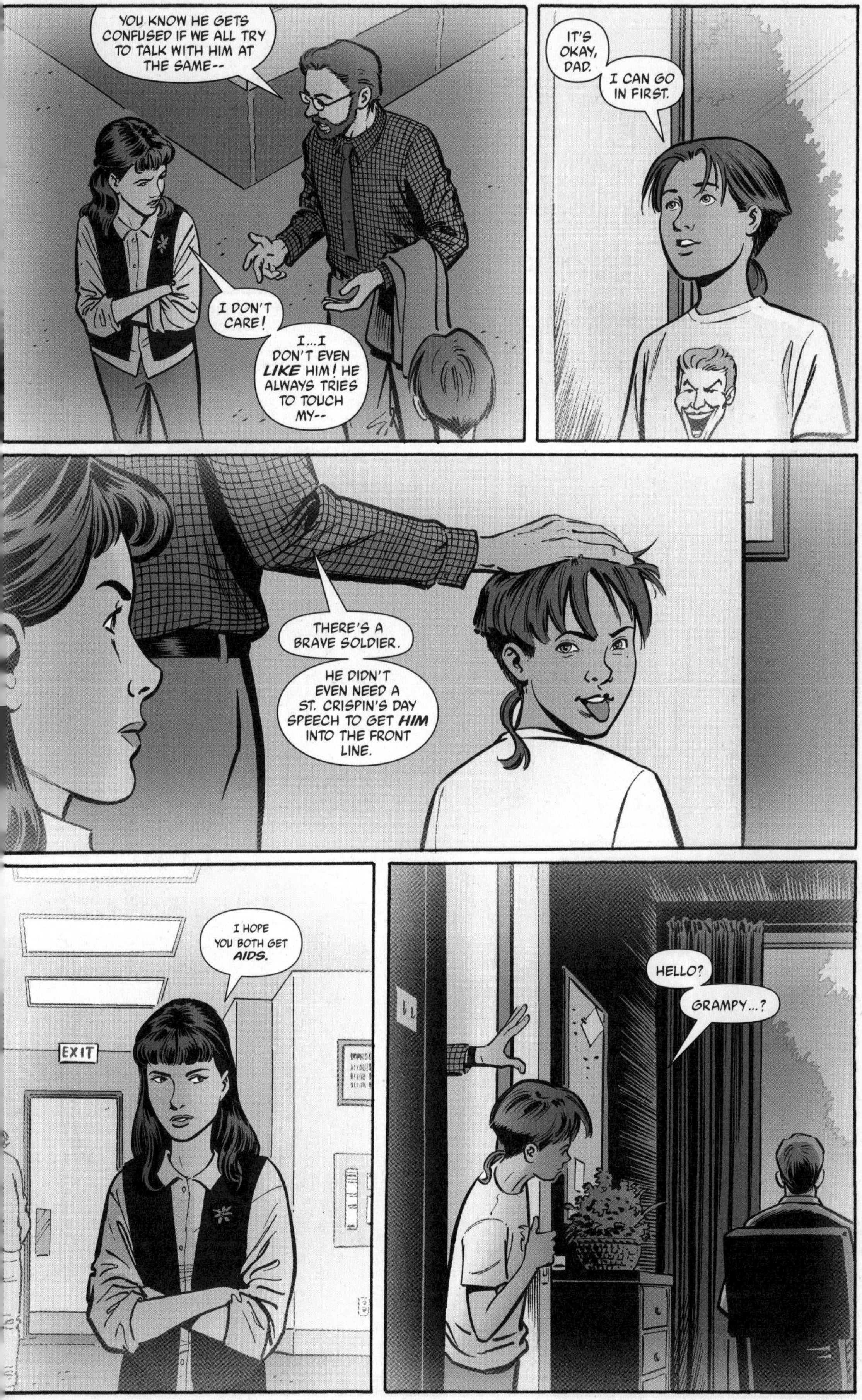

YOU KNOW HE GETS CONFUSED IF WE ALL TRY TO TALK WITH HIM AT THE SAME--
I DON'T CARE!
I...I DON'T EVEN LIKE HIM! HE ALWAYS TRIES TO TOUCH MY--
IT'S OKAY, DAD.
I CAN GO IN FIRST.
THERE'S A BRAVE SOLDIER.
HE DIDN'T EVEN NEED A ST. CRISPIN'S DAY SPEECH TO GET HIM INTO THE FRONT LINE.
I HOPE YOU BOTH GET AIDS.
EXIT
HELLO?
GRAMPY...?

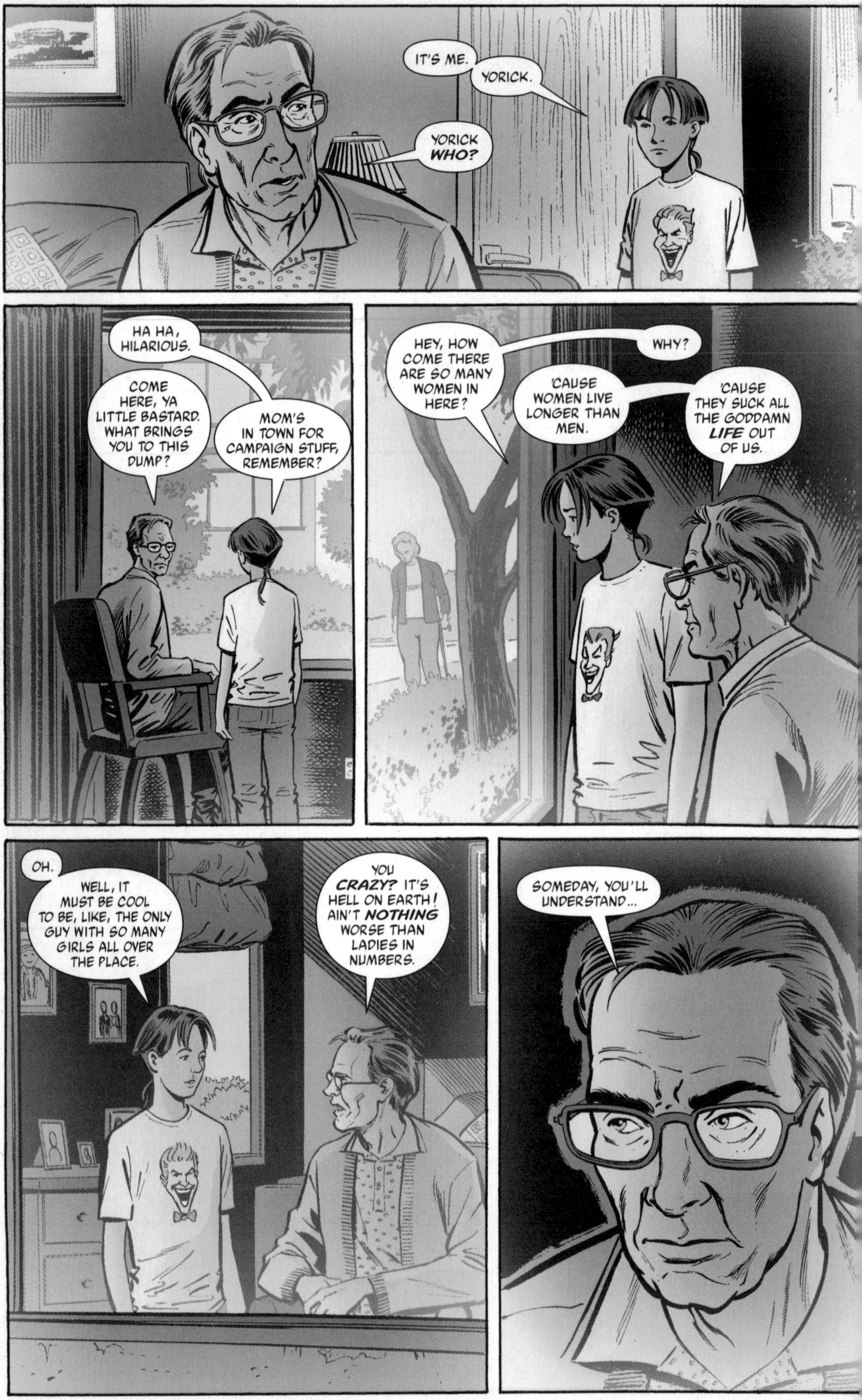

IT'S ME.
YORICK.
YORICK **WHO?**
HA HA, HILARIOUS.
COME HERE, YA LITTLE BASTARD. WHAT BRINGS YOU TO THIS DUMP?
MOM'S IN TOWN FOR CAMPAIGN STUFF, REMEMBER?
HEY, HOW COME THERE ARE SO MANY WOMEN IN HERE?
WHY?
'CAUSE WOMEN LIVE LONGER THAN MEN.
'CAUSE THEY SUCK ALL THE GODDAMN **LIFE** OUT OF US.
OH.
WELL, IT MUST BE COOL TO BE, LIKE, THE ONLY GUY WITH SO MANY GIRLS ALL OVER THE PLACE.
YOU **CRAZY?** IT'S HELL ON EARTH! AIN'T **NOTHING** WORSE THAN LADIES IN NUMBERS.
SOMEDAY, YOU'LL UNDERSTAND...

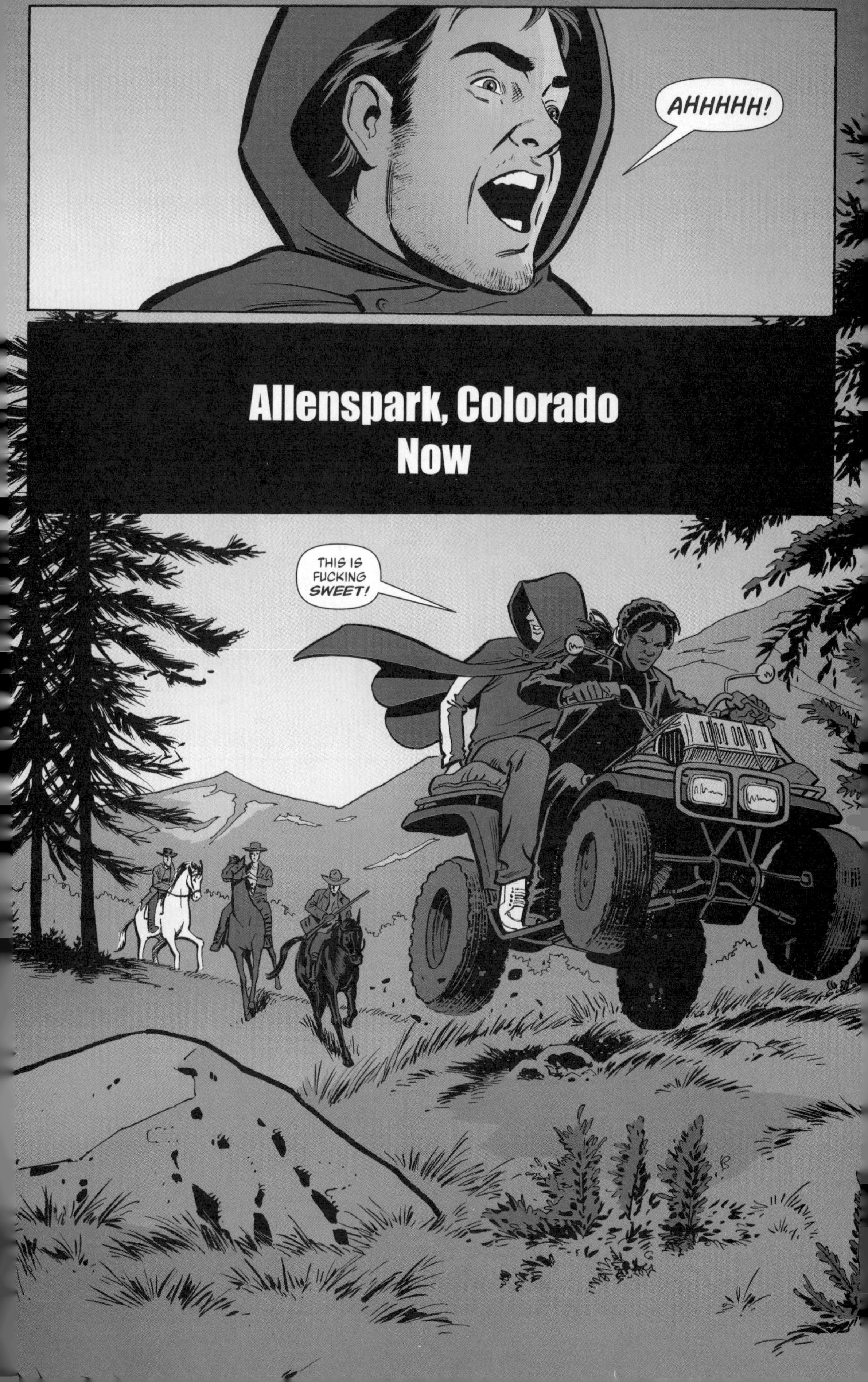
AHHHHH!
Allenspark, Colorado
Now
THIS IS FUCKING SWEET!

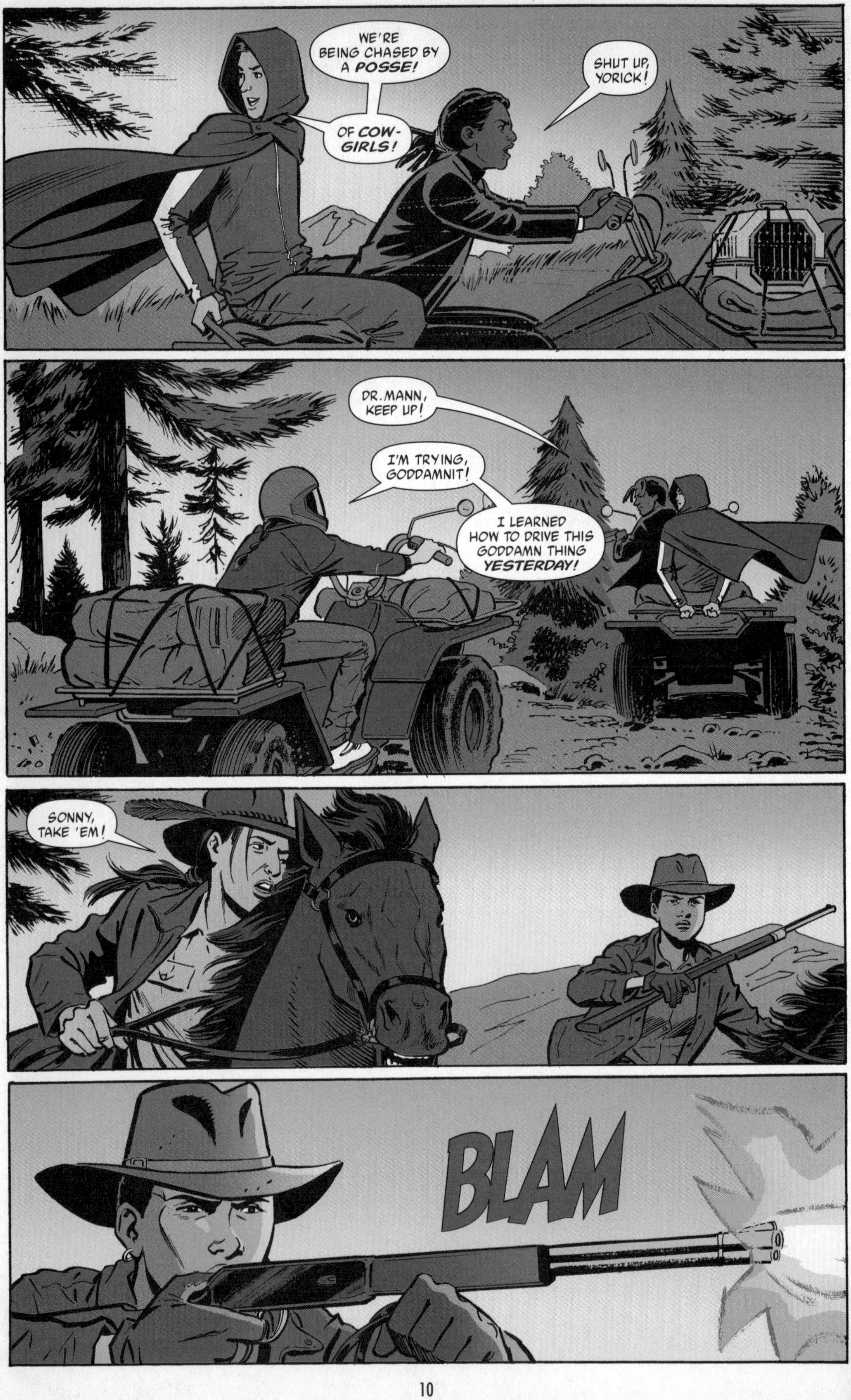
WE'RE BEING CHASED BY A POSSE!
OF COW-GIRLS!
SHUT UP, YORICK!
DR. MANN, KEEP UP!
I'M TRYING, GODDAMNIT!
I LEARNED HOW TO DRIVE THIS GODDAMN THING YESTERDAY!
SONNY, TAKE 'EM!
BLAM

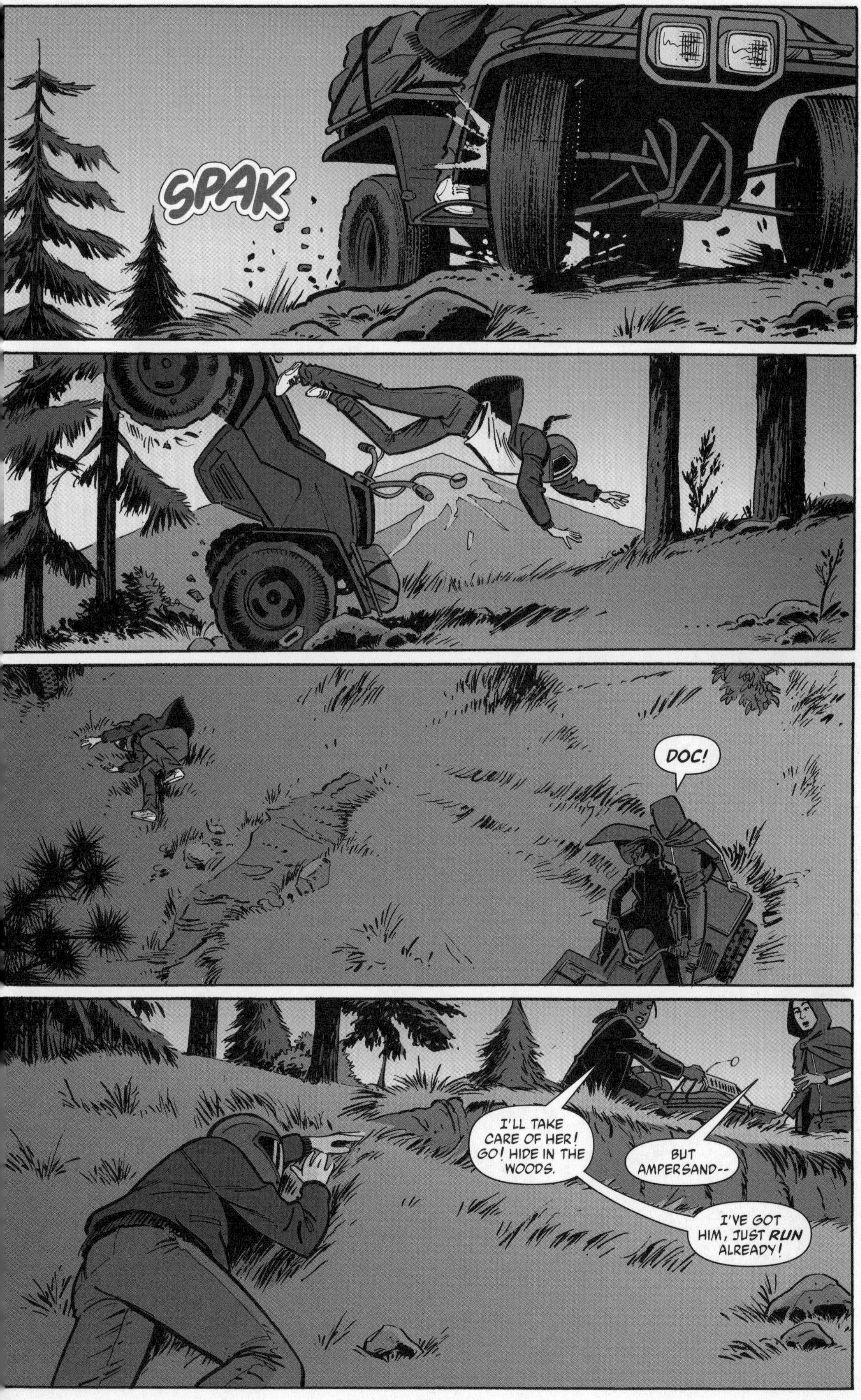
SPAK
DOC!
I'LL TAKE CARE OF HER! GO! HIDE IN THE WOODS.
BUT AMPERSAND--
I'VE GOT HIM, JUST RUN ALREADY!

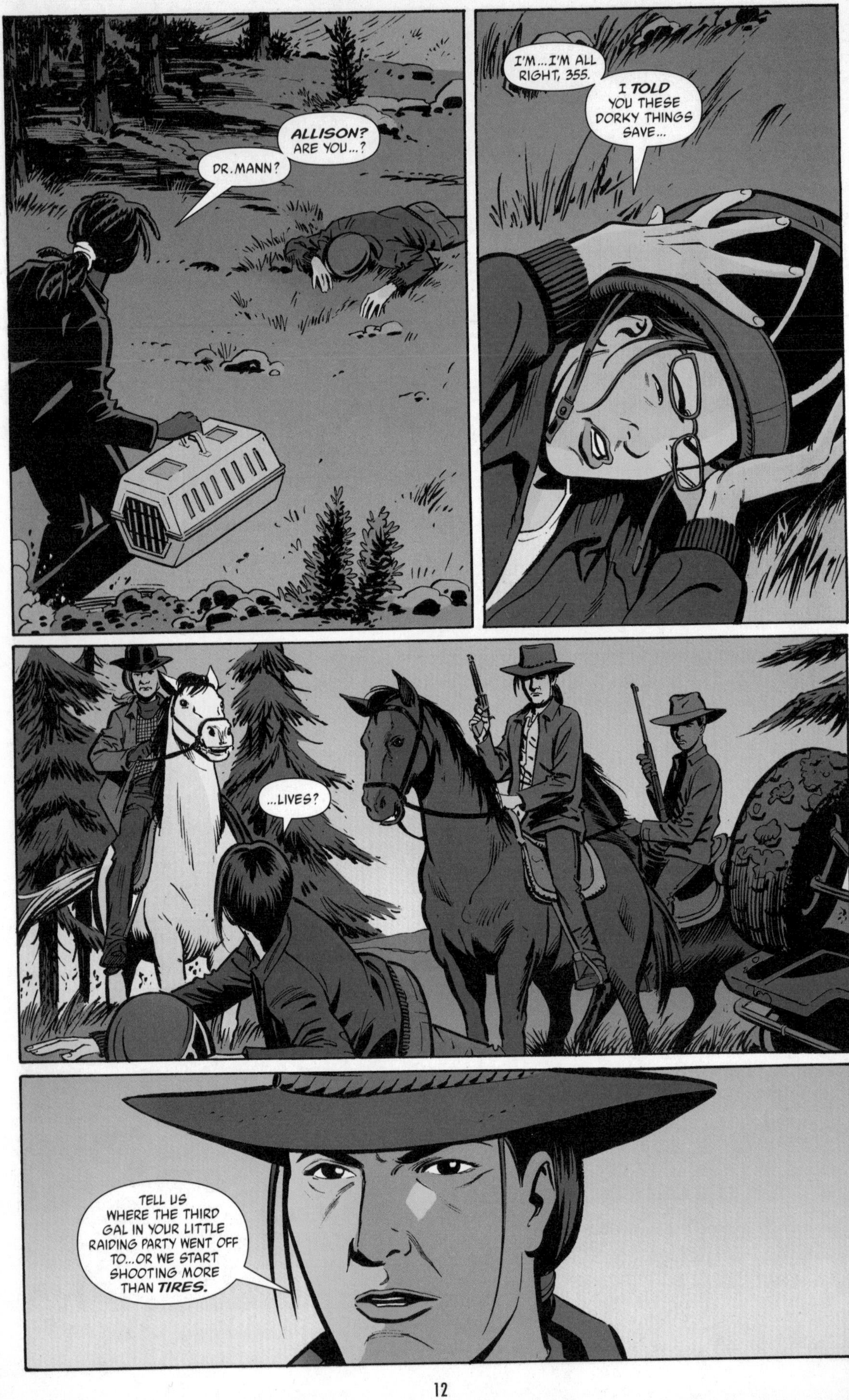
DR. MANN?
ALLISON? ARE YOU...?
I'M...I'M ALL RIGHT, 355.
I TOLD YOU THESE DORKY THINGS SAVE...
...LIVES?
TELL US WHERE THE THIRD GAL IN YOUR LITTLE RAIDING PARTY WENT OFF TO...OR WE START SHOOTING MORE THAN TIRES.

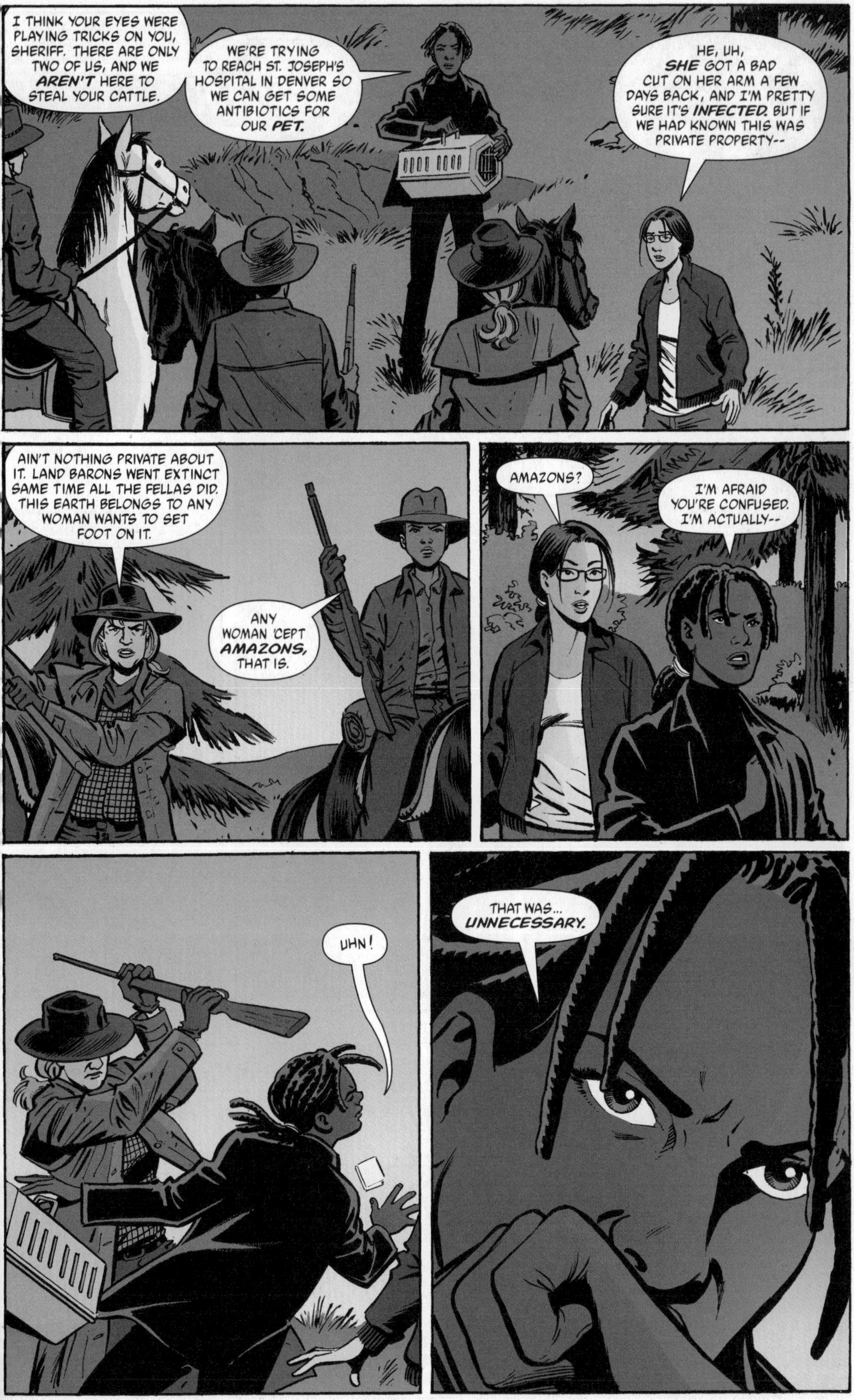
I THINK YOUR EYES WERE PLAYING TRICKS ON YOU, SHERIFF. THERE ARE ONLY TWO OF US, AND WE AREN'T HERE TO STEAL YOUR CATTLE.
WE'RE TRYING TO REACH ST. JOSEPH'S HOSPITAL IN DENVER SO WE CAN GET SOME ANTIBIOTICS FOR OUR PET.
HE, UH, SHE GOT A BAD CUT ON HER ARM A FEW DAYS BACK, AND I'M PRETTY SURE IT'S INFECTED. BUT IF WE HAD KNOWN THIS WAS PRIVATE PROPERTY--
AIN'T NOTHING PRIVATE ABOUT IT. LAND BARONS WENT EXTINCT SAME TIME ALL THE FELLAS DID. THIS EARTH BELONGS TO ANY WOMAN WANTS TO SET FOOT ON IT.
ANY WOMAN 'CEPT AMAZONS, THAT IS.
AMAZONS?
I'M AFRAID YOU'RE CONFUSED. I'M ACTUALLY--
UHN!
THAT WAS... UNNECESSARY.

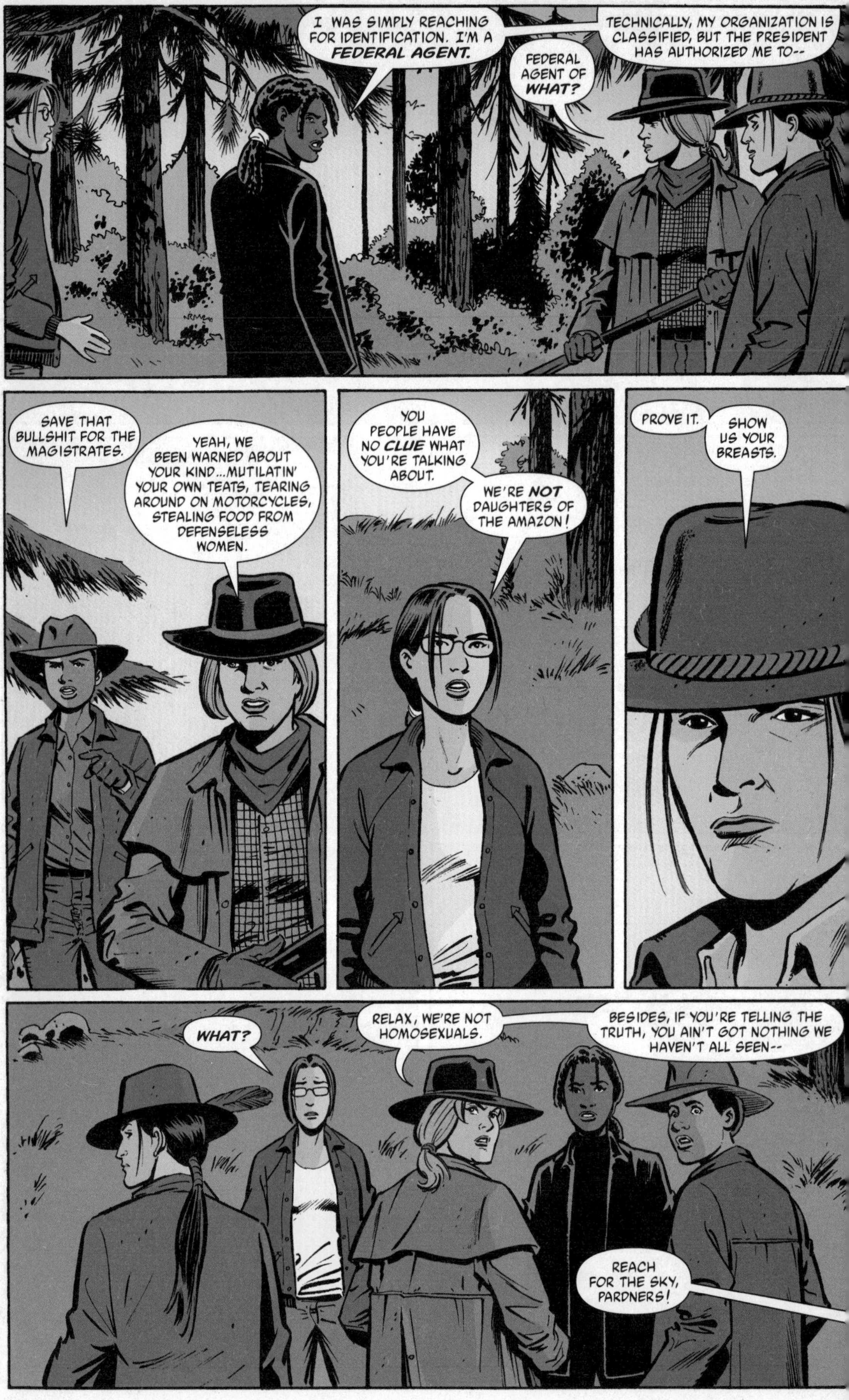
I WAS SIMPLY REACHING FOR IDENTIFICATION. I'M A FEDERAL AGENT.
FEDERAL AGENT OF WHAT?
TECHNICALLY, MY ORGANIZATION IS CLASSIFIED, BUT THE PRESIDENT HAS AUTHORIZED ME TO--
SAVE THAT BULLSHIT FOR THE MAGISTRATES.
YEAH, WE BEEN WARNED ABOUT YOUR KIND...MUTILATIN' YOUR OWN TEATS, TEARING AROUND ON MOTORCYCLES, STEALING FOOD FROM DEFENSELESS WOMEN.
YOU PEOPLE HAVE NO CLUE WHAT YOU'RE TALKING ABOUT.
WE'RE NOT DAUGHTERS OF THE AMAZON!
PROVE IT.
SHOW US YOUR BREASTS.
WHAT?
RELAX, WE'RE NOT HOMOSEXUALS.
BESIDES, IF YOU'RE TELLING THE TRUTH, YOU AIN'T GOT NOTHING WE HAVEN'T ALL SEEN--
REACH FOR THE SKY, PARDNERS!

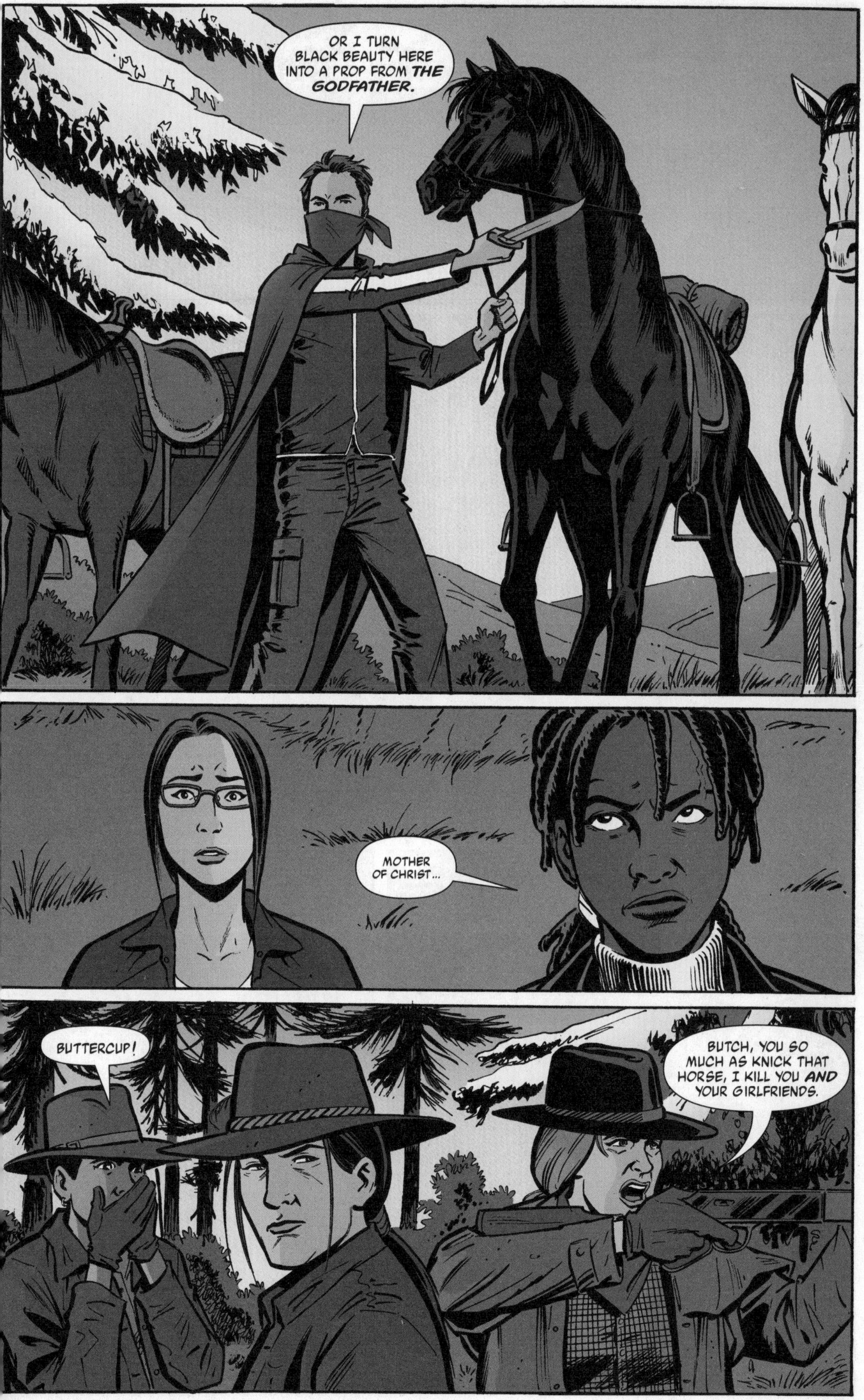
OR I TURN BLACK BEAUTY HERE INTO A PROP FROM THE GODFATHER.
MOTHER OF CHRIST...
BUTTERCUP!
BUTCH, YOU SO MUCH AS KNICK THAT HORSE, I KILL YOU AND YOUR GIRLFRIENDS.

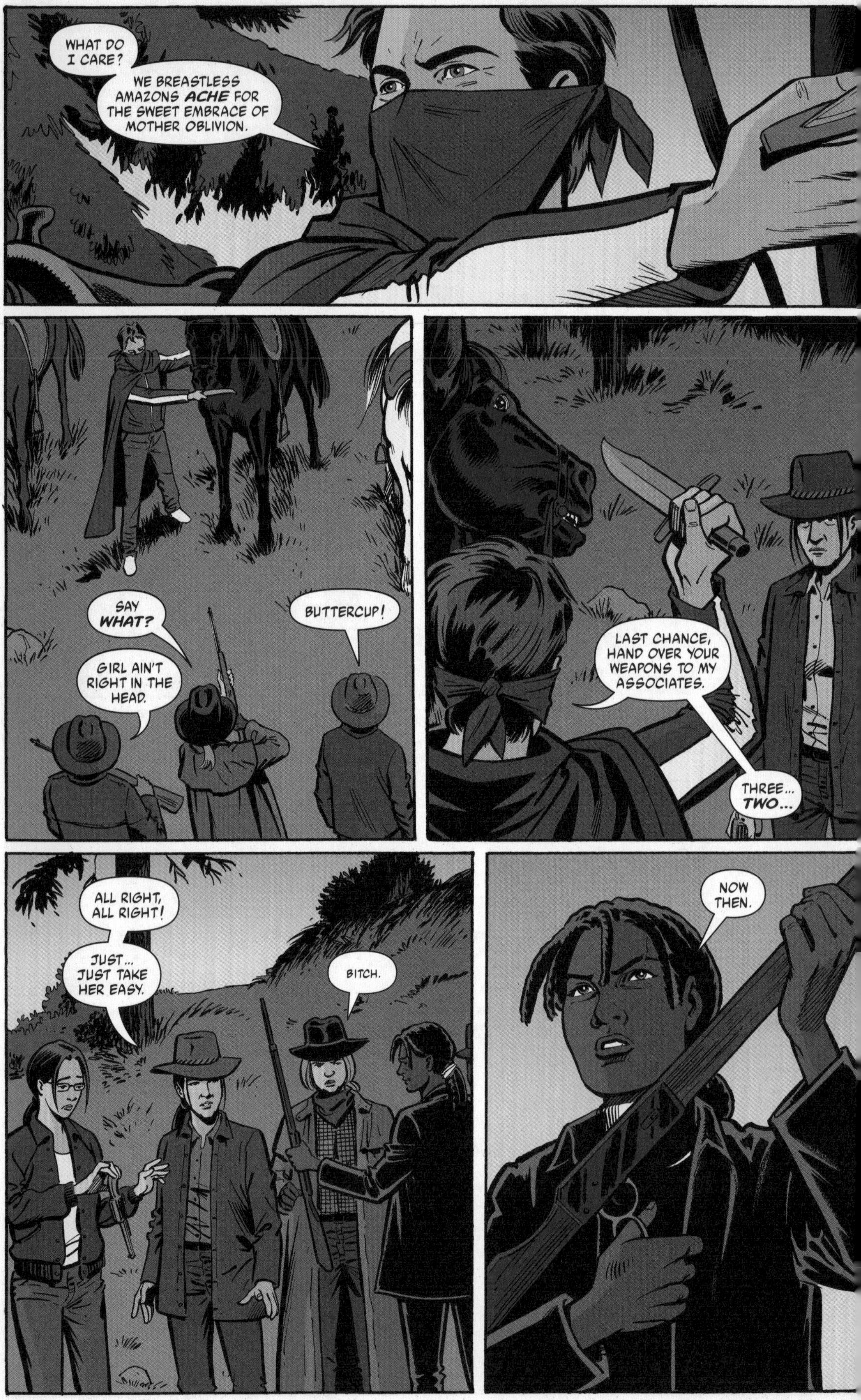
WHAT DO I CARE?
WE BREASTLESS AMAZONS ***ACHE*** FOR THE SWEET EMBRACE OF MOTHER OBLIVION.
SAY ***WHAT?***
GIRL AIN'T RIGHT IN THE HEAD.
BUTTERCUP!
LAST CHANCE, HAND OVER YOUR WEAPONS TO MY ASSOCIATES.
THREE... ***TWO...***
ALL RIGHT, ALL RIGHT!
JUST... JUST TAKE HER EASY.
BITCH.
NOW THEN.

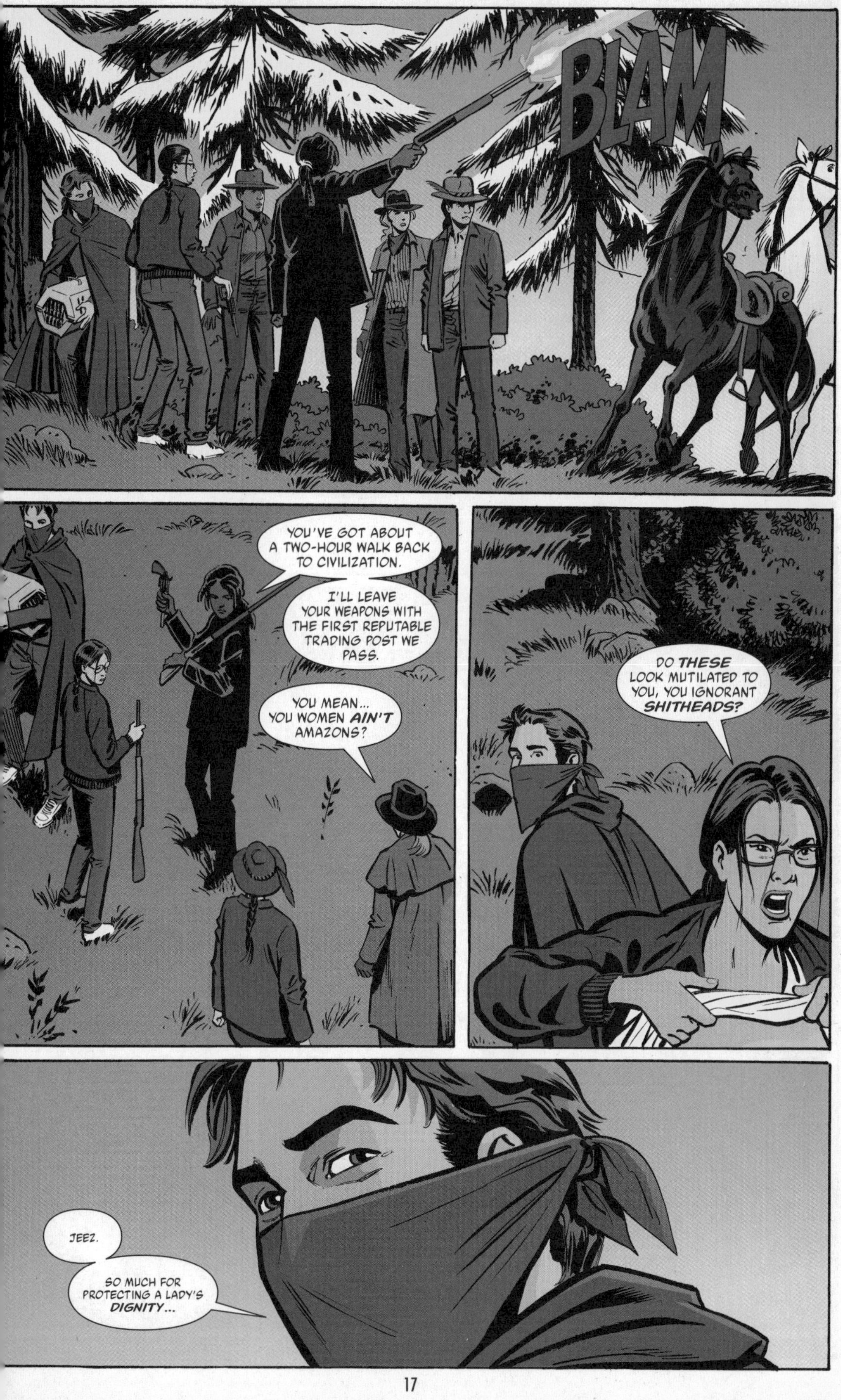
BLAM
YOU'VE GOT ABOUT A TWO-HOUR WALK BACK TO CIVILIZATION.
I'LL LEAVE YOUR WEAPONS WITH THE FIRST REPUTABLE TRADING POST WE PASS.
YOU MEAN... YOU WOMEN AIN'T AMAZONS?
DO THESE LOOK MUTILATED TO YOU, YOU IGNORANT SHITHEADS?
JEEZ.
SO MUCH FOR PROTECTING A LADY'S DIGNITY...

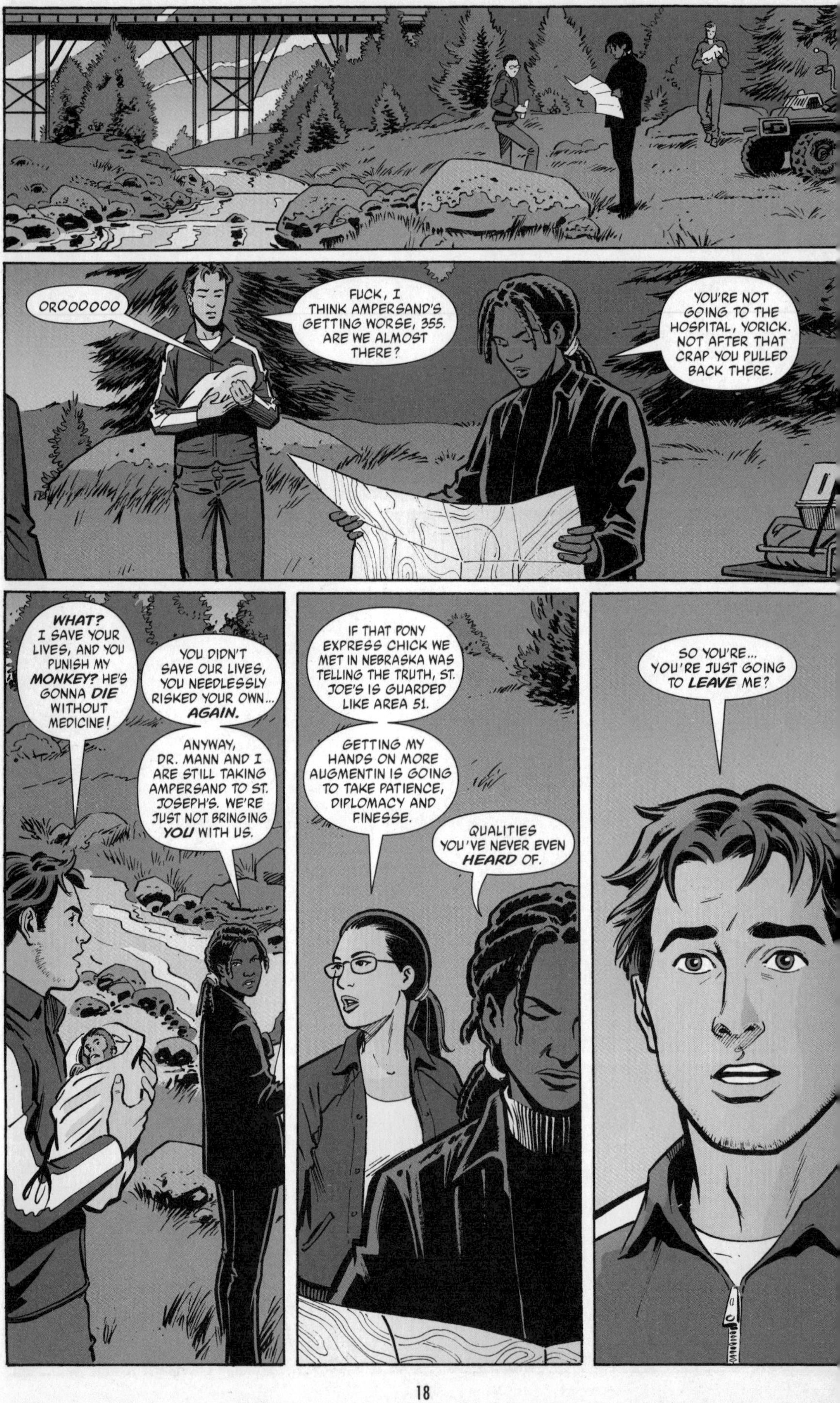
OROOOOOO
FUCK, I THINK AMPERSAND'S GETTING WORSE, 355. ARE WE ALMOST THERE?
YOU'RE NOT GOING TO THE HOSPITAL, YORICK. NOT AFTER THAT CRAP YOU PULLED BACK THERE.
WHAT? I SAVE YOUR LIVES, AND YOU PUNISH MY MONKEY? HE'S GONNA DIE WITHOUT MEDICINE!
YOU DIDN'T SAVE OUR LIVES, YOU NEEDLESSLY RISKED YOUR OWN... AGAIN.
ANYWAY, DR. MANN AND I ARE STILL TAKING AMPERSAND TO ST. JOSEPH'S. WE'RE JUST NOT BRINGING YOU WITH US.
IF THAT PONY EXPRESS CHICK WE MET IN NEBRASKA WAS TELLING THE TRUTH, ST. JOE'S IS GUARDED LIKE AREA 51.
GETTING MY HANDS ON MORE AUGMENTIN IS GOING TO TAKE PATIENCE, DIPLOMACY AND FINESSE.
QUALITIES YOU'VE NEVER EVEN HEARD OF.
SO YOU'RE... YOU'RE JUST GOING TO LEAVE ME?

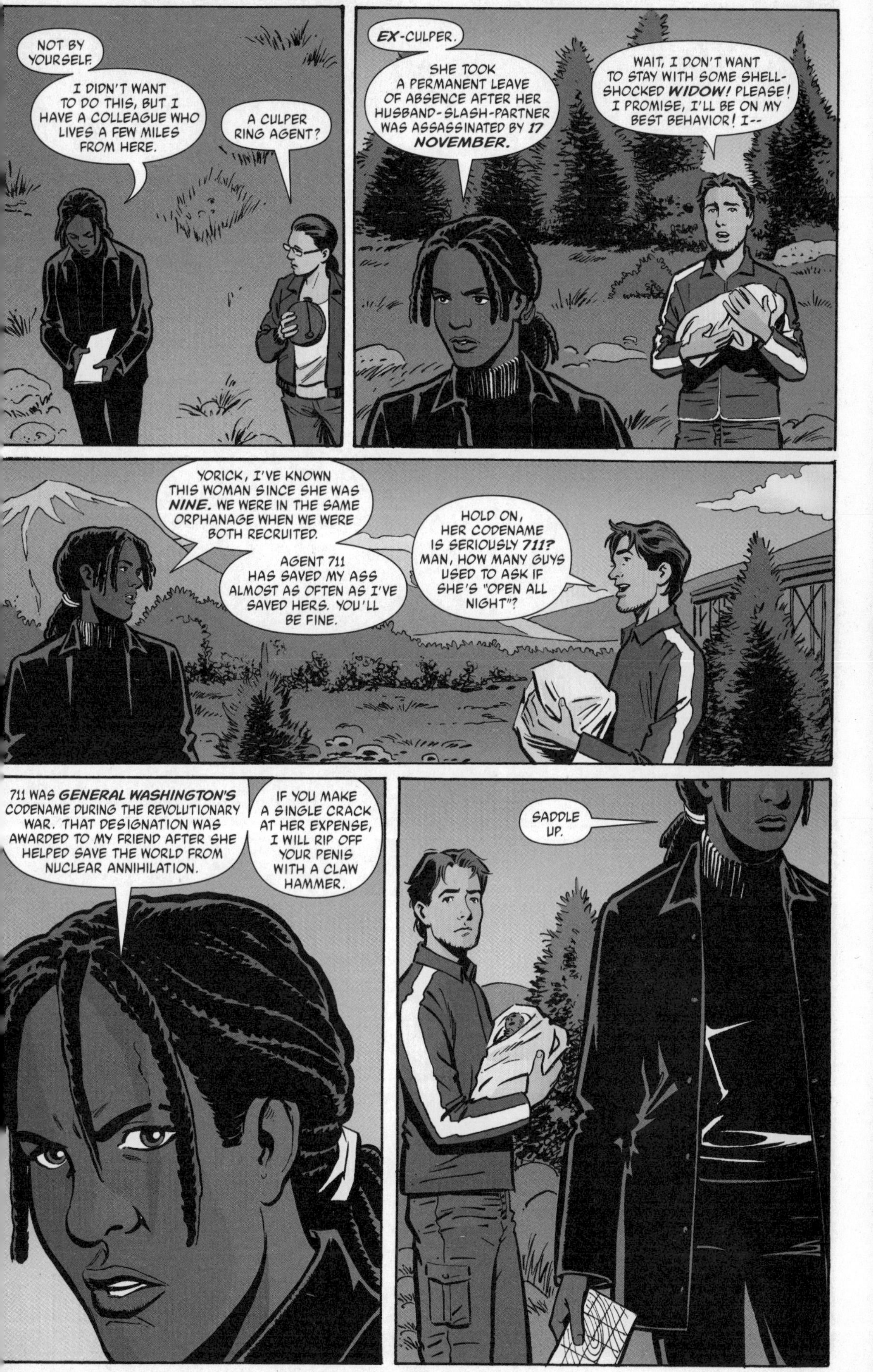
NOT BY YOURSELF.
I DIDN'T WANT TO DO THIS, BUT I HAVE A COLLEAGUE WHO LIVES A FEW MILES FROM HERE.
A CULPER RING AGENT?
EX-CULPER.
SHE TOOK A PERMANENT LEAVE OF ABSENCE AFTER HER HUSBAND-SLASH-PARTNER WAS ASSASSINATED BY 17 NOVEMBER.
WAIT, I DON'T WANT TO STAY WITH SOME SHELL-SHOCKED WIDOW! PLEASE! I PROMISE, I'LL BE ON MY BEST BEHAVIOR! I--
YORICK, I'VE KNOWN THIS WOMAN SINCE SHE WAS NINE. WE WERE IN THE SAME ORPHANAGE WHEN WE WERE BOTH RECRUITED.
AGENT 711 HAS SAVED MY ASS ALMOST AS OFTEN AS I'VE SAVED HERS. YOU'LL BE FINE.
HOLD ON, HER CODENAME IS SERIOUSLY 711? MAN, HOW MANY GUYS USED TO ASK IF SHE'S "OPEN ALL NIGHT"?
711 WAS GENERAL WASHINGTON'S CODENAME DURING THE REVOLUTIONARY WAR. THAT DESIGNATION WAS AWARDED TO MY FRIEND AFTER SHE HELPED SAVE THE WORLD FROM NUCLEAR ANNIHILATION.
IF YOU MAKE A SINGLE CRACK AT HER EXPENSE, I WILL RIP OFF YOUR PENIS WITH A CLAW HAMMER.
SADDLE UP.

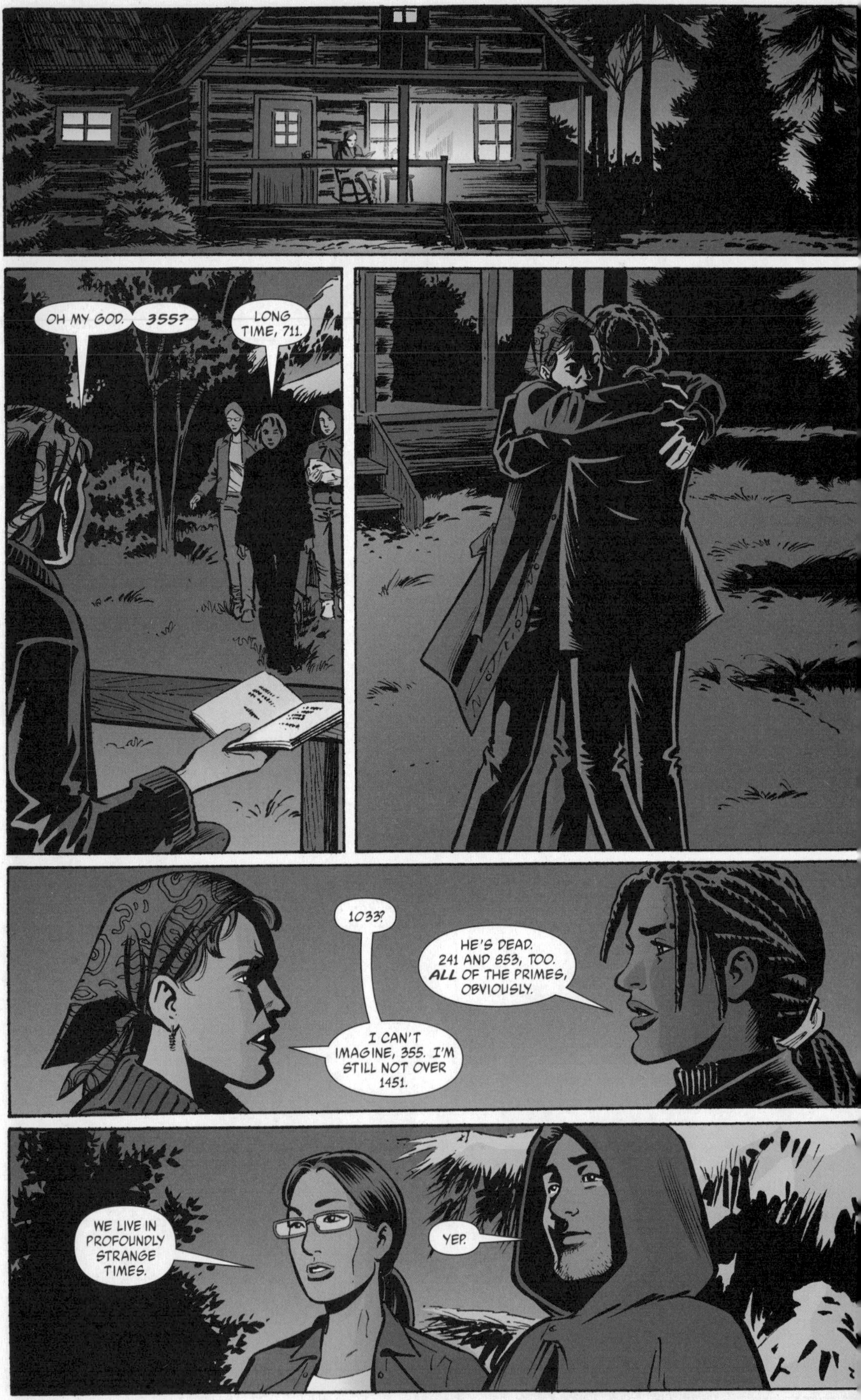
OH MY GOD.
355?
LONG TIME, 711.
1033?
HE'S DEAD. 241 AND 853, TOO. ALL OF THE PRIMES, OBVIOUSLY.
I CAN'T IMAGINE, 355. I'M STILL NOT OVER 1451.
WE LIVE IN PROFOUNDLY STRANGE TIMES.
YEP.

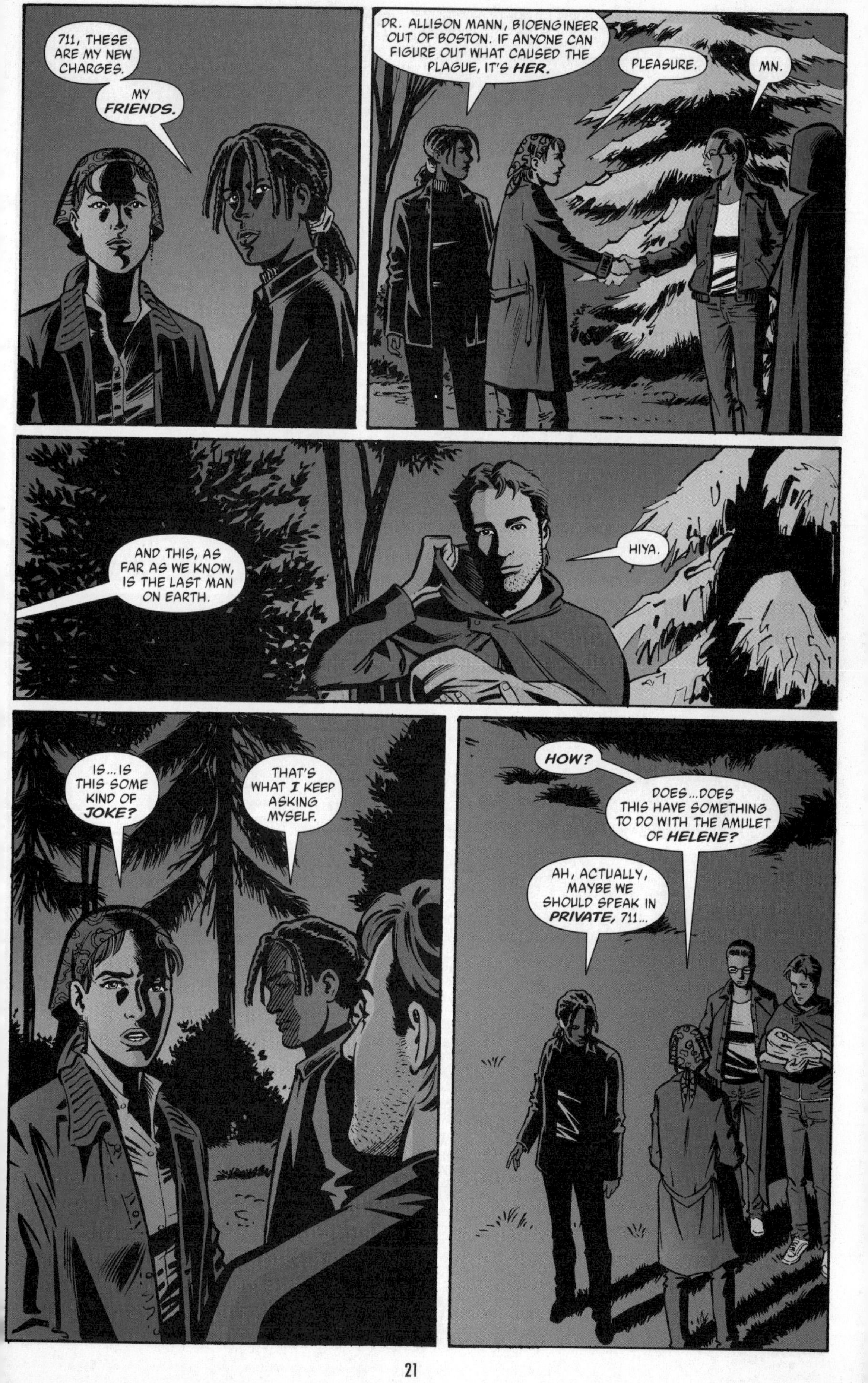
711, THESE ARE MY NEW CHARGES.
MY FRIENDS.
DR. ALLISON MANN, BIOENGINEER OUT OF BOSTON. IF ANYONE CAN FIGURE OUT WHAT CAUSED THE PLAGUE, IT'S HER.
PLEASURE.
MN.
AND THIS, AS FAR AS WE KNOW, IS THE LAST MAN ON EARTH.
HIYA.
IS...IS THIS SOME KIND OF JOKE?
THAT'S WHAT I KEEP ASKING MYSELF.
HOW?
DOES...DOES THIS HAVE SOMETHING TO DO WITH THE AMULET OF HELENE?
AH, ACTUALLY, MAYBE WE SHOULD SPEAK IN PRIVATE, 711...

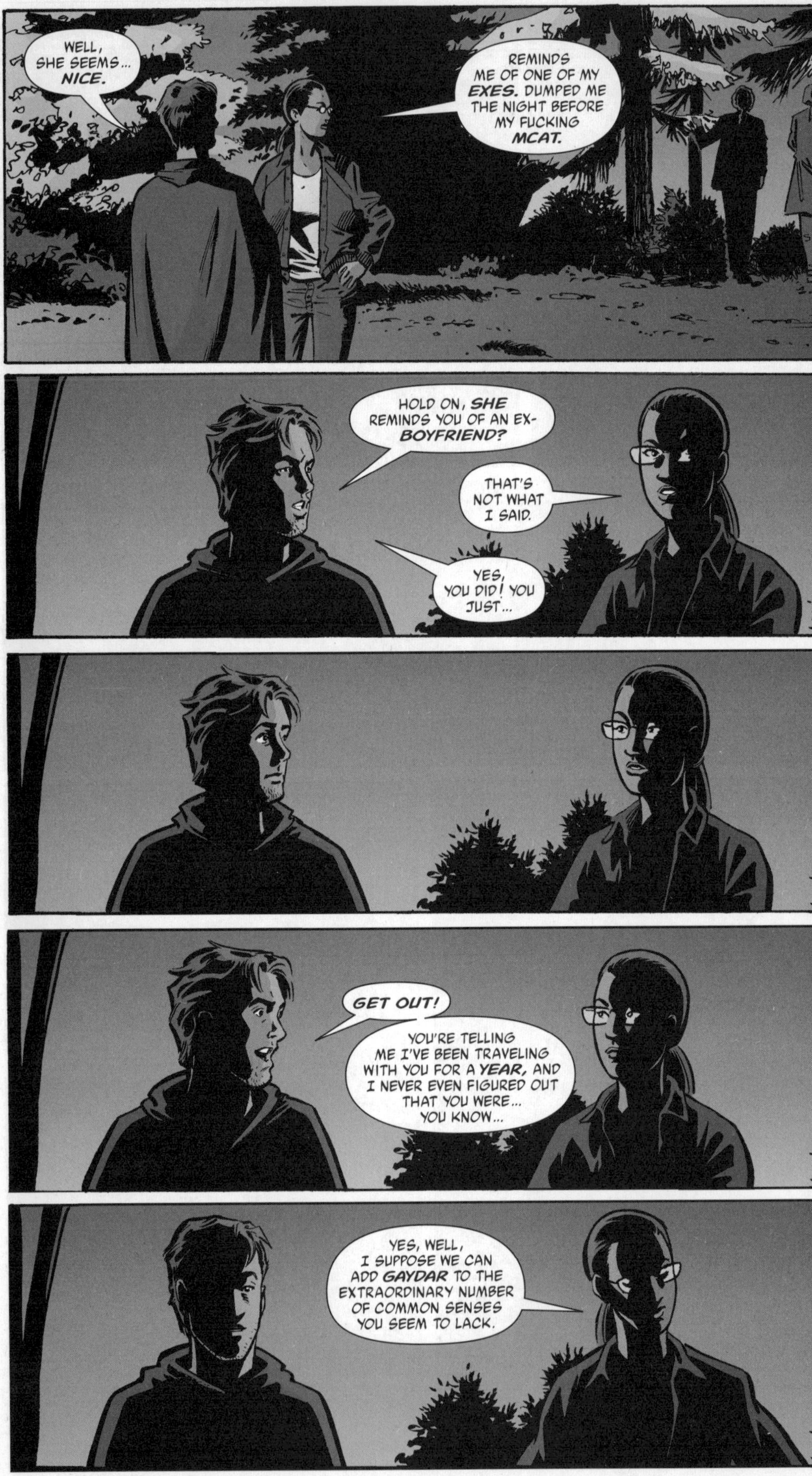
WELL, SHE SEEMS... NICE.
REMINDS ME OF ONE OF MY EXES. DUMPED ME THE NIGHT BEFORE MY FUCKING MCAT.
HOLD ON, SHE REMINDS YOU OF AN EX-BOYFRIEND?
THAT'S NOT WHAT I SAID.
YES, YOU DID! YOU JUST...
GET OUT!
YOU'RE TELLING ME I'VE BEEN TRAVELING WITH YOU FOR A YEAR, AND I NEVER EVEN FIGURED OUT THAT YOU WERE... YOU KNOW...
YES, WELL, I SUPPOSE WE CAN ADD GAYDAR TO THE EXTRAORDINARY NUMBER OF COMMON SENSES YOU SEEM TO LACK.

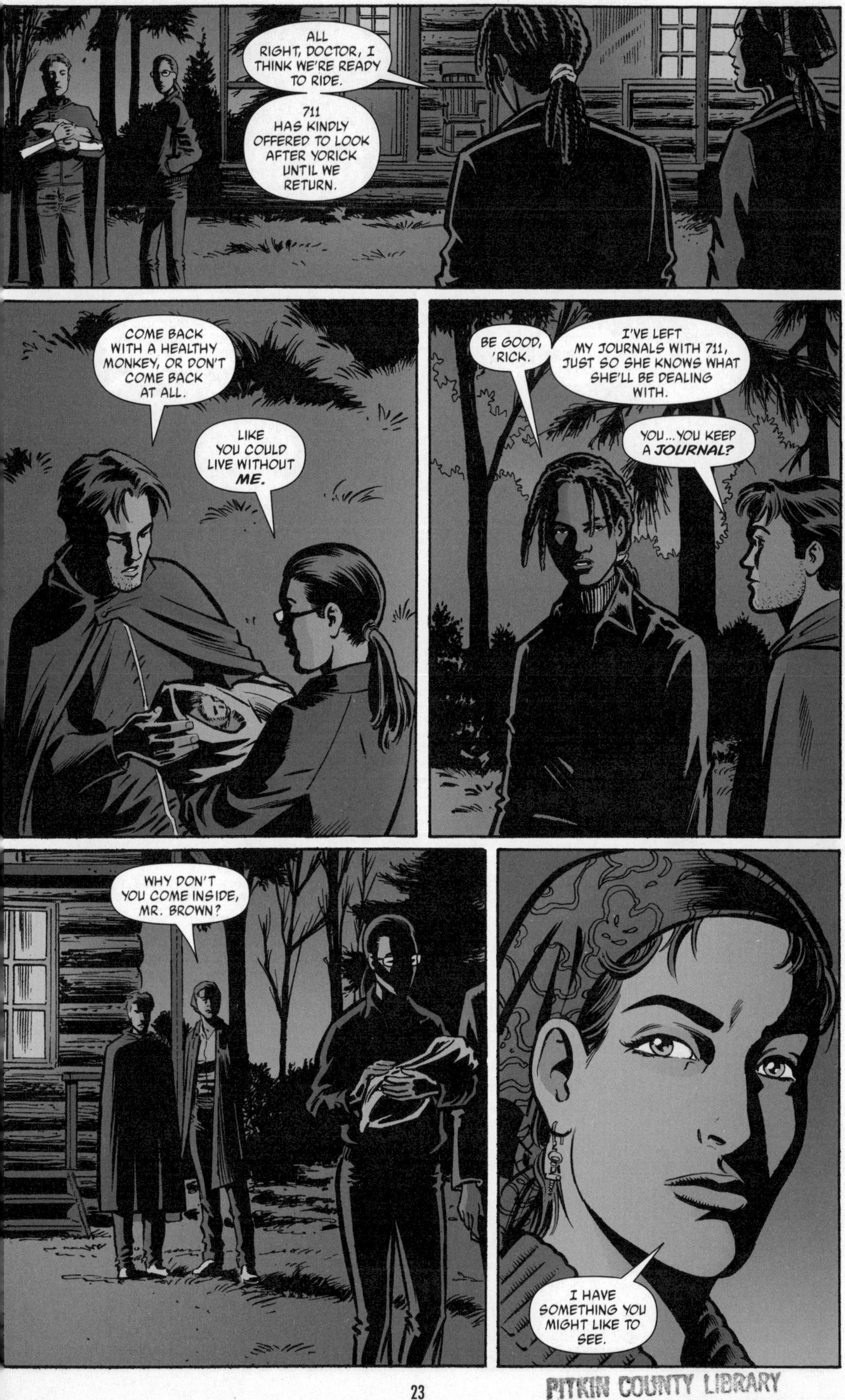
ALL RIGHT, DOCTOR, I THINK WE'RE READY TO RIDE.
711 HAS KINDLY OFFERED TO LOOK AFTER YORICK UNTIL WE RETURN.
COME BACK WITH A HEALTHY MONKEY, OR DON'T COME BACK AT ALL.
LIKE YOU COULD LIVE WITHOUT **ME.**
BE GOOD, 'RICK.
I'VE LEFT MY JOURNALS WITH 711, JUST SO SHE KNOWS WHAT SHE'LL BE DEALING WITH.
YOU...YOU KEEP A ***JOURNAL?***
WHY DON'T YOU COME INSIDE, MR. BROWN?
I HAVE SOMETHING YOU MIGHT LIKE TO SEE.

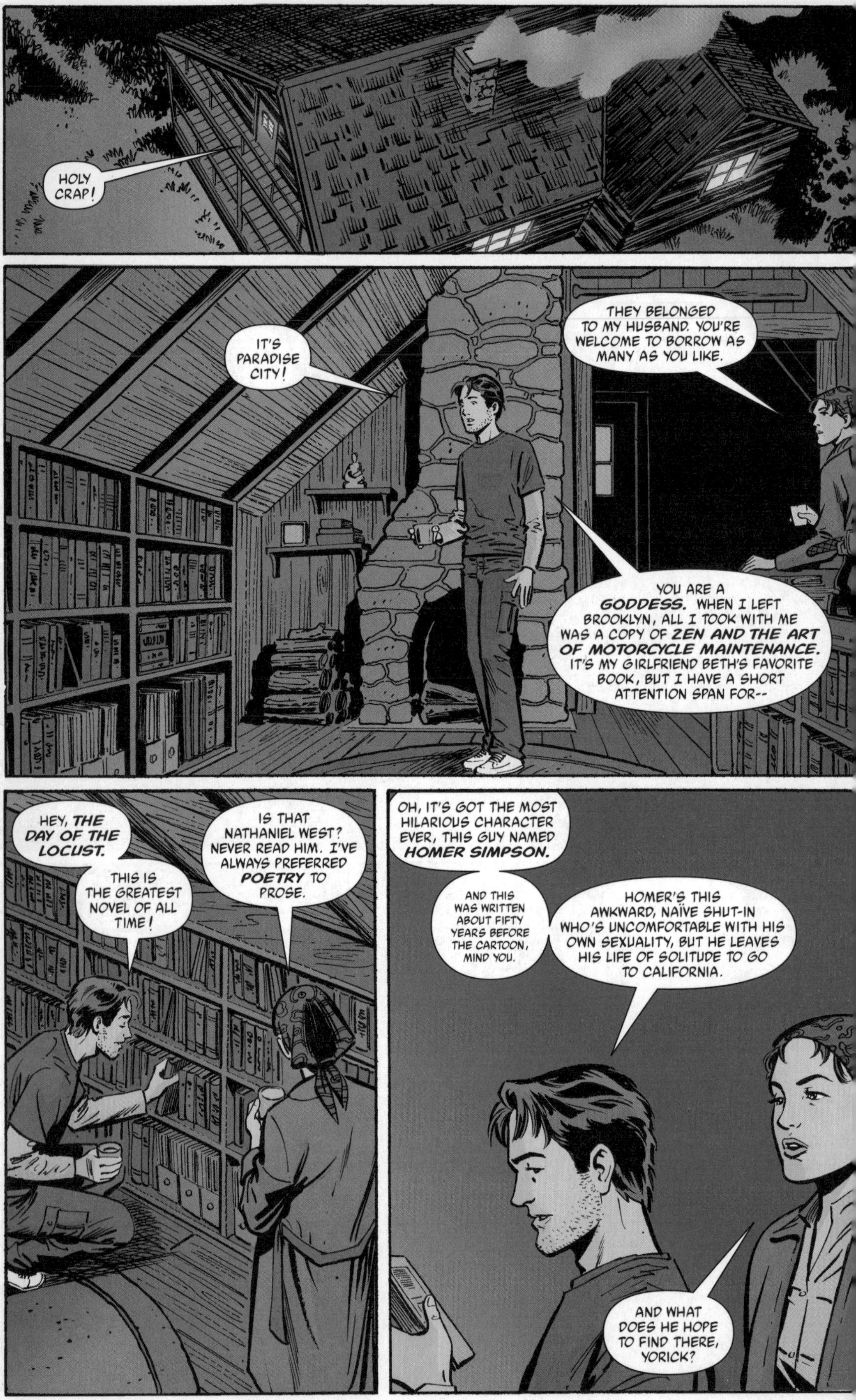

HOLY CRAP!
IT'S PARADISE CITY!
THEY BELONGED TO MY HUSBAND. YOU'RE WELCOME TO BORROW AS MANY AS YOU LIKE.
YOU ARE A **GODDESS.** WHEN I LEFT BROOKLYN, ALL I TOOK WITH ME WAS A COPY OF ***ZEN AND THE ART OF MOTORCYCLE MAINTENANCE.*** IT'S MY GIRLFRIEND BETH'S FAVORITE BOOK, BUT I HAVE A SHORT ATTENTION SPAN FOR--
HEY, ***THE DAY OF THE LOCUST.***
THIS IS THE GREATEST NOVEL OF ALL TIME!
IS THAT NATHANIEL WEST? NEVER READ HIM. I'VE ALWAYS PREFERRED ***POETRY*** TO PROSE.
OH, IT'S GOT THE MOST HILARIOUS CHARACTER EVER, THIS GUY NAMED ***HOMER SIMPSON.***
AND THIS WAS WRITTEN ABOUT FIFTY YEARS BEFORE THE CARTOON, MIND YOU.
HOMER'S THIS AWKWARD, NAÏVE SHUT-IN WHO'S UNCOMFORTABLE WITH HIS OWN SEXUALITY, BUT HE LEAVES HIS LIFE OF SOLITUDE TO GO TO CALIFORNIA.
AND WHAT DOES HE HOPE TO FIND THERE, YORICK?

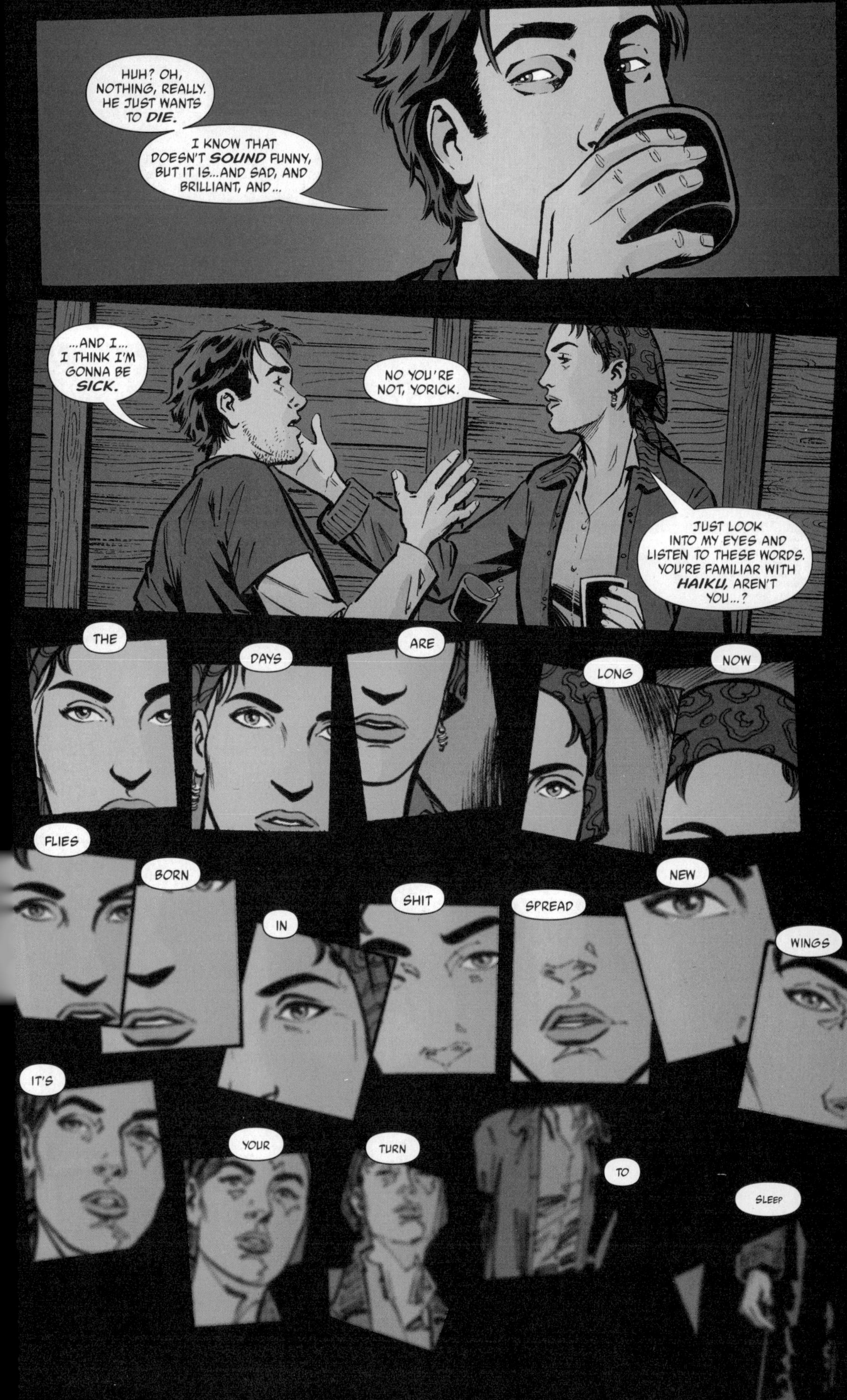
HUH? OH, NOTHING, REALLY. HE JUST WANTS TO **DIE.**
I KNOW THAT DOESN'T **SOUND** FUNNY, BUT IT IS...AND SAD, AND BRILLIANT, AND...
...AND I... I THINK I'M GONNA BE **SICK.**
NO YOU'RE NOT, YORICK.
JUST LOOK INTO MY EYES AND LISTEN TO THESE WORDS. YOU'RE FAMILIAR WITH **HAIKU**, AREN'T YOU...?
THE
DAYS
ARE
LONG
NOW
FLIES
BORN
IN
SHIT
SPREAD
NEW
WINGS
IT'S
YOUR
TURN
TO
SLEEP

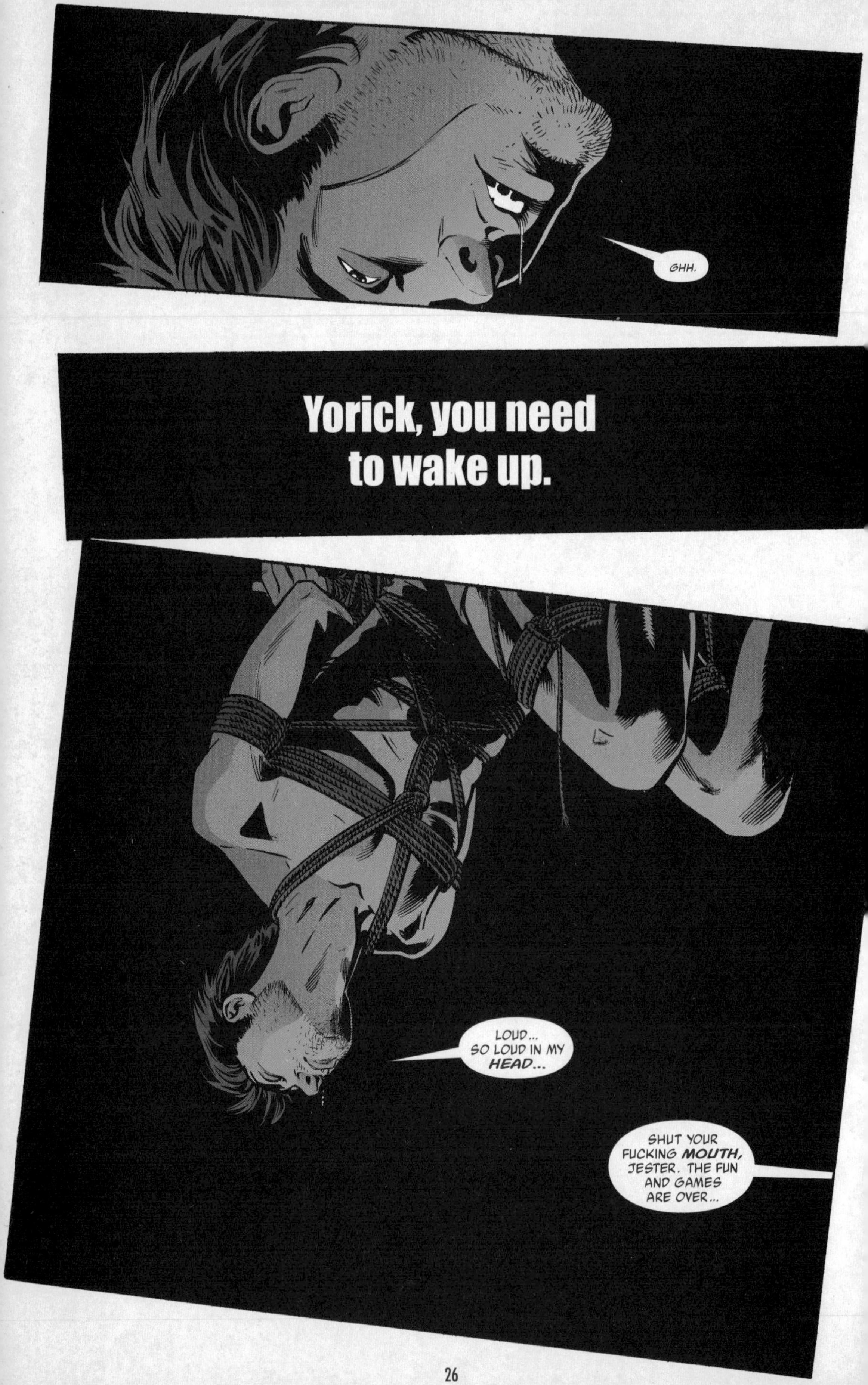
GHH.
Yorick, you need to wake up.
LOUD... SO LOUD IN MY HEAD...
SHUT YOUR FUCKING MOUTH, JESTER. THE FUN AND GAMES ARE OVER...

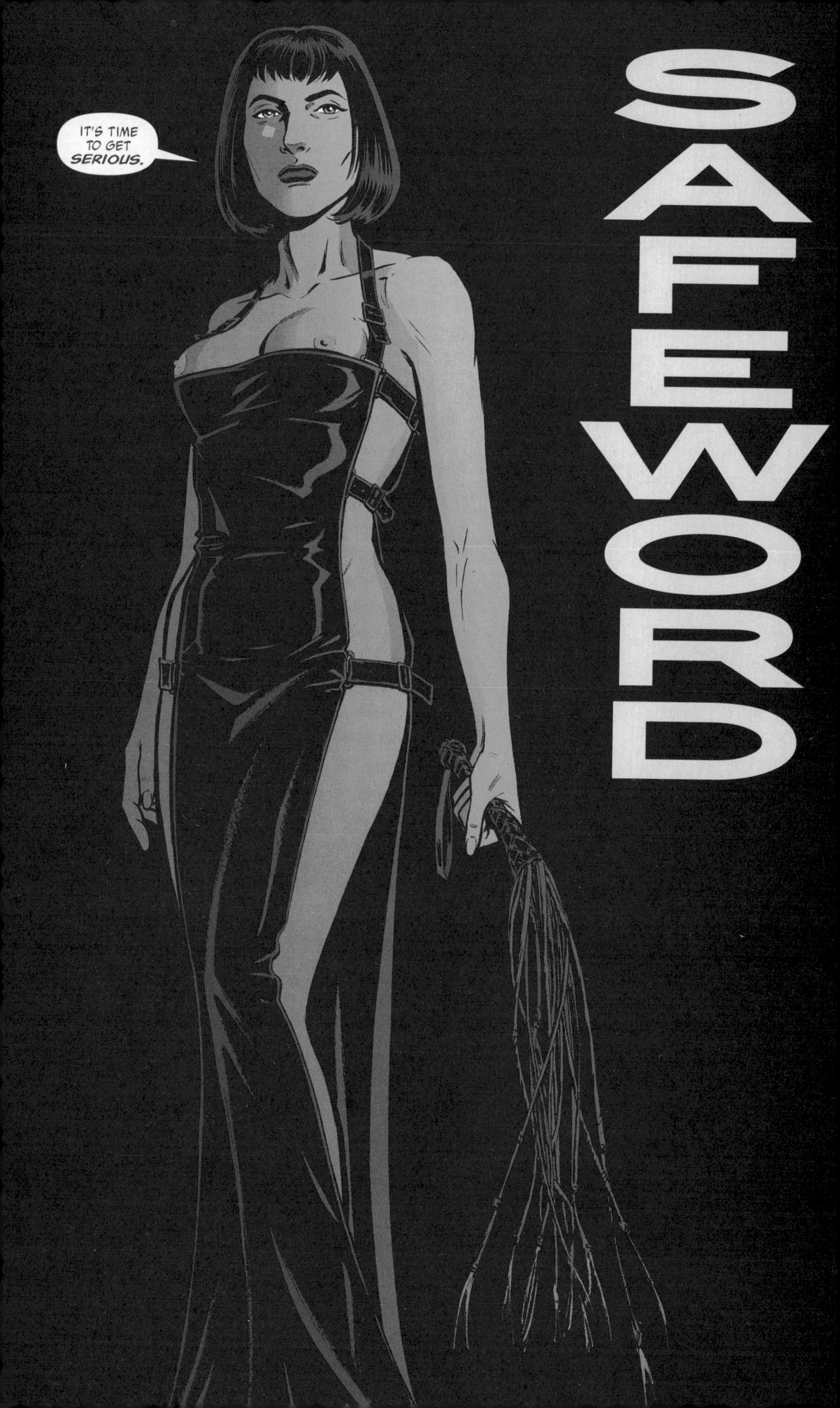
IT'S TIME TO GET SERIOUS.
SAFEWORD

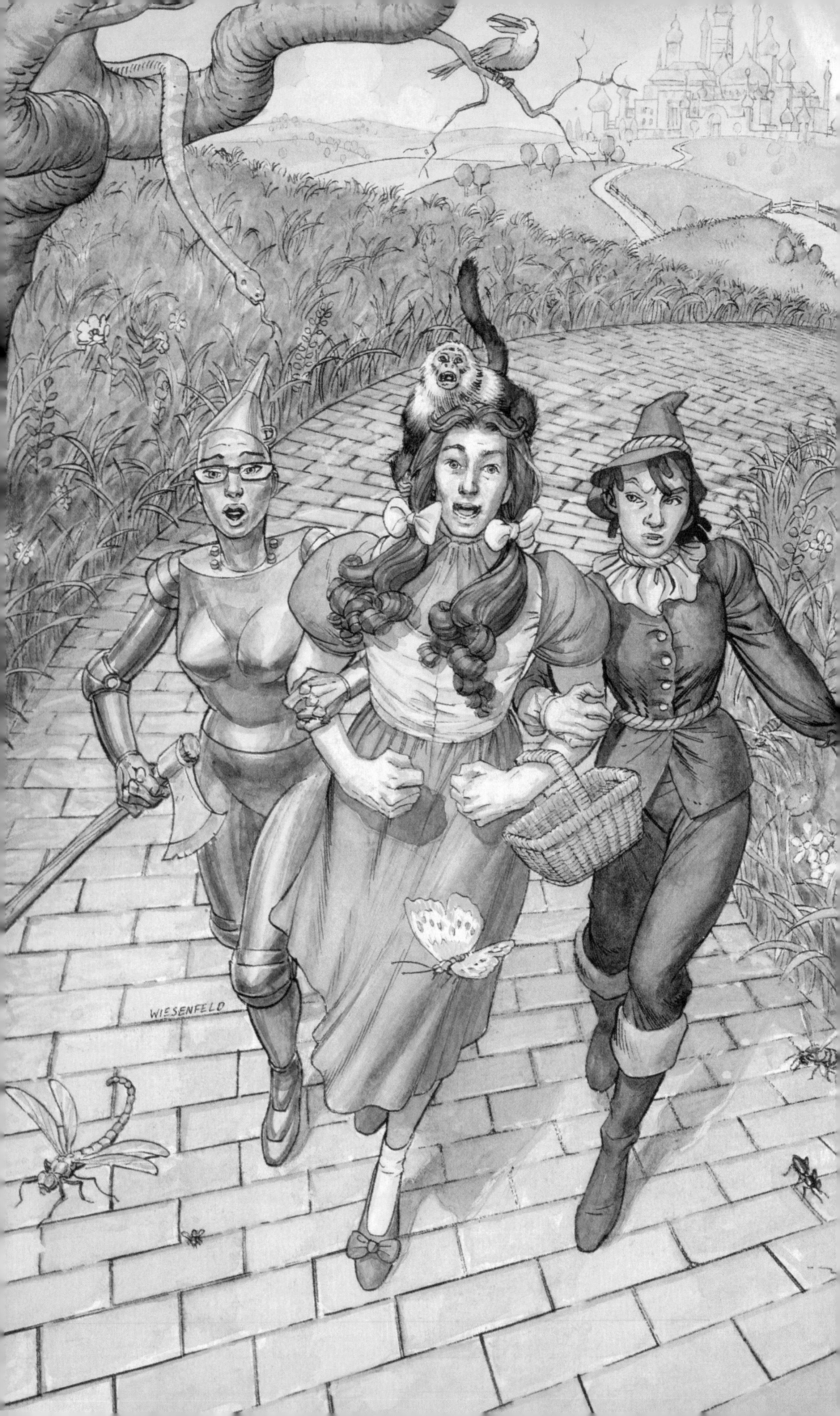
WIESENFELD

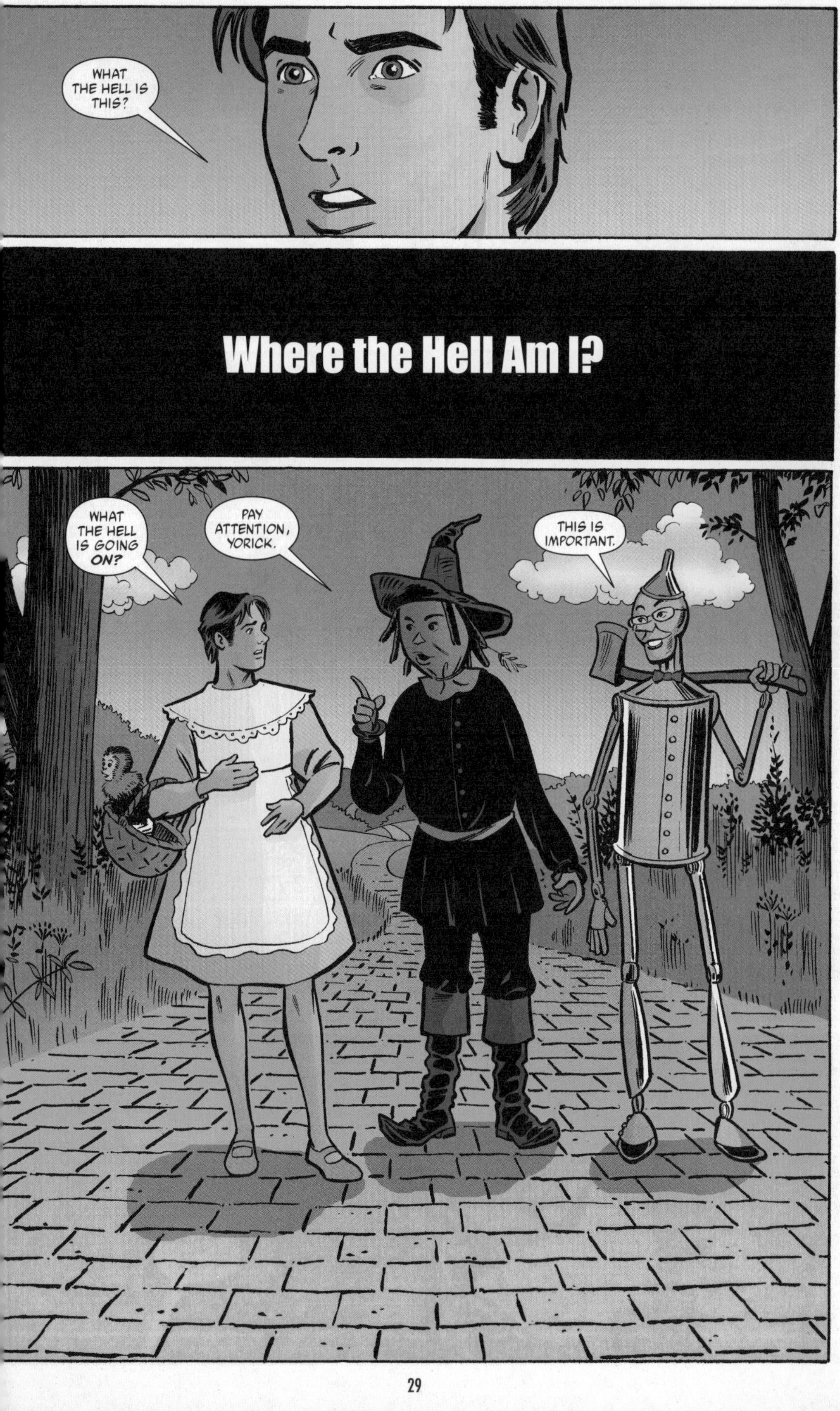
WHAT THE HELL IS THIS?
Where the Hell Am I?
WHAT THE HELL IS GOING ON?
PAY ATTENTION, YORICK.
THIS IS IMPORTANT.

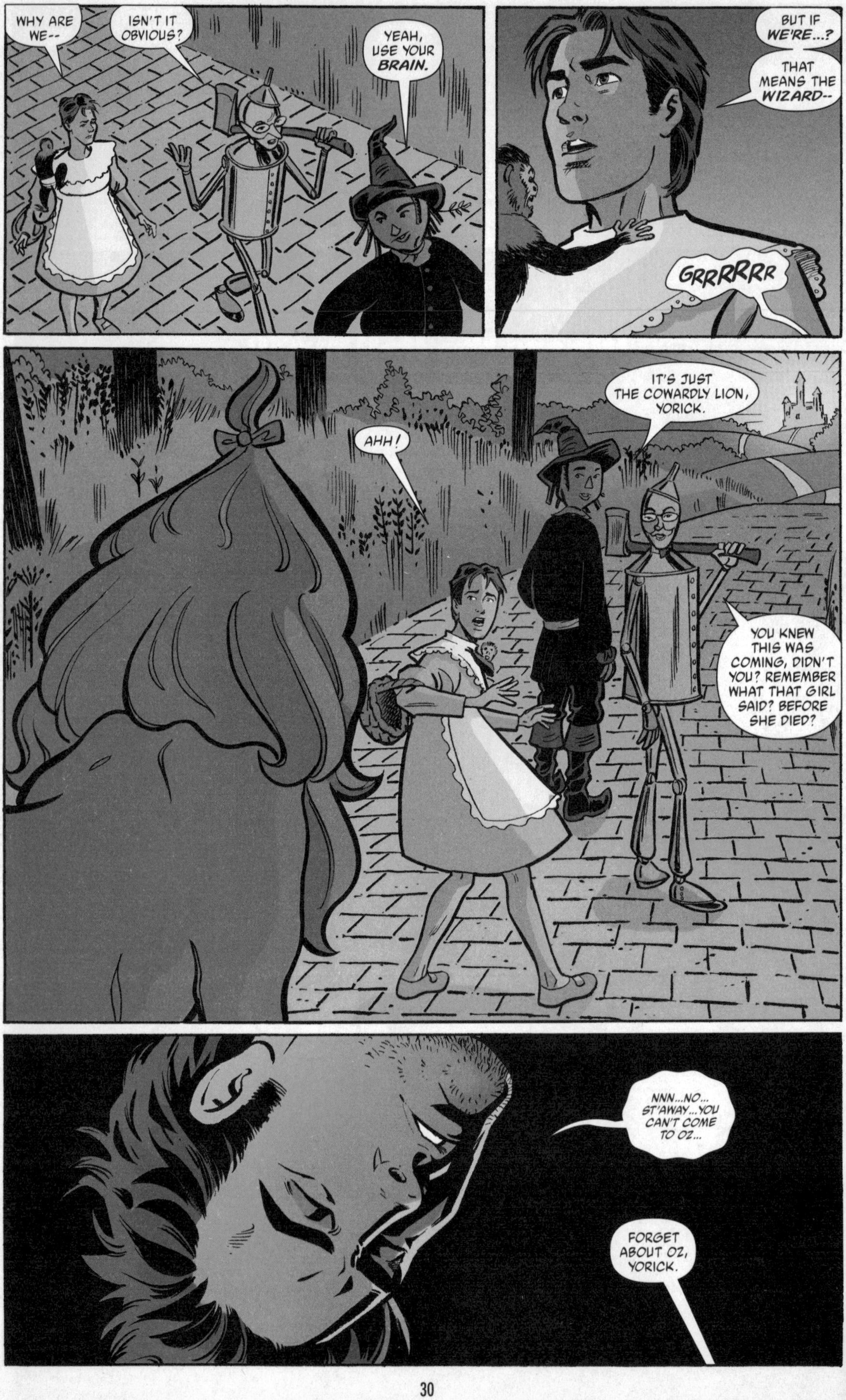
WHY ARE WE--
ISN'T IT OBVIOUS?
YEAH, USE YOUR **BRAIN.**
BUT IF **WE'RE...?**
THAT MEANS THE **WIZARD--**
GRRRRRR
IT'S JUST THE COWARDLY LION, YORICK.
AHH!
YOU KNEW THIS WAS COMING, DIDN'T YOU? REMEMBER WHAT THAT GIRL SAID? BEFORE SHE DIED?
NNN...NO... ST'AWAY...YOU CAN'T COME TO OZ...
FORGET ABOUT OZ, YORICK.

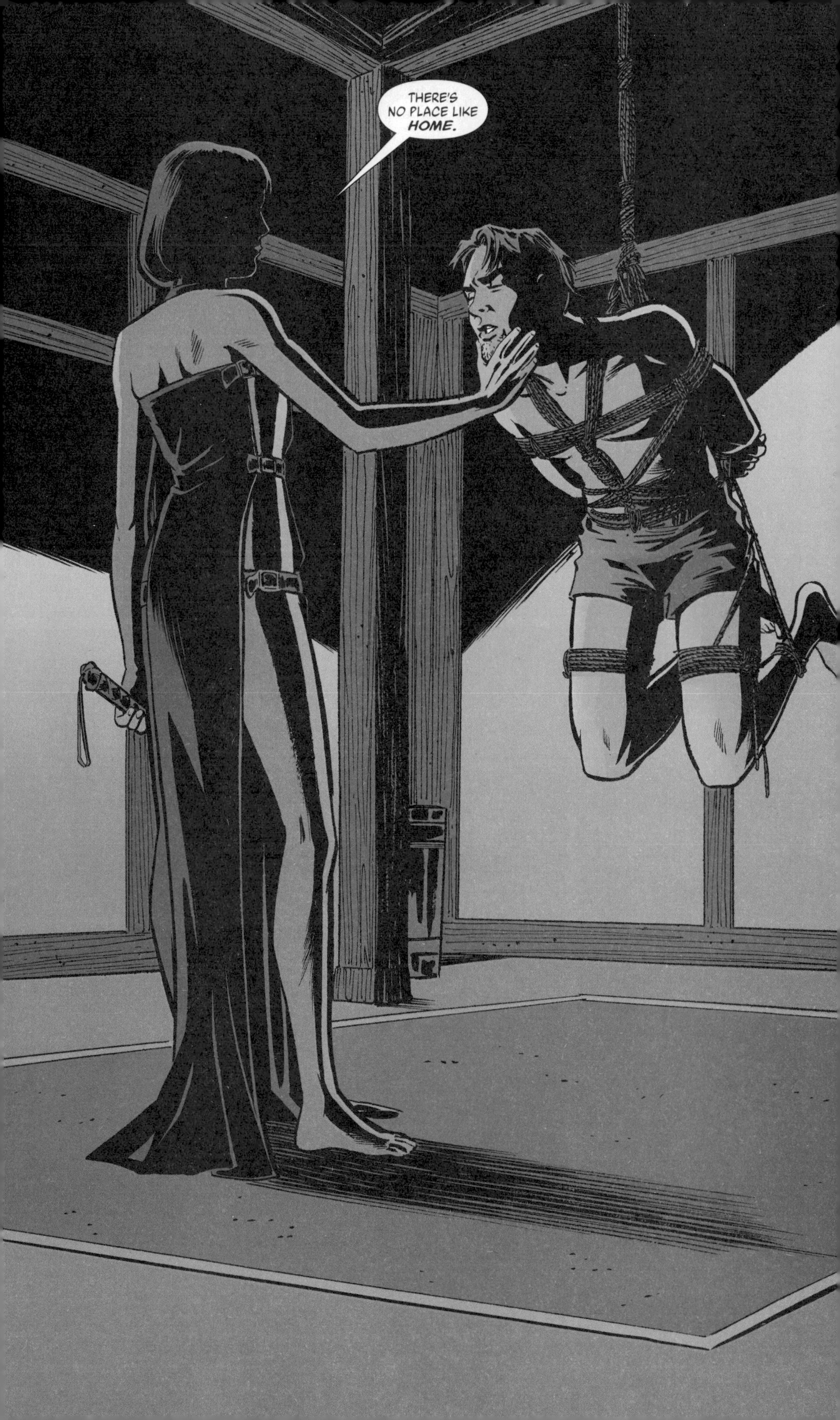
THERE'S NO PLACE LIKE *HOME.*

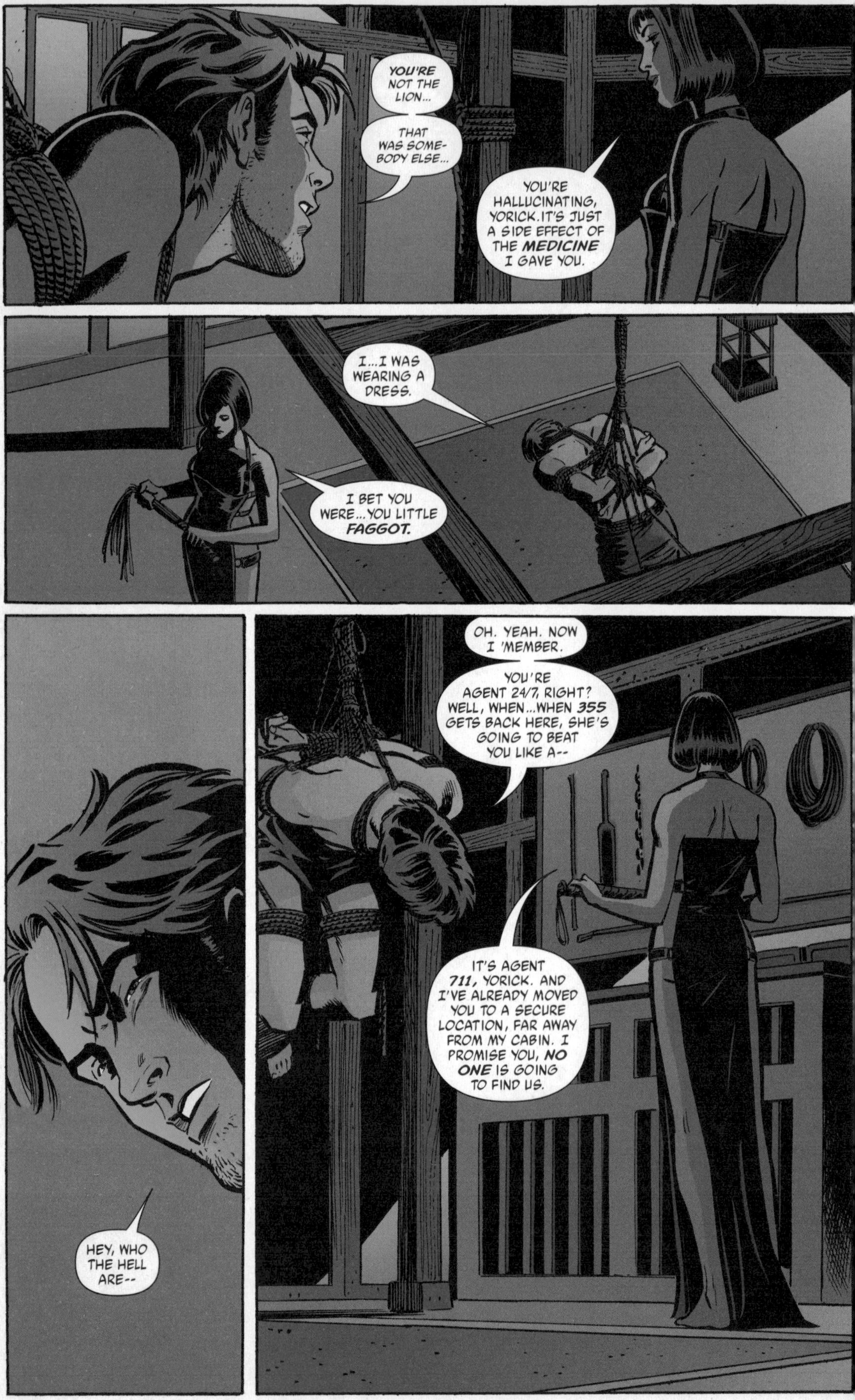

YOU'RE NOT THE LION...
THAT WAS SOMEBODY ELSE...
YOU'RE HALLUCINATING, YORICK. IT'S JUST A SIDE EFFECT OF THE MEDICINE I GAVE YOU.
I...I WAS WEARING A DRESS.
I BET YOU WERE...YOU LITTLE FAGGOT.
HEY, WHO THE HELL ARE--
OH. YEAH. NOW I 'MEMBER.
YOU'RE AGENT 24/7, RIGHT? WELL, WHEN...WHEN 355 GETS BACK HERE, SHE'S GOING TO BEAT YOU LIKE A--
IT'S AGENT 711, YORICK. AND I'VE ALREADY MOVED YOU TO A SECURE LOCATION, FAR AWAY FROM MY CABIN. I PROMISE YOU, NO ONE IS GOING TO FIND US.

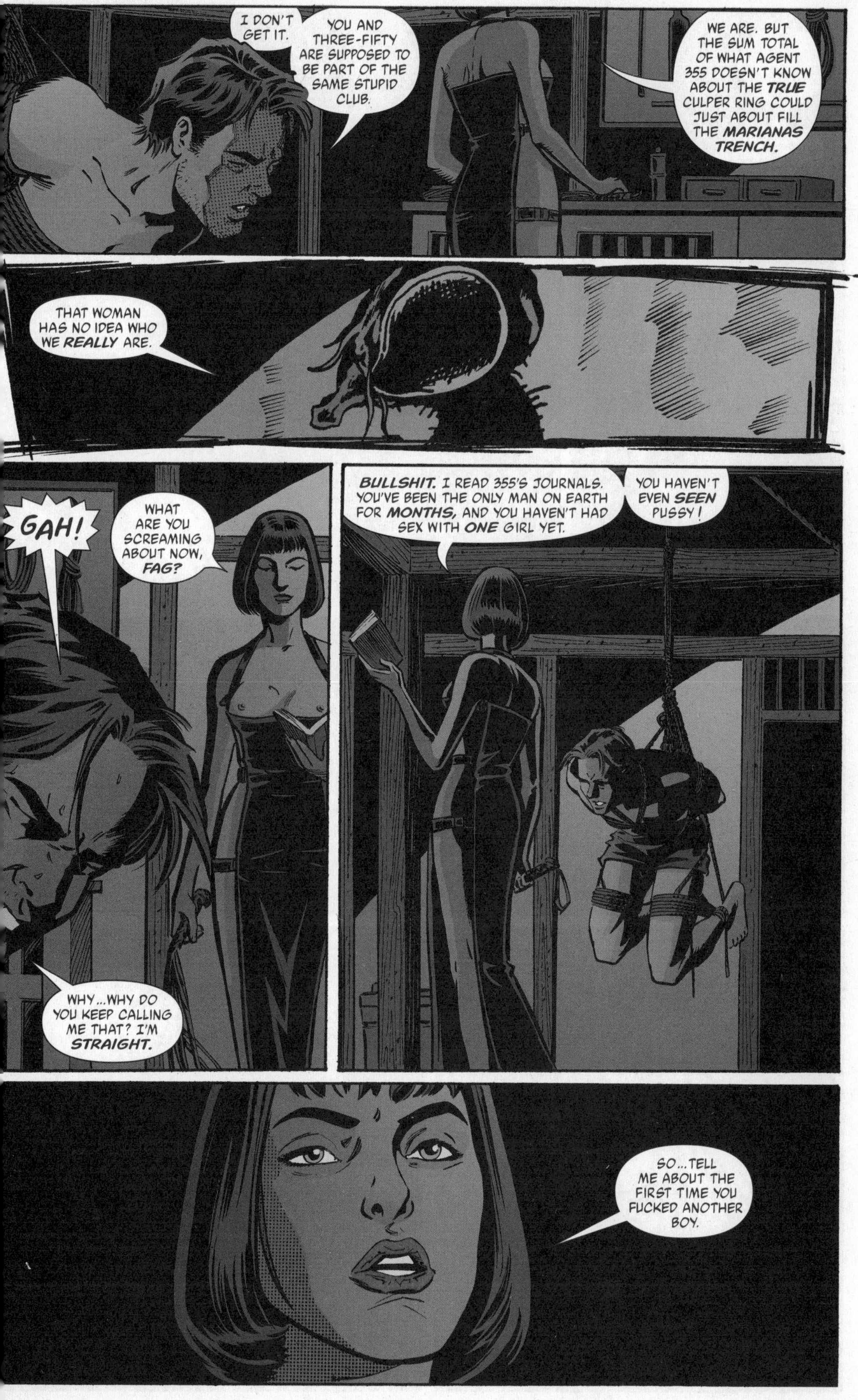
I DON'T GET IT.
YOU AND THREE-FIFTY ARE SUPPOSED TO BE PART OF THE SAME STUPID CLUB.
WE ARE. BUT THE SUM TOTAL OF WHAT AGENT 355 DOESN'T KNOW ABOUT THE TRUE CULPER RING COULD JUST ABOUT FILL THE MARIANAS TRENCH.
THAT WOMAN HAS NO IDEA WHO WE REALLY ARE.
GAH!
WHAT ARE YOU SCREAMING ABOUT NOW, FAG?
WHY...WHY DO YOU KEEP CALLING ME THAT? I'M STRAIGHT.
BULLSHIT. I READ 355'S JOURNALS. YOU'VE BEEN THE ONLY MAN ON EARTH FOR MONTHS, AND YOU HAVEN'T HAD SEX WITH ONE GIRL YET.
YOU HAVEN'T EVEN SEEN PUSSY!
SO...TELL ME ABOUT THE FIRST TIME YOU FUCKED ANOTHER BOY.

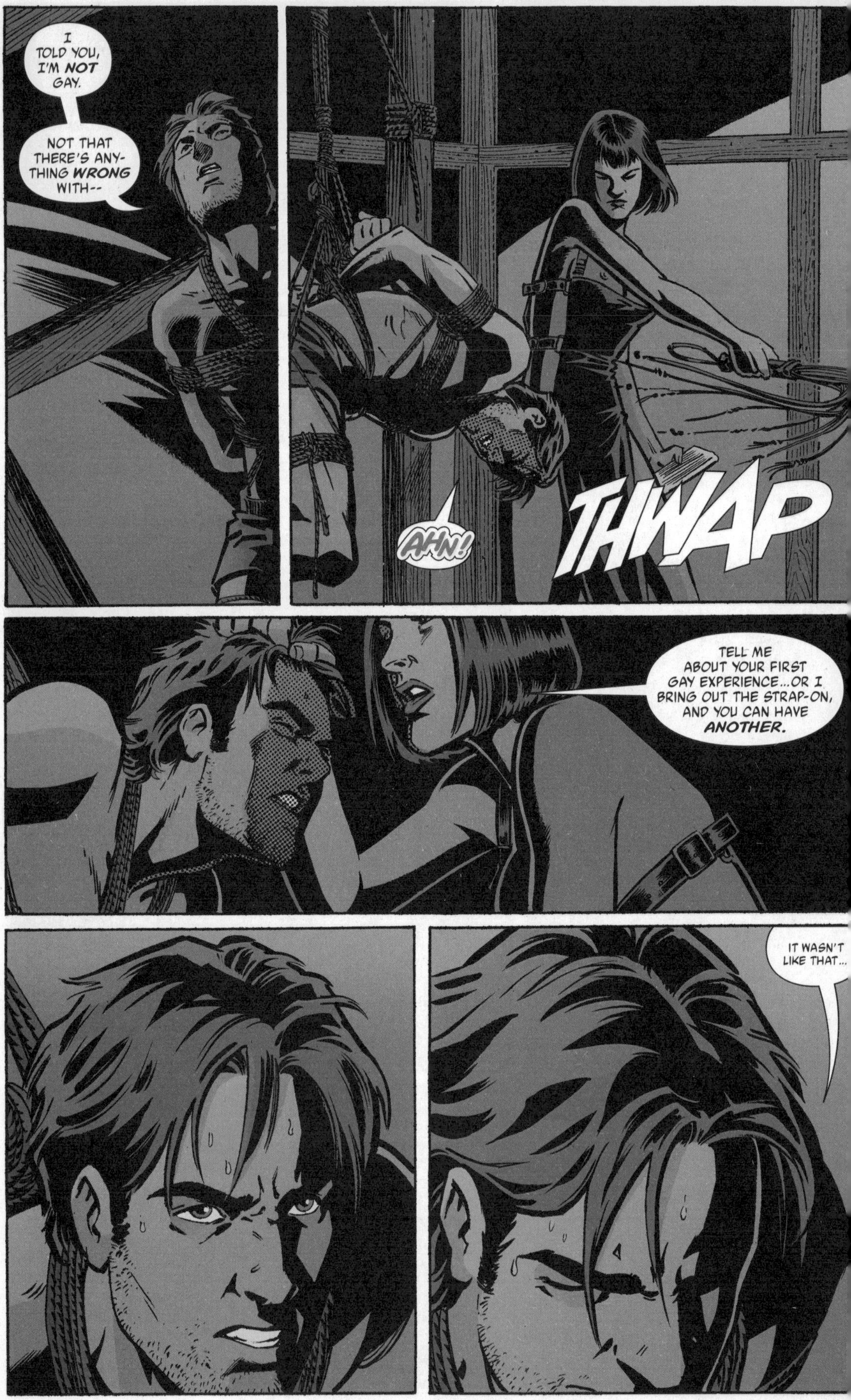
I TOLD YOU, I'M NOT GAY.
NOT THAT THERE'S ANYTHING WRONG WITH--
AHN!
THWAP
TELL ME ABOUT YOUR FIRST GAY EXPERIENCE...OR I BRING OUT THE STRAP-ON, AND YOU CAN HAVE ANOTHER.
IT WASN'T LIKE THAT...

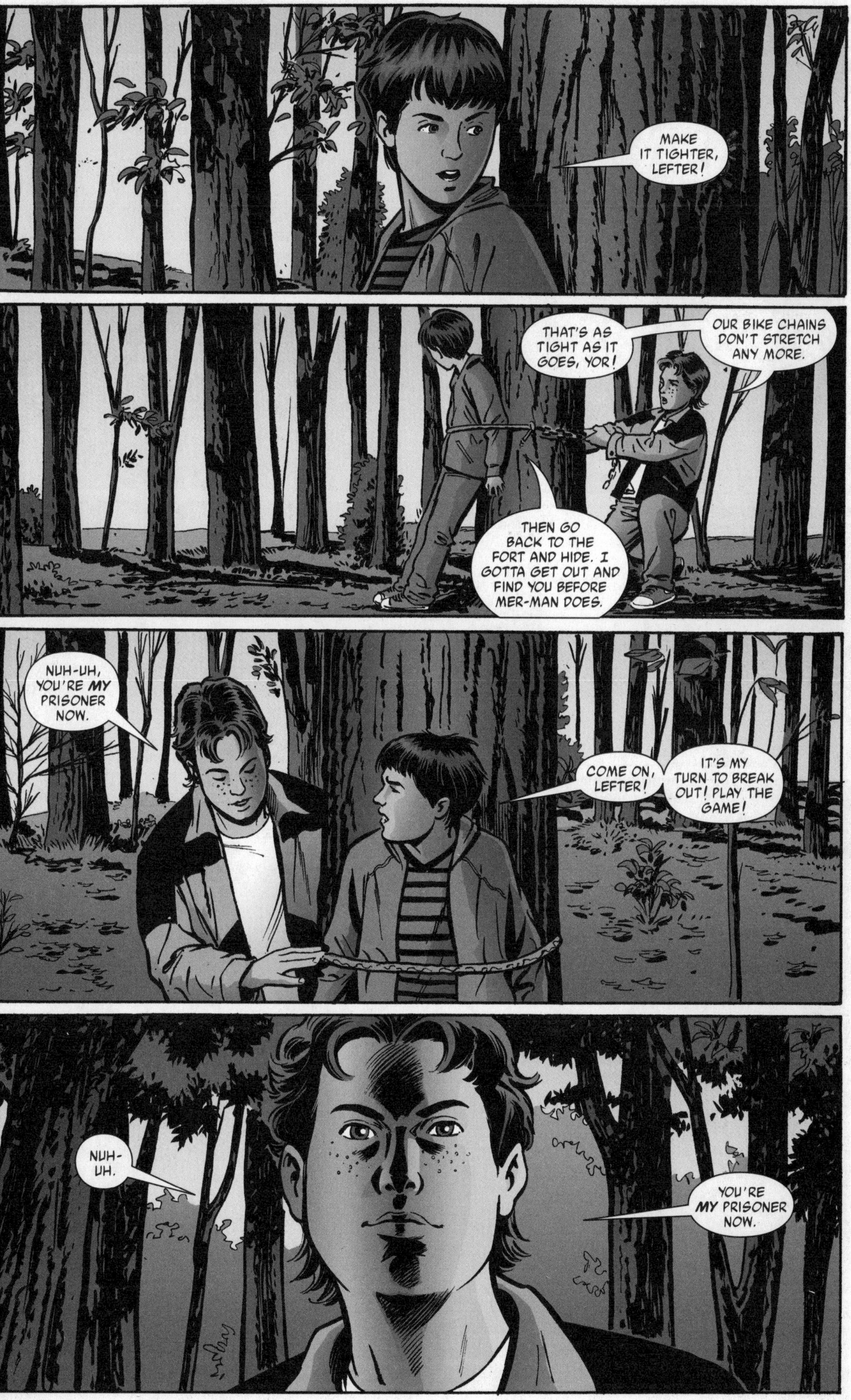
MAKE IT TIGHTER, LEFTER!
THAT'S AS TIGHT AS IT GOES, YOR!
OUR BIKE CHAINS DON'T STRETCH ANY MORE.
THEN GO BACK TO THE FORT AND HIDE. I GOTTA GET OUT AND FIND YOU BEFORE MER-MAN DOES.
NUH-UH, YOU'RE *MY* PRISONER NOW.
COME ON, LEFTER!
IT'S MY TURN TO BREAK OUT! PLAY THE GAME!
NUH-UH.
YOU'RE *MY* PRISONER NOW.

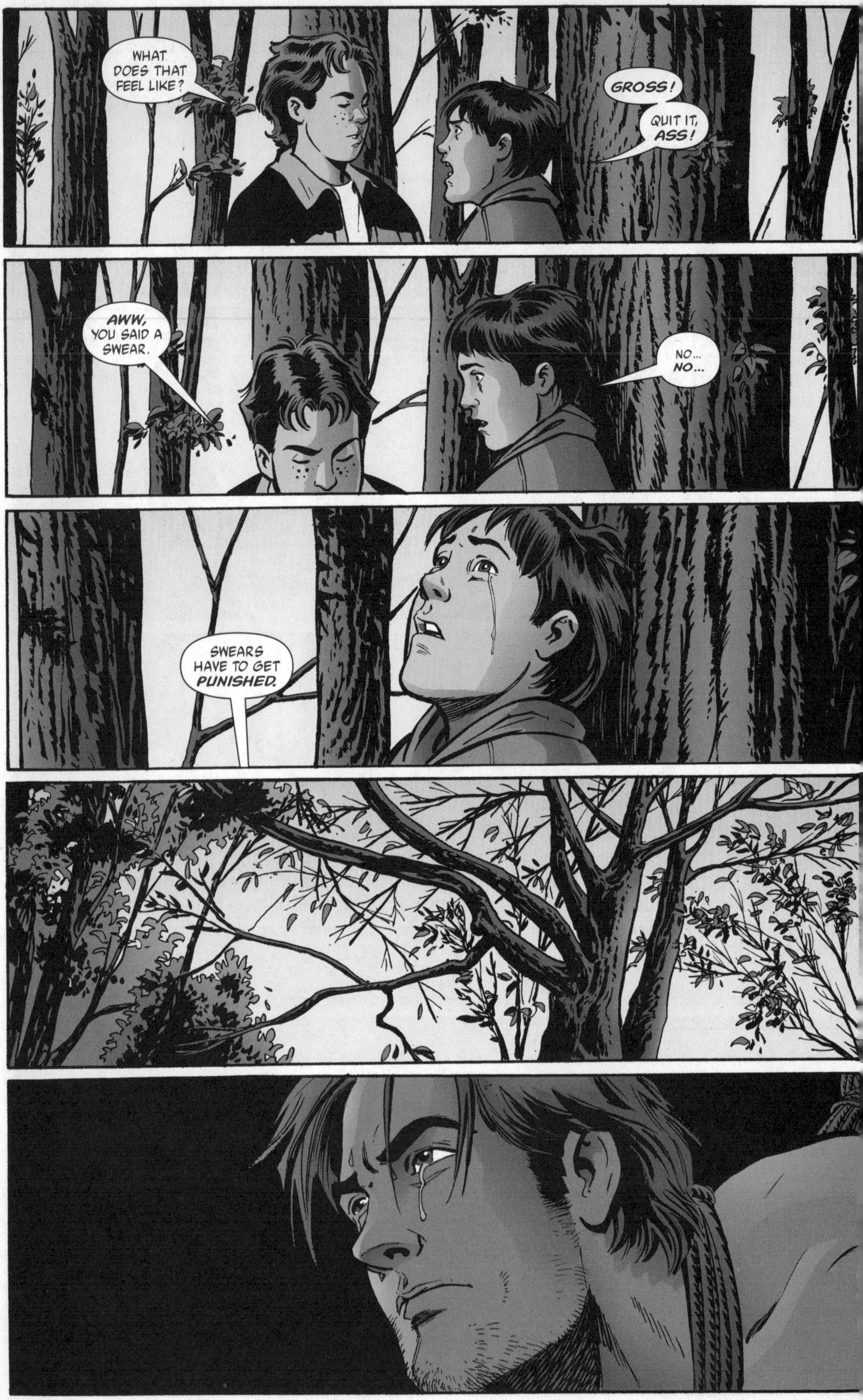
WHAT DOES THAT FEEL LIKE?
GROSS!
QUIT IT, ASS!
AWW, YOU SAID A SWEAR.
NO... NO...
SWEARS HAVE TO GET PUNISHED.

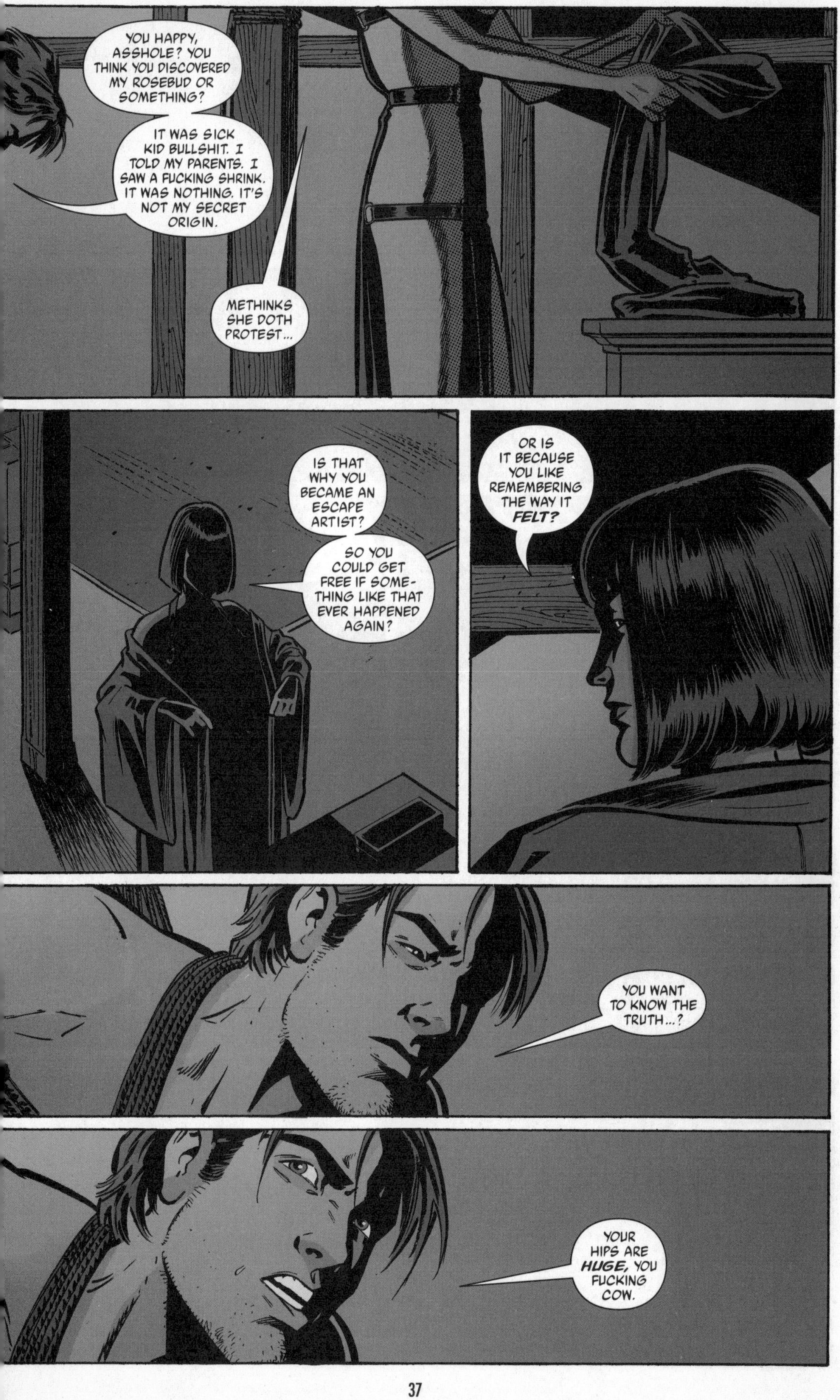

YOU HAPPY, ASSHOLE? YOU THINK YOU DISCOVERED MY ROSEBUD OR SOMETHING?
IT WAS SICK KID BULLSHIT. I TOLD MY PARENTS. I SAW A FUCKING SHRINK. IT WAS NOTHING. IT'S NOT MY SECRET ORIGIN.
METHINKS SHE DOTH PROTEST...
IS THAT WHY YOU BECAME AN ESCAPE ARTIST?
SO YOU COULD GET FREE IF SOME-THING LIKE THAT EVER HAPPENED AGAIN?
OR IS IT BECAUSE YOU LIKE REMEMBERING THE WAY IT *FELT?*
YOU WANT TO KNOW THE TRUTH...?
YOUR HIPS ARE *HUGE,* YOU FUCKING COW.

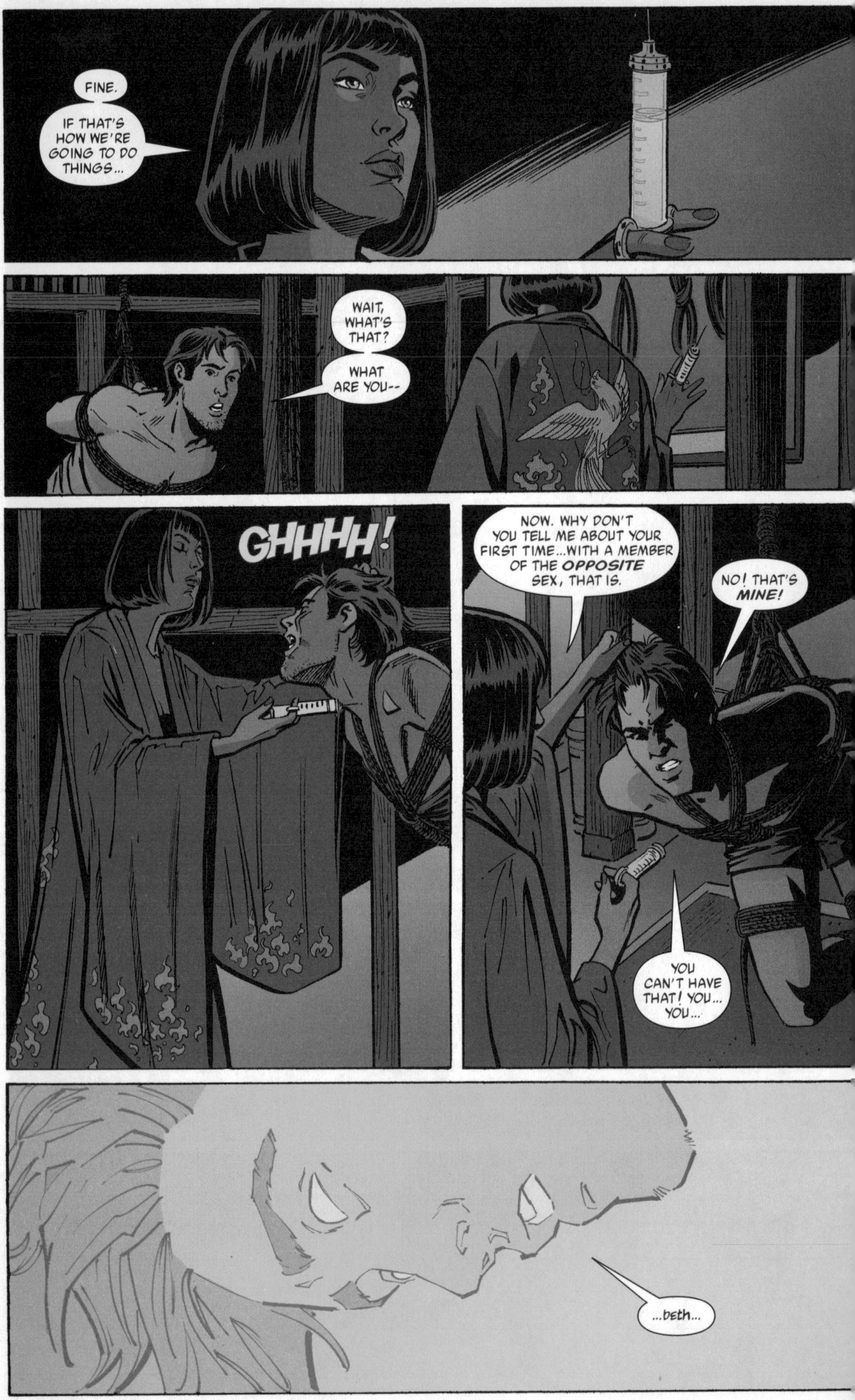
FINE.
IF THAT'S HOW WE'RE GOING TO DO THINGS...
WAIT, WHAT'S THAT?
WHAT ARE YOU--
GHHHH!
NOW. WHY DON'T YOU TELL ME ABOUT YOUR FIRST TIME...WITH A MEMBER OF THE OPPOSITE SEX, THAT IS.
NO! THAT'S MINE!
YOU CAN'T HAVE THAT! YOU... YOU...
...beth...

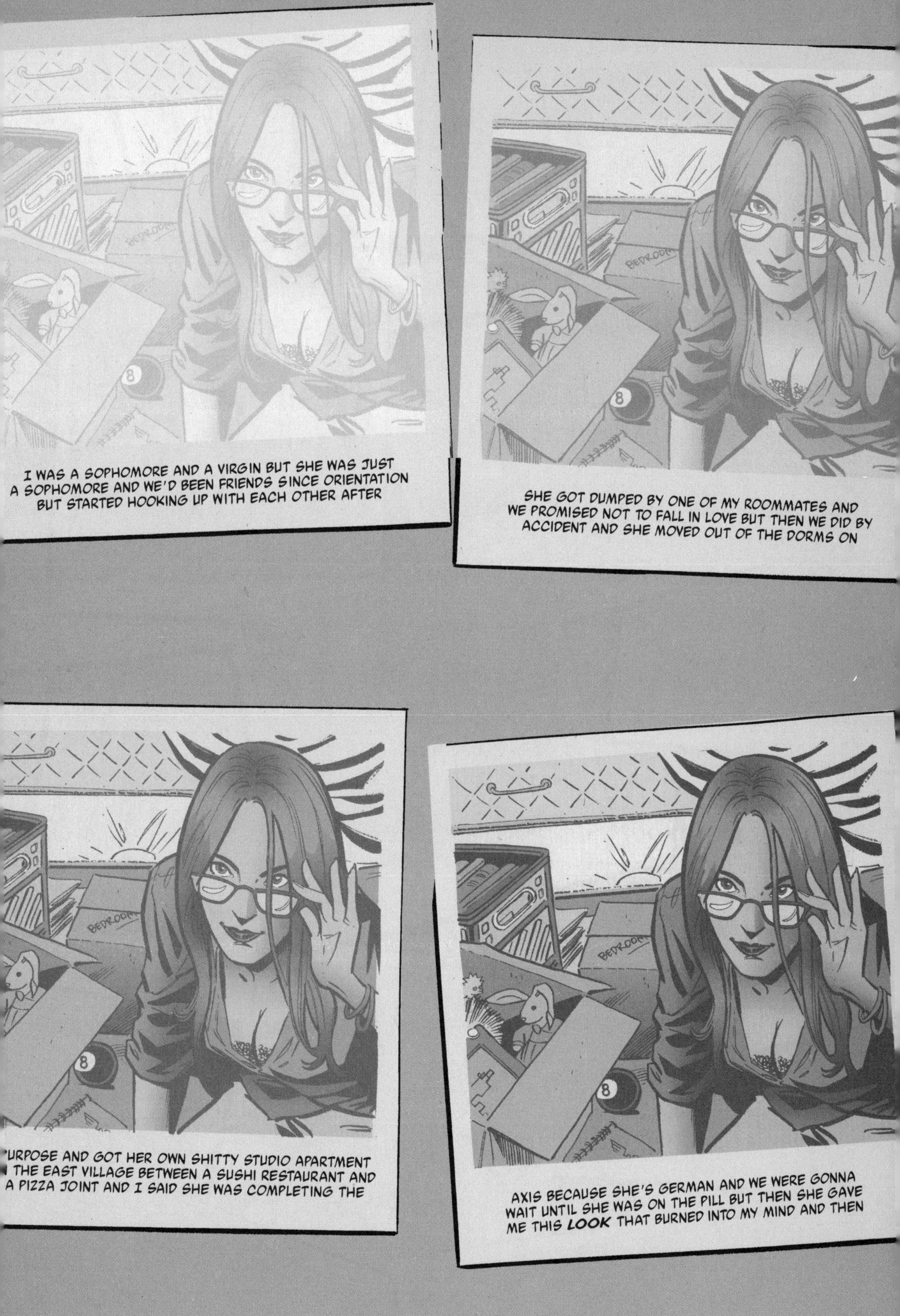
I WAS A SOPHOMORE AND A VIRGIN BUT SHE WAS JUST A SOPHOMORE AND WE'D BEEN FRIENDS SINCE ORIENTATION BUT STARTED HOOKING UP WITH EACH OTHER AFTER
SHE GOT DUMPED BY ONE OF MY ROOMMATES AND WE PROMISED NOT TO FALL IN LOVE BUT THEN WE DID BY ACCIDENT AND SHE MOVED OUT OF THE DORMS ON
URPOSE AND GOT HER OWN SHITTY STUDIO APARTMENT THE EAST VILLAGE BETWEEN A SUSHI RESTAURANT AND A PIZZA JOINT AND I SAID SHE WAS COMPLETING THE
AXIS BECAUSE SHE'S GERMAN AND WE WERE GONNA WAIT UNTIL SHE WAS ON THE PILL BUT THEN SHE GAVE ME THIS LOOK THAT BURNED INTO MY MIND AND THEN

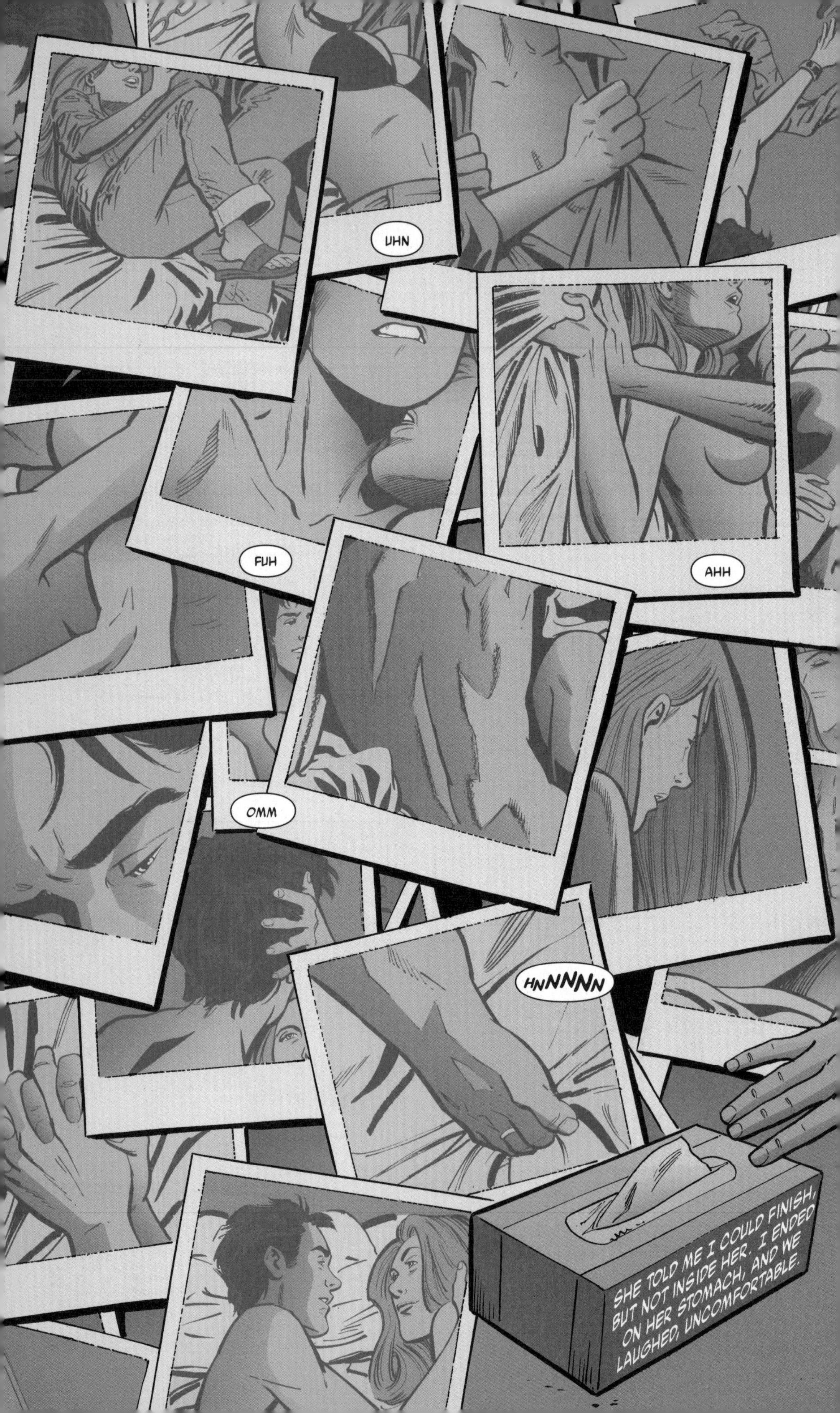
UHN
FUH
AHH
OMM
HNNNNN
SHE TOLD ME I COULD FINISH, BUT NOT INSIDE HER. I ENDED ON HER STOMACH, AND WE LAUGHED, UNCOMFORTABLE.

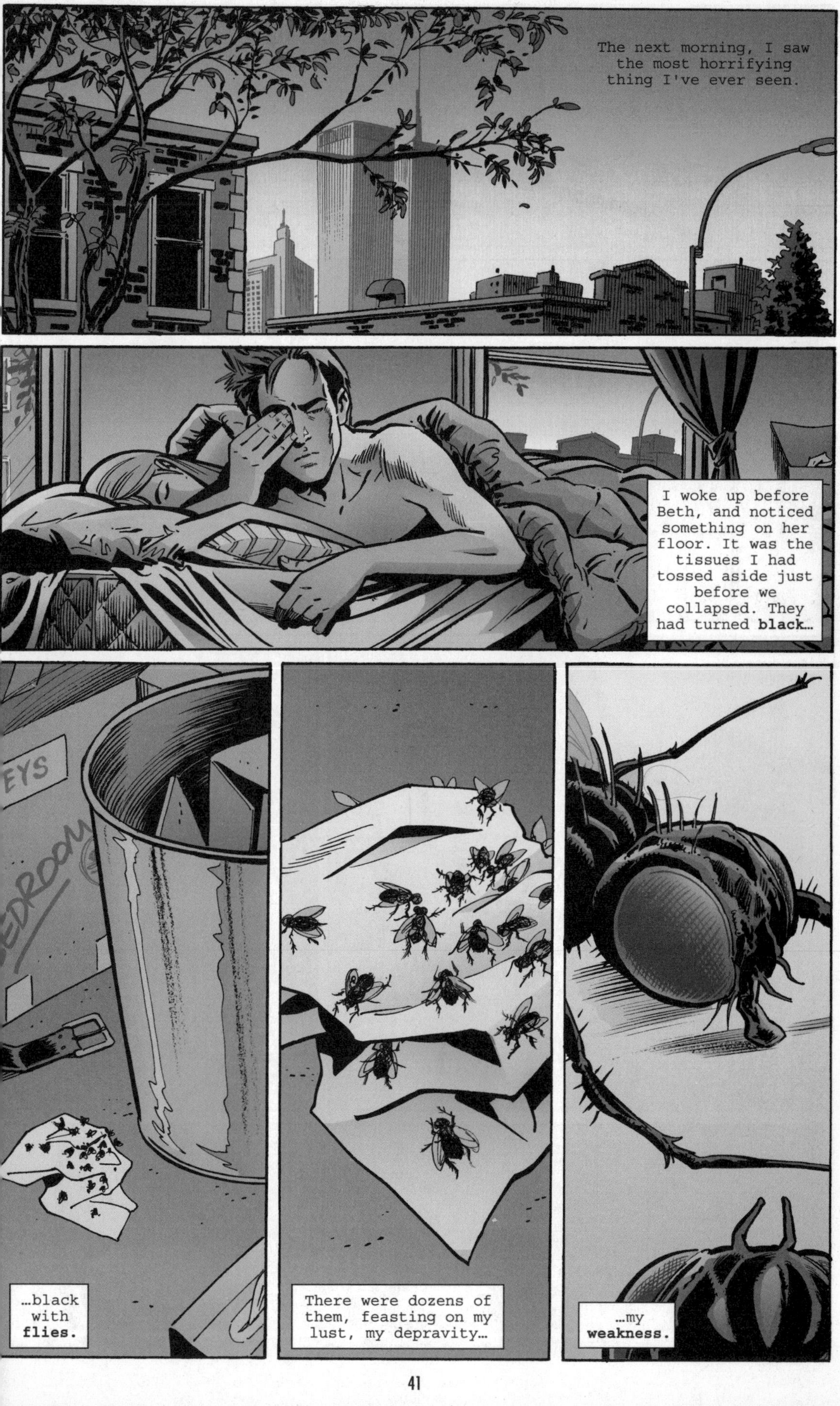
The next morning, I saw the most horrifying thing I've ever seen.
I woke up before Beth, and noticed something on her floor. It was the tissues I had tossed aside just before we collapsed. They had turned **black**...
EYS
EDROOM
...black with **flies.**
There were dozens of them, feasting on my lust, my depravity...
...my **weakness.**

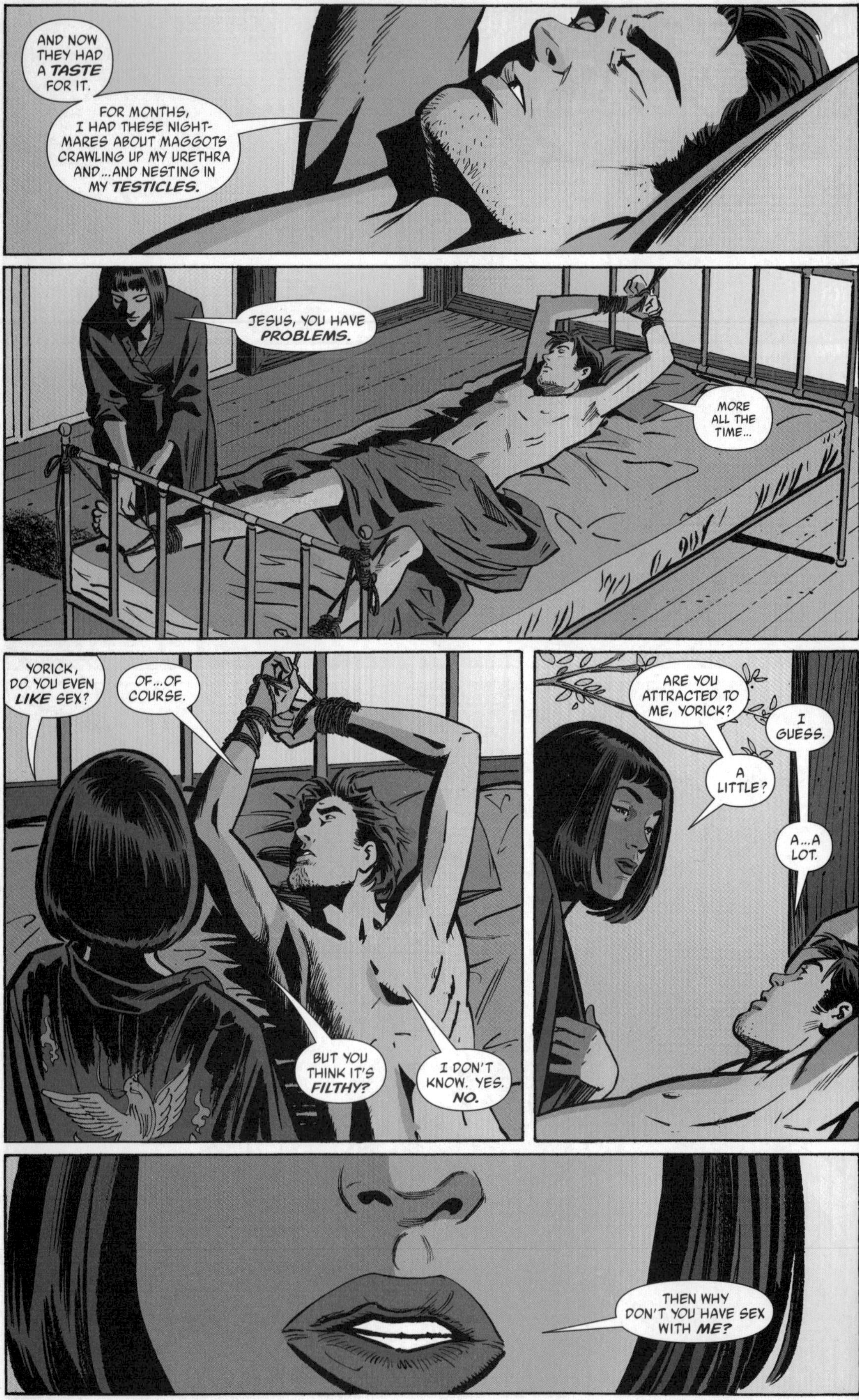
AND NOW THEY HAD A *TASTE* FOR IT.
FOR MONTHS, I HAD THESE NIGHT-MARES ABOUT MAGGOTS CRAWLING UP MY URETHRA AND...AND NESTING IN MY *TESTICLES.*
JESUS, YOU HAVE *PROBLEMS.*
MORE ALL THE TIME...
YORICK, DO YOU EVEN *LIKE* SEX?
OF...OF COURSE.
BUT YOU THINK IT'S *FILTHY?*
I DON'T KNOW. YES. *NO.*
ARE YOU ATTRACTED TO ME, YORICK?
I GUESS.
A LITTLE?
A...A LOT.
THEN WHY DON'T YOU HAVE SEX WITH *ME?*

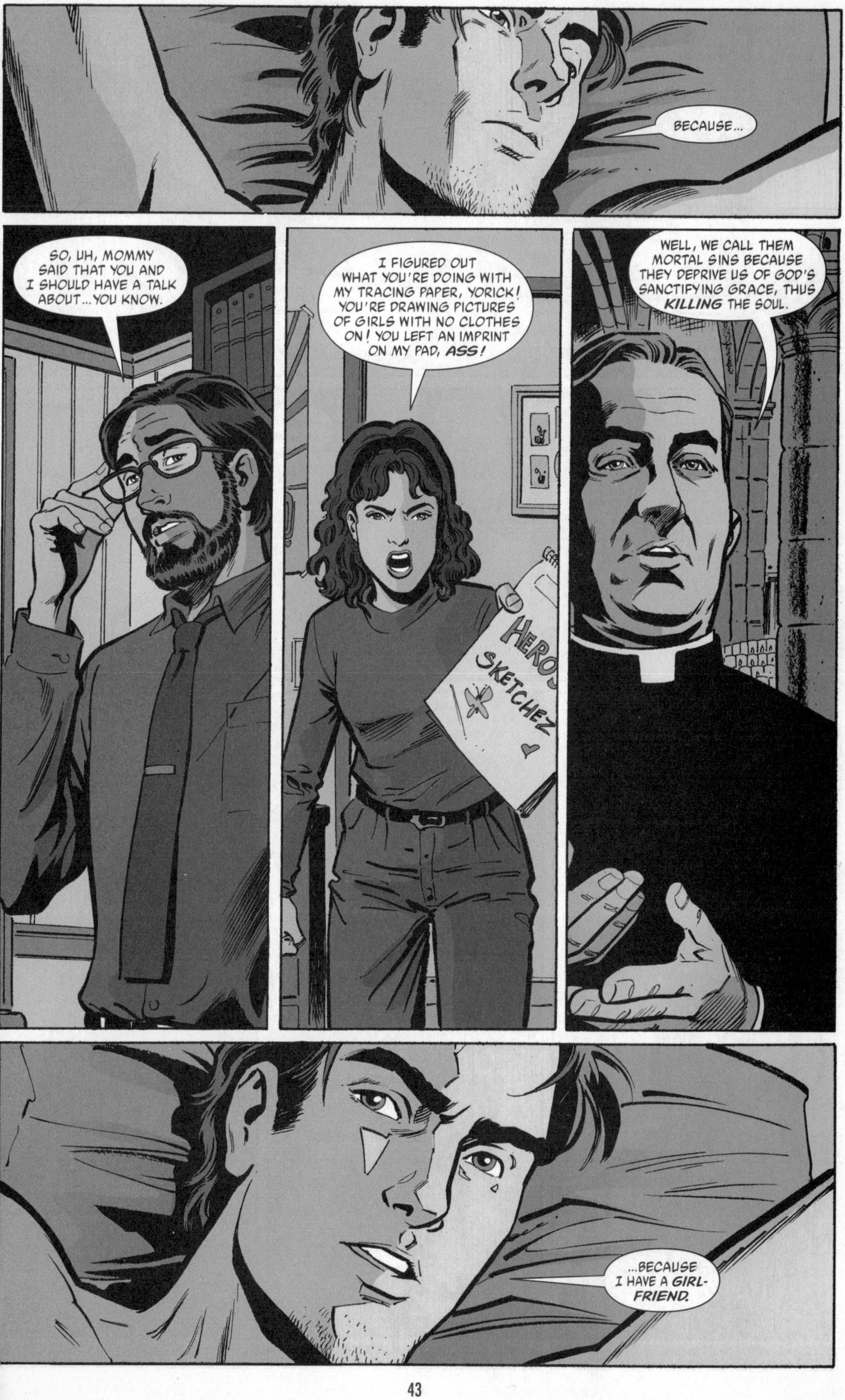
BECAUSE...
SO, UH, MOMMY SAID THAT YOU AND I SHOULD HAVE A TALK ABOUT...YOU KNOW.
I FIGURED OUT WHAT YOU'RE DOING WITH MY TRACING PAPER, YORICK! YOU'RE DRAWING PICTURES OF GIRLS WITH NO CLOTHES ON! YOU LEFT AN IMPRINT ON MY PAD, ASS!
HERO'S SKETCHEZ
WELL, WE CALL THEM MORTAL SINS BECAUSE THEY DEPRIVE US OF GOD'S SANCTIFYING GRACE, THUS KILLING THE SOUL.
...BECAUSE I HAVE A GIRL-FRIEND.

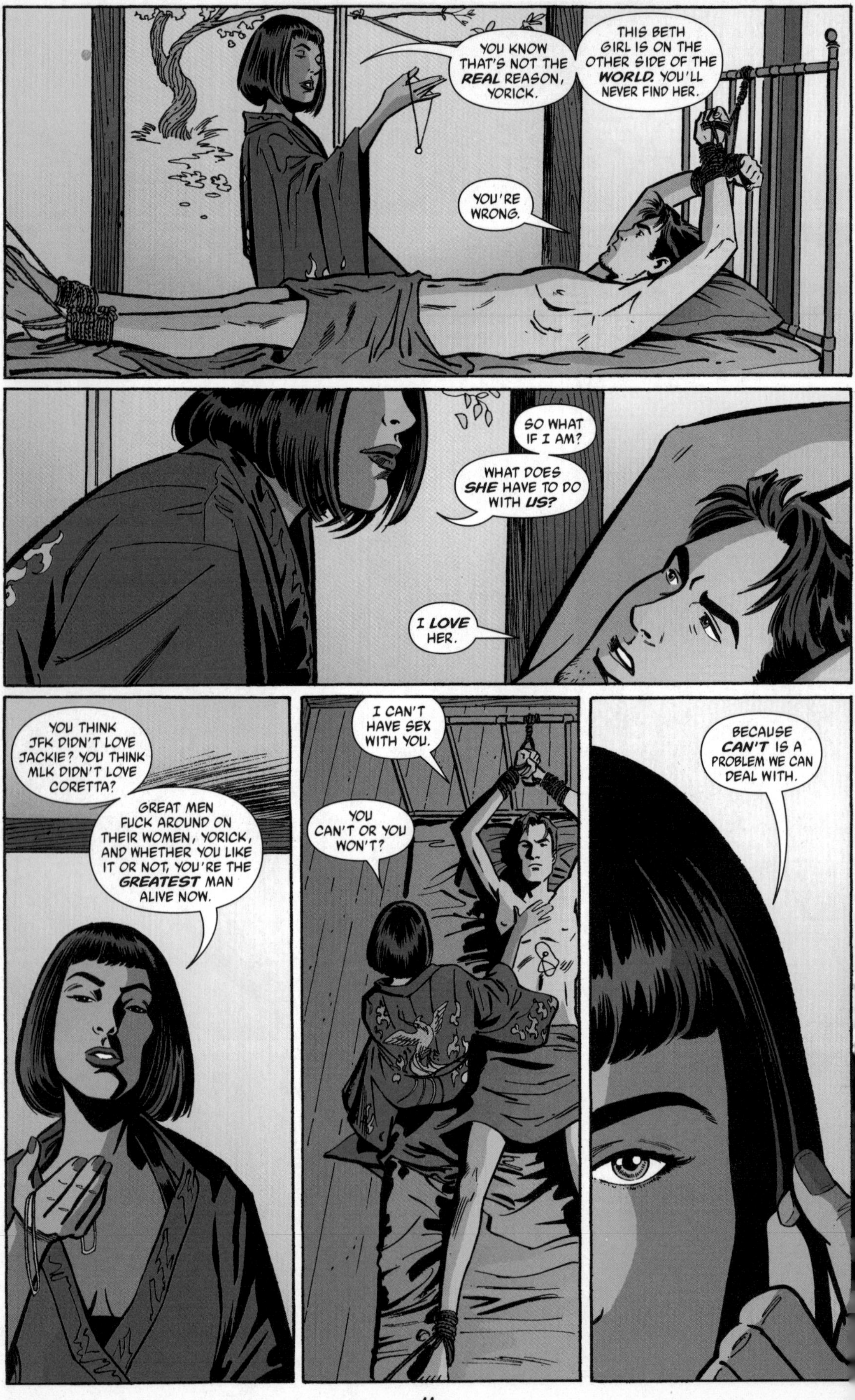

YOU KNOW THAT'S NOT THE REAL REASON, YORICK.
THIS BETH GIRL IS ON THE OTHER SIDE OF THE WORLD. YOU'LL NEVER FIND HER.
YOU'RE WRONG.
SO WHAT IF I AM?
WHAT DOES SHE HAVE TO DO WITH US?
I LOVE HER.
YOU THINK JFK DIDN'T LOVE JACKIE? YOU THINK MLK DIDN'T LOVE CORETTA?
GREAT MEN FUCK AROUND ON THEIR WOMEN, YORICK, AND WHETHER YOU LIKE IT OR NOT, YOU'RE THE GREATEST MAN ALIVE NOW.
I CAN'T HAVE SEX WITH YOU.
YOU CAN'T OR YOU WON'T?
BECAUSE CAN'T IS A PROBLEM WE CAN DEAL WITH.

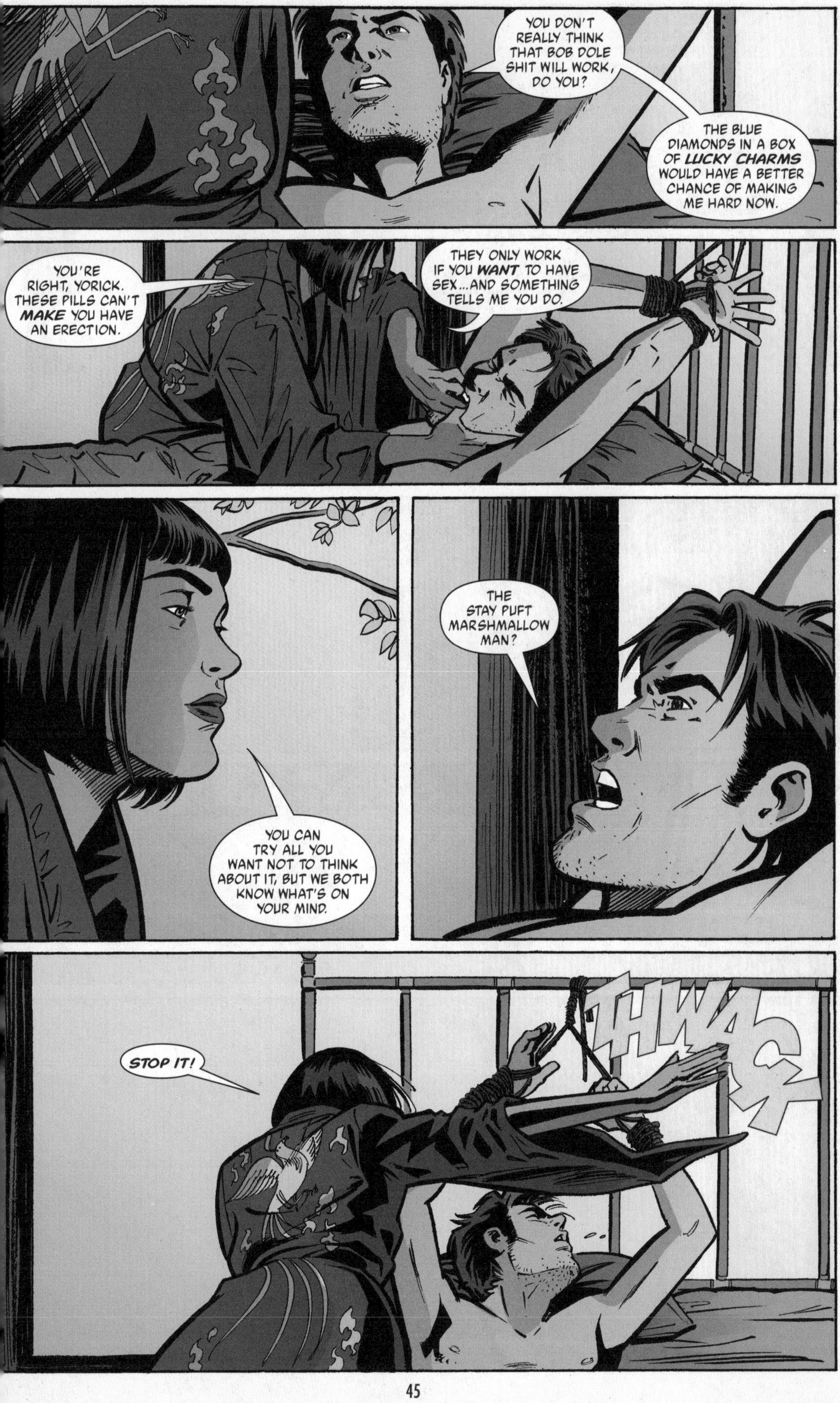
YOU DON'T REALLY THINK THAT BOB DOLE SHIT WILL WORK, DO YOU?
THE BLUE DIAMONDS IN A BOX OF LUCKY CHARMS WOULD HAVE A BETTER CHANCE OF MAKING ME HARD NOW.
YOU'RE RIGHT, YORICK. THESE PILLS CAN'T MAKE YOU HAVE AN ERECTION.
THEY ONLY WORK IF YOU WANT TO HAVE SEX...AND SOMETHING TELLS ME YOU DO.
YOU CAN TRY ALL YOU WANT NOT TO THINK ABOUT IT, BUT WE BOTH KNOW WHAT'S ON YOUR MIND.
THE STAY PUFT MARSHMALLOW MAN?
STOP IT!
THWACK

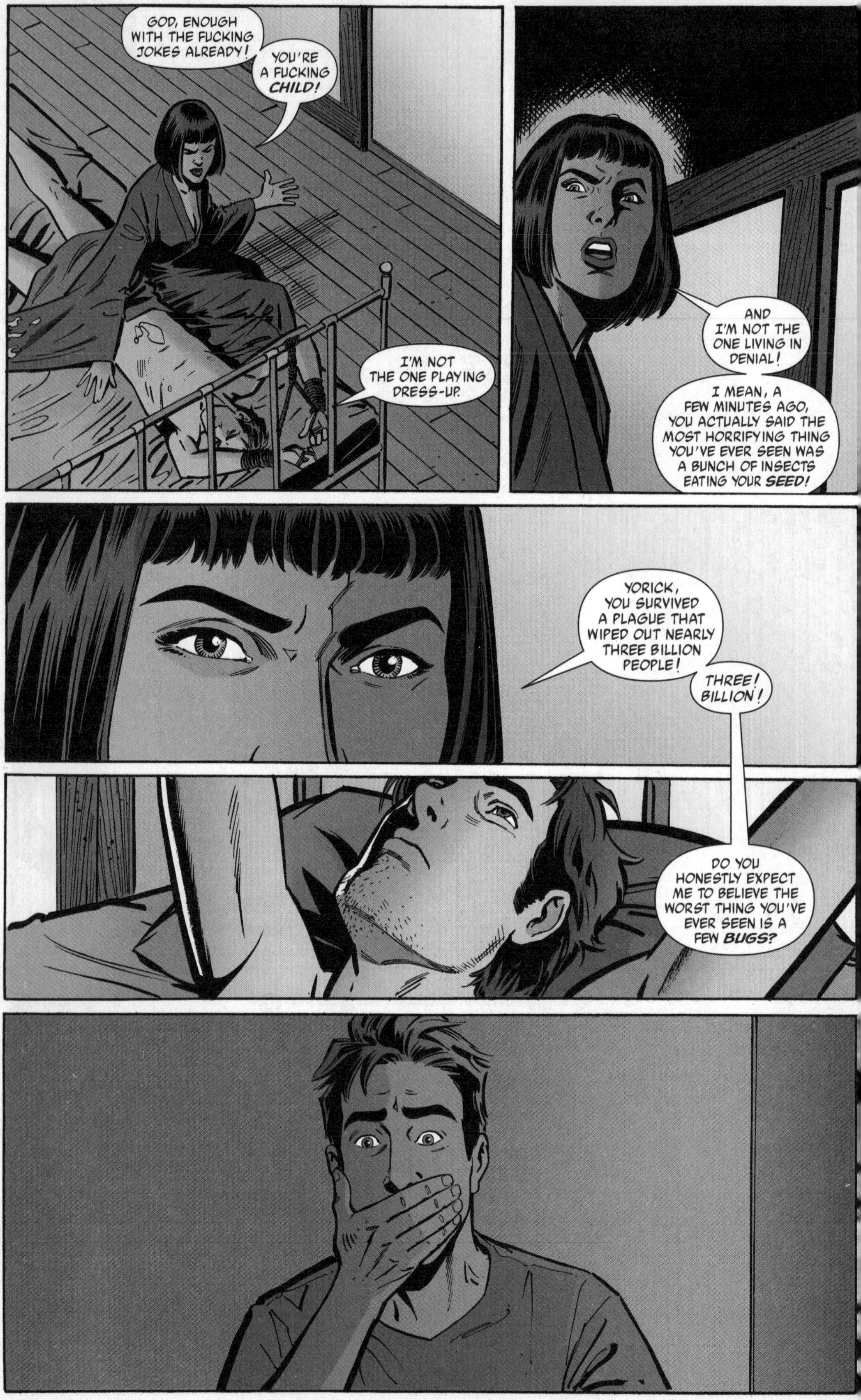
GOD, ENOUGH WITH THE FUCKING JOKES ALREADY!
YOU'RE A FUCKING CHILD!
I'M NOT THE ONE PLAYING DRESS-UP.
AND I'M NOT THE ONE LIVING IN DENIAL!
I MEAN, A FEW MINUTES AGO, YOU ACTUALLY SAID THE MOST HORRIFYING THING YOU'VE EVER SEEN WAS A BUNCH OF INSECTS EATING YOUR SEED!
YORICK, YOU SURVIVED A PLAGUE THAT WIPED OUT NEARLY THREE BILLION PEOPLE!
THREE! BILLION!
DO YOU HONESTLY EXPECT ME TO BELIEVE THE WORST THING YOU'VE EVER SEEN IS A FEW BUGS?

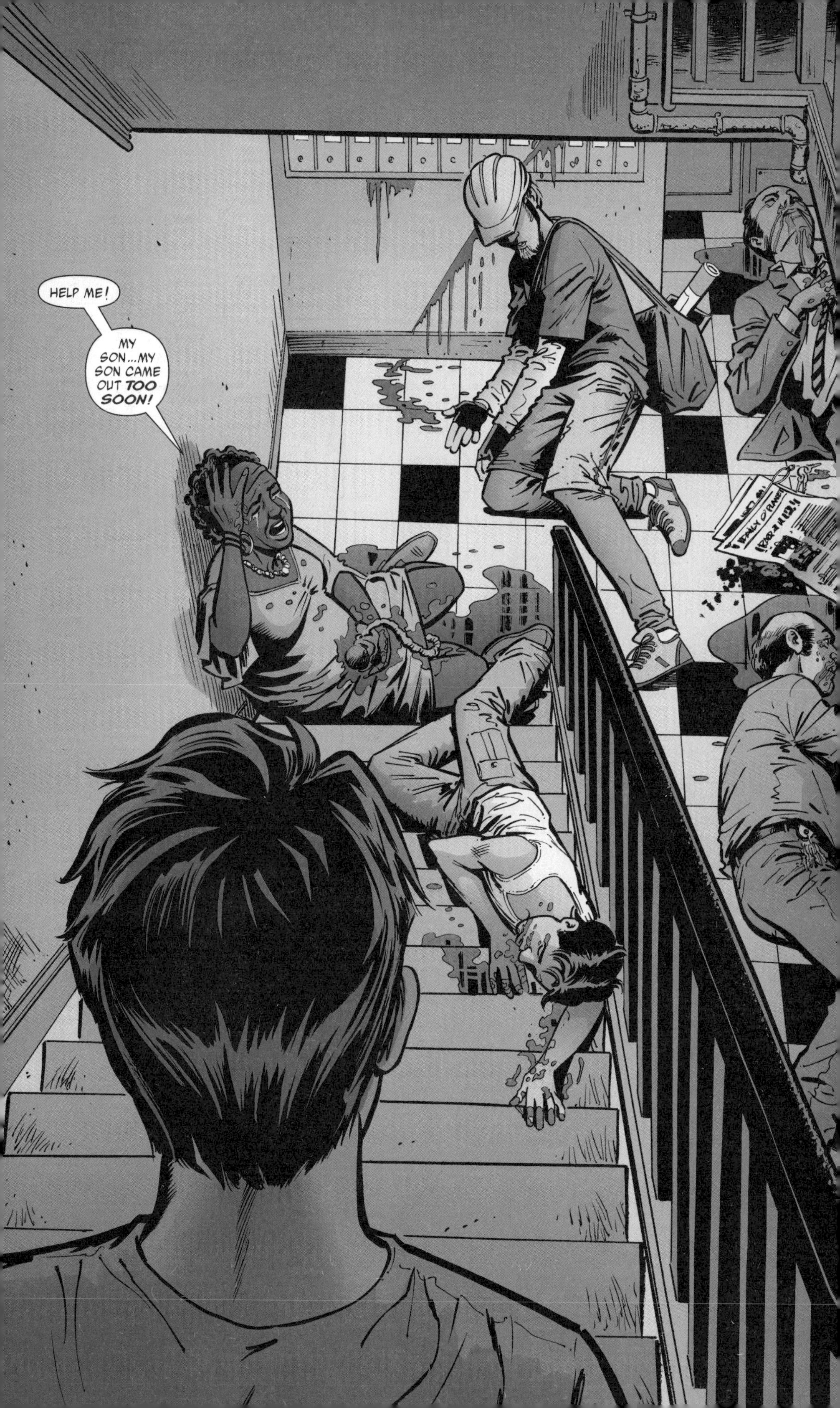
HELP ME!
MY SON...MY SON CAME OUT TOO SOON!

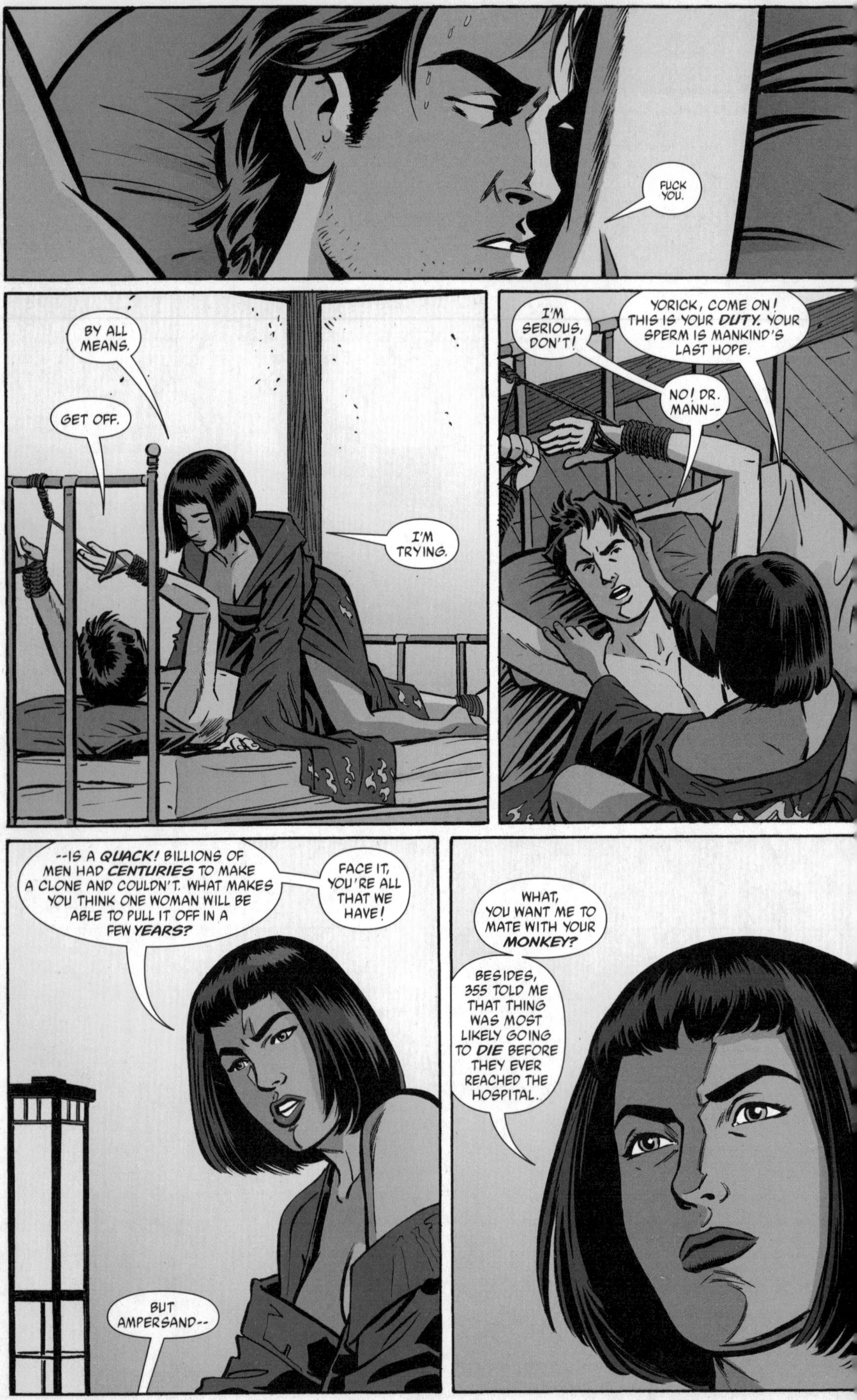
FUCK YOU.
BY ALL MEANS.
GET OFF.
I'M TRYING.
I'M SERIOUS, DON'T!
YORICK, COME ON! THIS IS YOUR DUTY. YOUR SPERM IS MANKIND'S LAST HOPE.
NO! DR. MANN--
--IS A QUACK! BILLIONS OF MEN HAD CENTURIES TO MAKE A CLONE AND COULDN'T. WHAT MAKES YOU THINK ONE WOMAN WILL BE ABLE TO PULL IT OFF IN A FEW YEARS?
FACE IT, YOU'RE ALL THAT WE HAVE!
BUT AMPERSAND--
WHAT, YOU WANT ME TO MATE WITH YOUR MONKEY?
BESIDES, 355 TOLD ME THAT THING WAS MOST LIKELY GOING TO DIE BEFORE THEY EVER REACHED THE HOSPITAL.

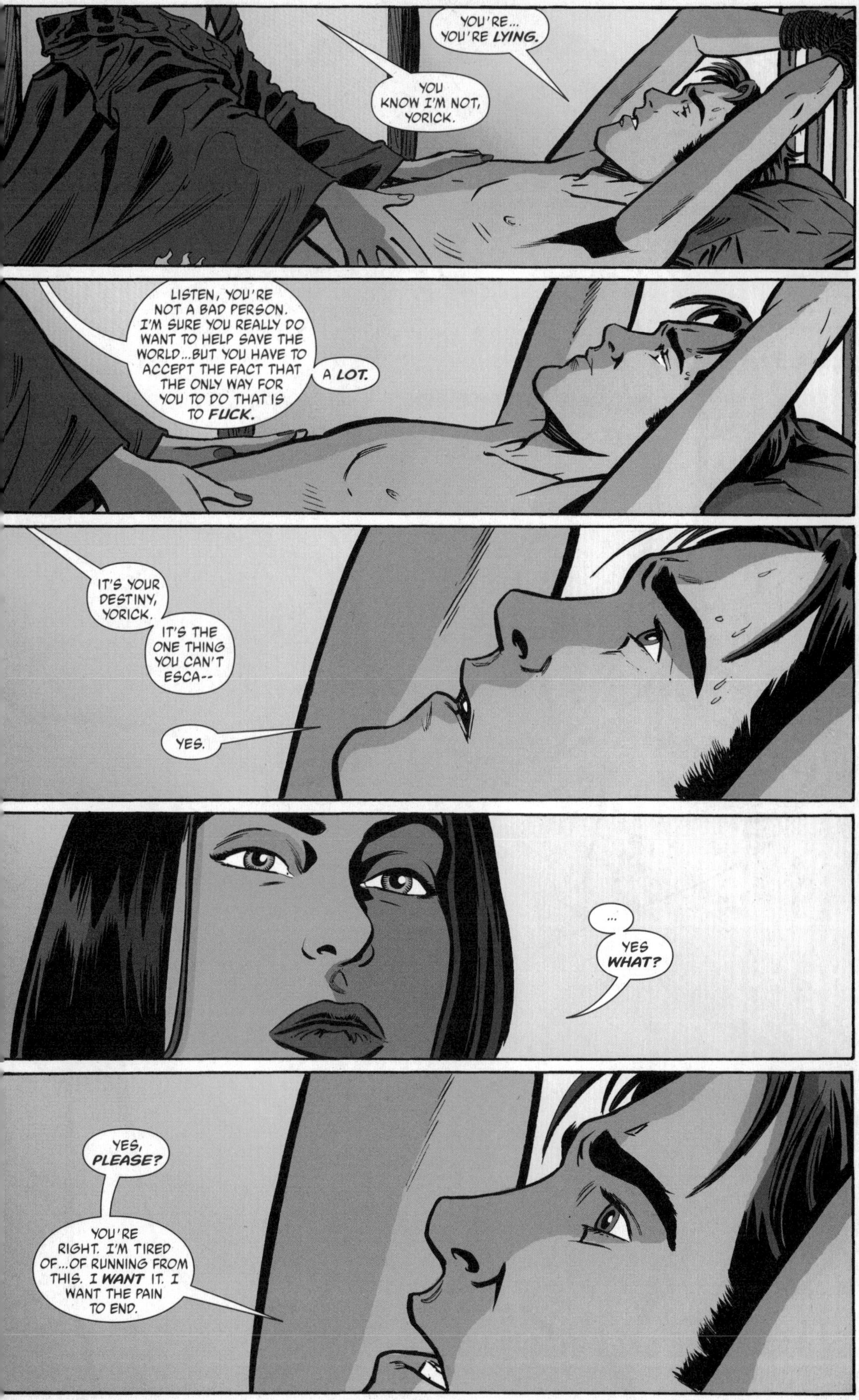
YOU'RE...
YOU'RE LYING.
YOU KNOW I'M NOT, YORICK.
LISTEN, YOU'RE NOT A BAD PERSON. I'M SURE YOU REALLY DO WANT TO HELP SAVE THE WORLD...BUT YOU HAVE TO ACCEPT THE FACT THAT THE ONLY WAY FOR YOU TO DO THAT IS TO FUCK.
A LOT.
IT'S YOUR DESTINY, YORICK.
IT'S THE ONE THING YOU CAN'T ESCA--
YES.
...
YES WHAT?
YES, PLEASE?
YOU'RE RIGHT. I'M TIRED OF...OF RUNNING FROM THIS. I WANT IT. I WANT THE PAIN TO END.

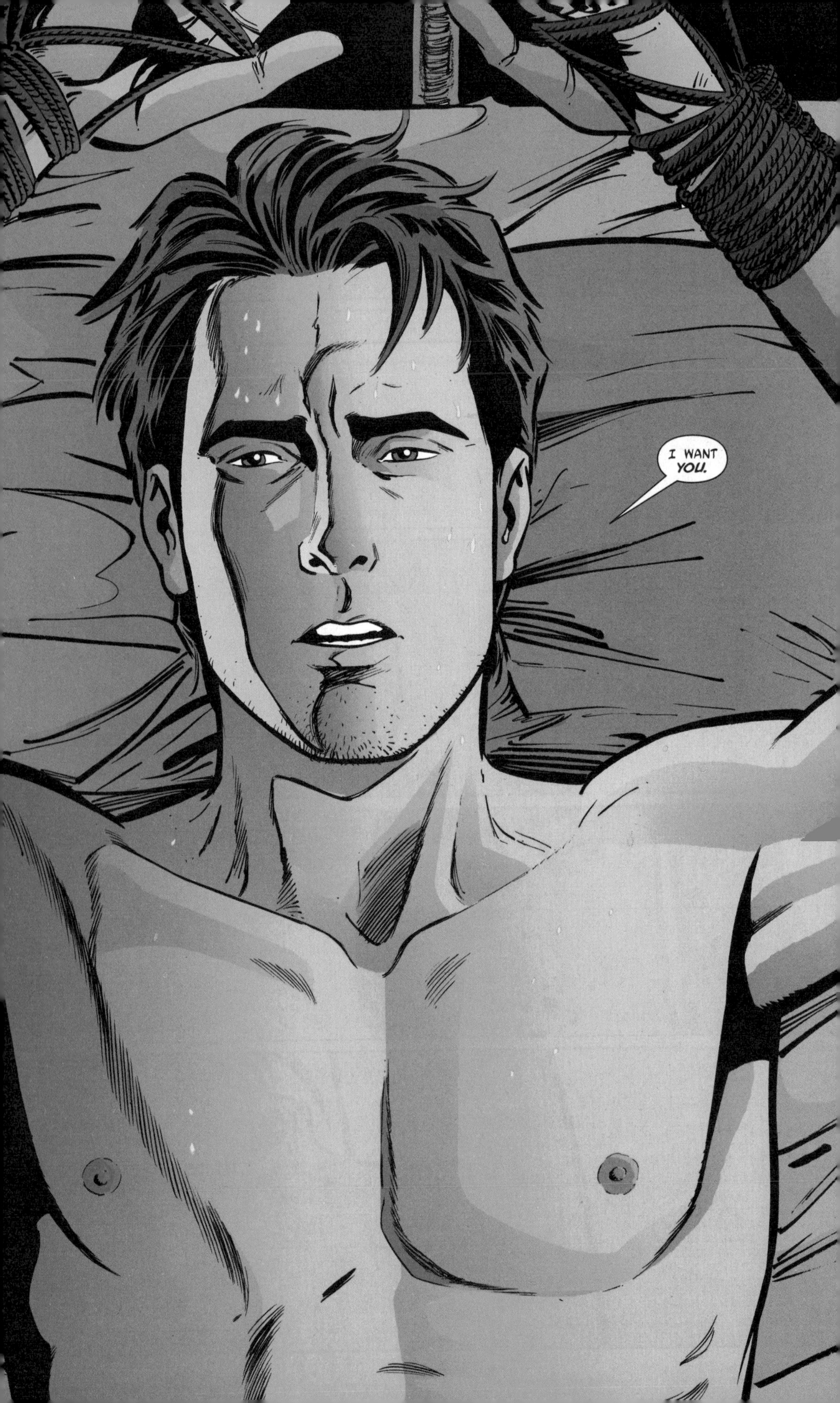
I WANT YOU.

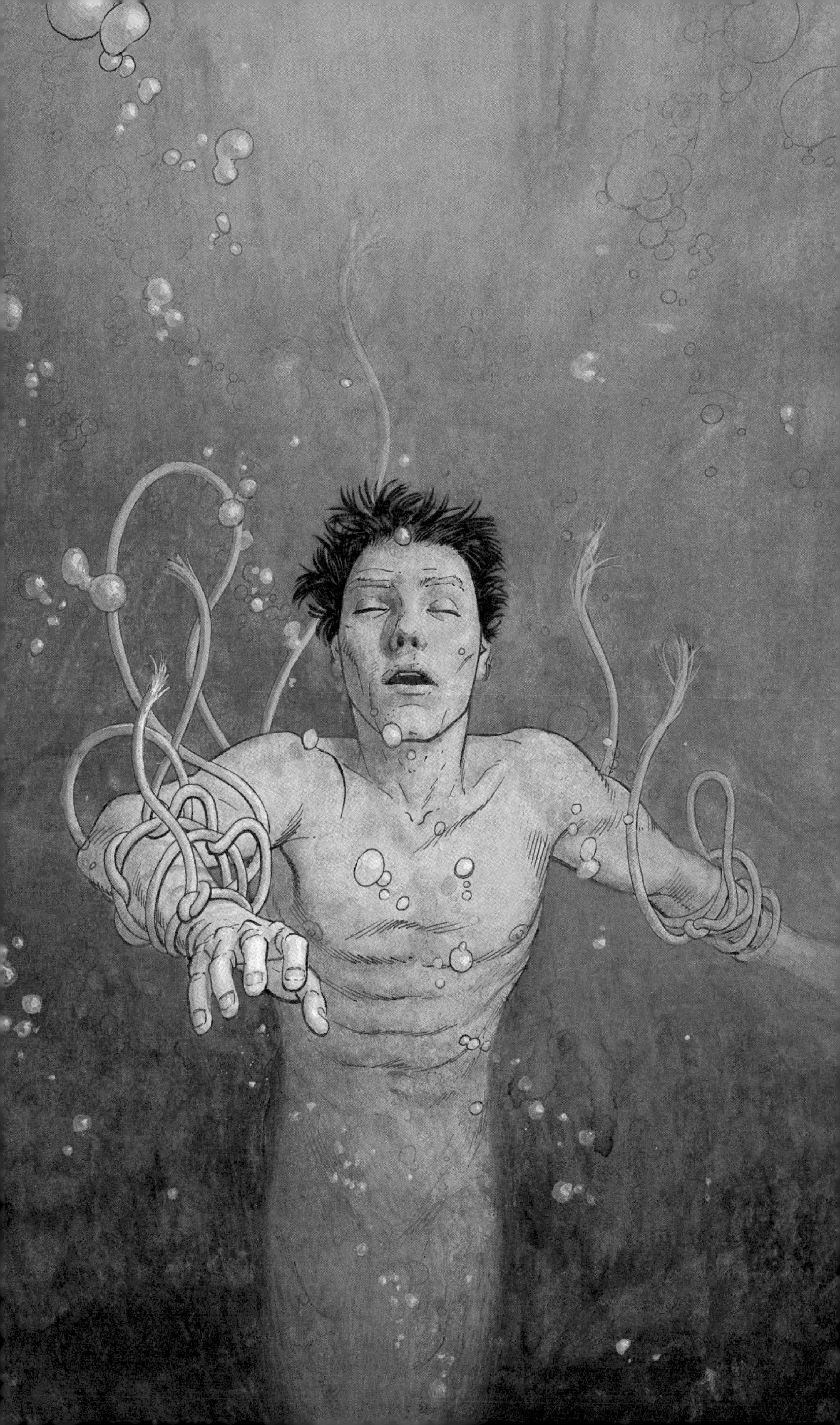

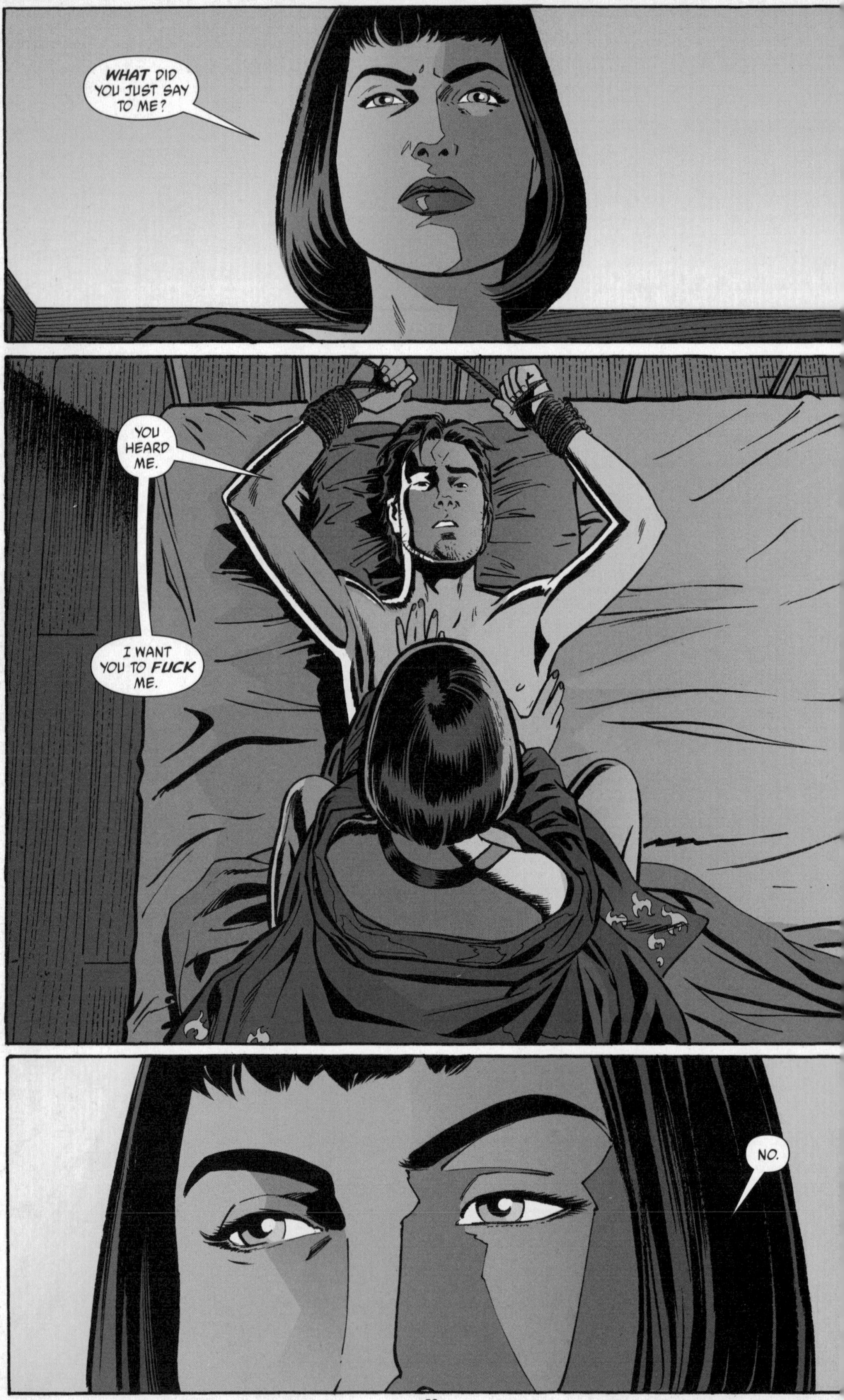
WHAT DID YOU JUST SAY TO ME?
YOU HEARD ME.
I WANT YOU TO FUCK ME.
NO.

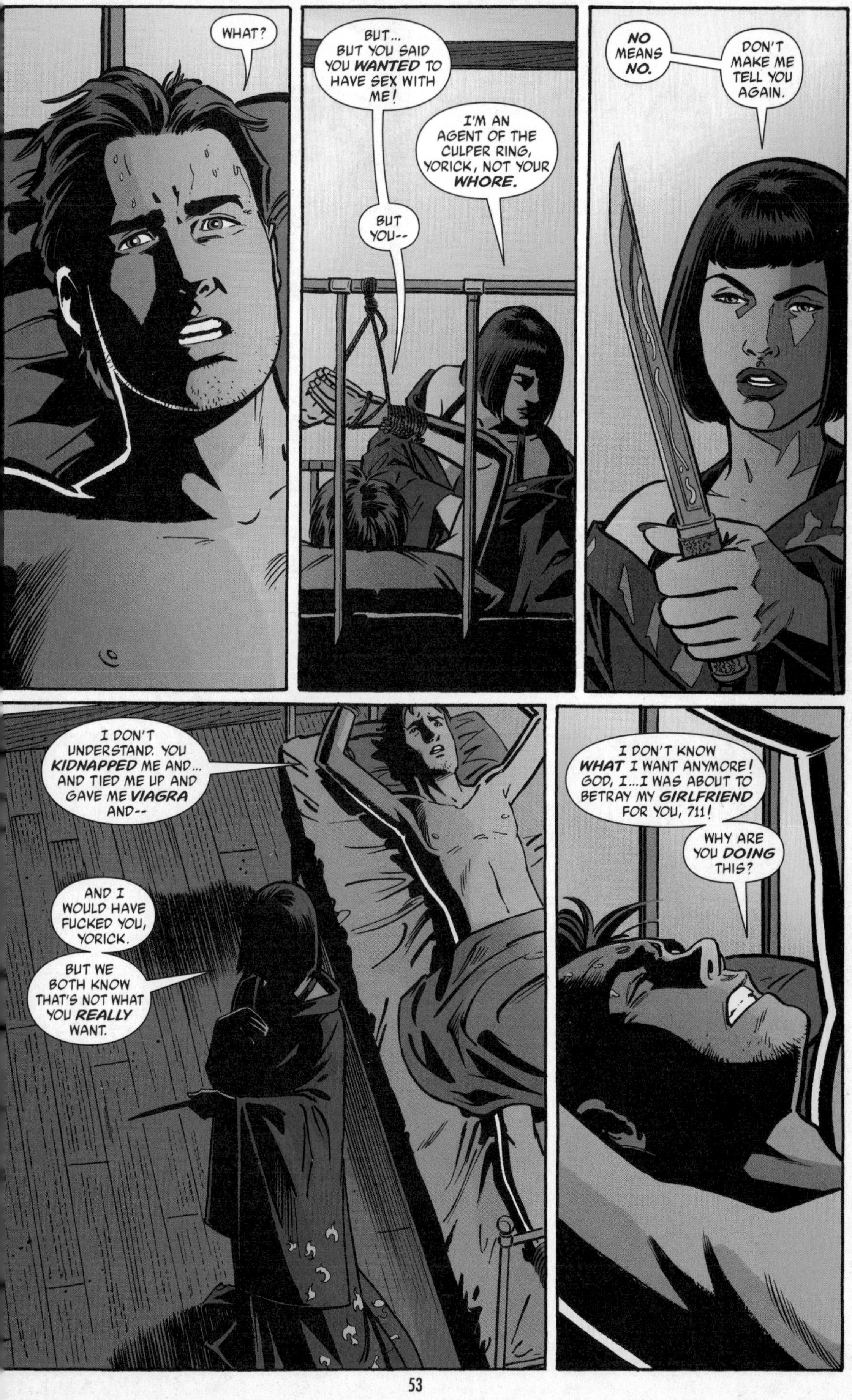
WHAT?
BUT... BUT YOU SAID YOU WANTED TO HAVE SEX WITH ME!
I'M AN AGENT OF THE CULPER RING, YORICK, NOT YOUR WHORE.
BUT YOU--
NO MEANS NO.
DON'T MAKE ME TELL YOU AGAIN.
I DON'T UNDERSTAND. YOU KIDNAPPED ME AND... AND TIED ME UP AND GAVE ME VIAGRA AND--
AND I WOULD HAVE FUCKED YOU, YORICK.
BUT WE BOTH KNOW THAT'S NOT WHAT YOU REALLY WANT.
I DON'T KNOW WHAT I WANT ANYMORE! GOD, I...I WAS ABOUT TO BETRAY MY GIRLFRIEND FOR YOU, 711!
WHY ARE YOU DOING THIS?

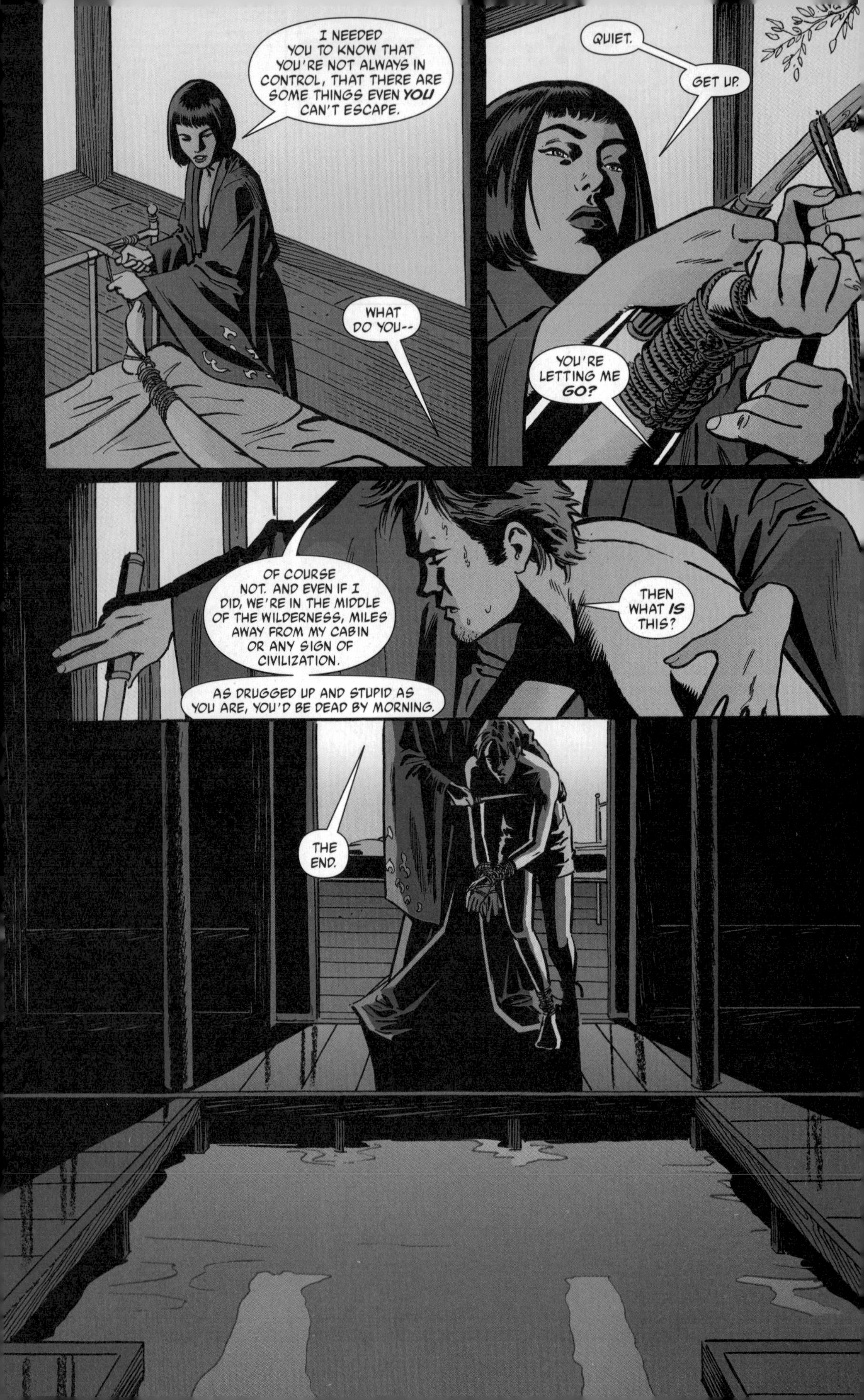
I NEEDED YOU TO KNOW THAT YOU'RE NOT ALWAYS IN CONTROL, THAT THERE ARE SOME THINGS EVEN ***YOU*** CAN'T ESCAPE.
WHAT DO YOU--
QUIET.
GET UP.
YOU'RE LETTING ME ***GO?***
OF COURSE NOT. AND EVEN IF I DID, WE'RE IN THE MIDDLE OF THE WILDERNESS, MILES AWAY FROM MY CABIN OR ANY SIGN OF CIVILIZATION.
AS DRUGGED UP AND STUPID AS YOU ARE, YOU'D BE DEAD BY MORNING.
THEN WHAT ***IS*** THIS?
THE END.

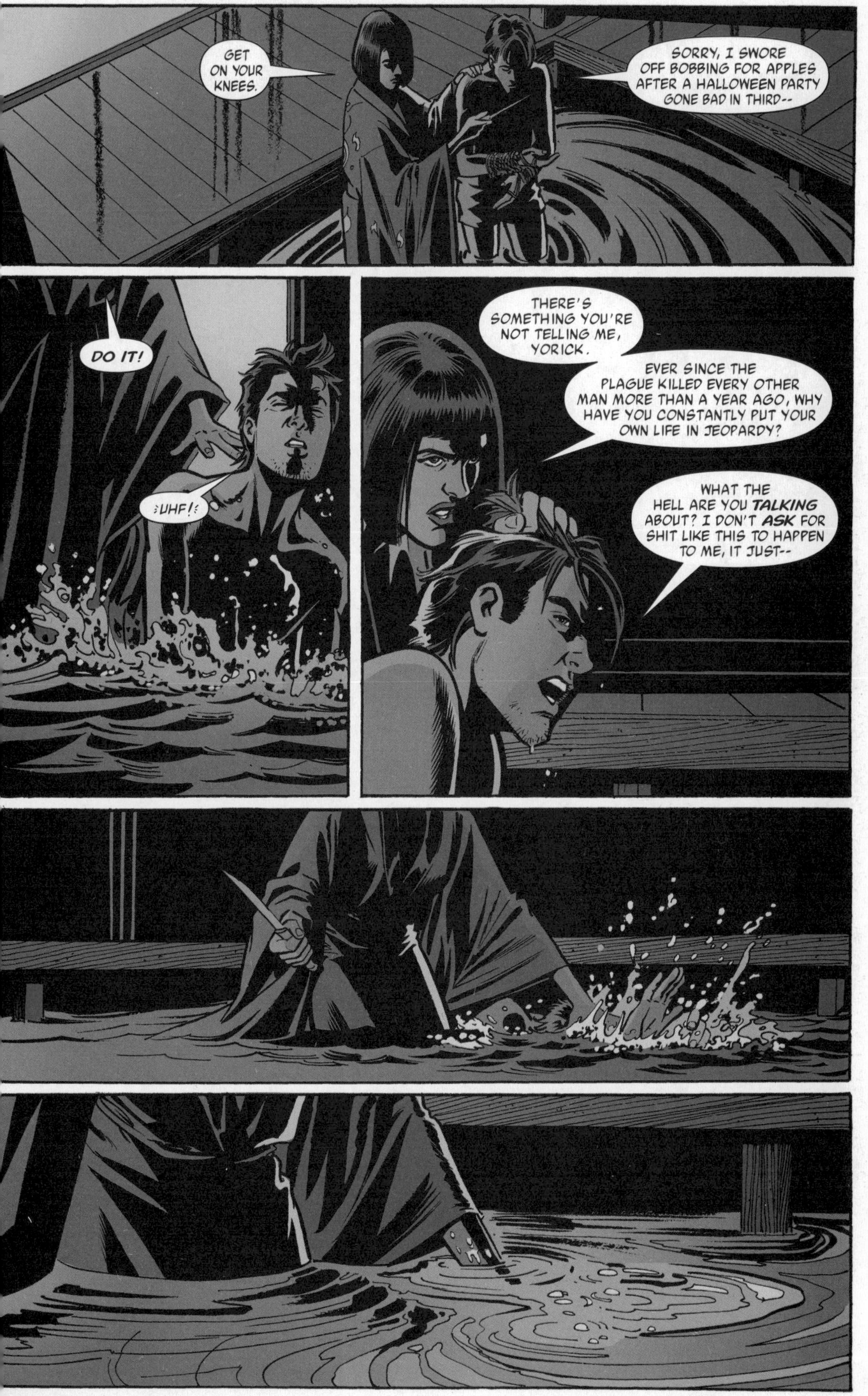
GET ON YOUR KNEES.
SORRY, I SWORE OFF BOBBING FOR APPLES AFTER A HALLOWEEN PARTY GONE BAD IN THIRD--
DO IT!
UHF!
THERE'S SOMETHING YOU'RE NOT TELLING ME, YORICK.
EVER SINCE THE PLAGUE KILLED EVERY OTHER MAN MORE THAN A YEAR AGO, WHY HAVE YOU CONSTANTLY PUT YOUR OWN LIFE IN JEOPARDY?
WHAT THE HELL ARE YOU TALKING ABOUT? I DON'T ASK FOR SHIT LIKE THIS TO HAPPEN TO ME, IT JUST--

HWUUUHHHH

KOFF KOFF KOFF

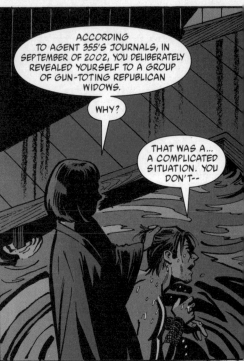

ACCORDING TO AGENT 355'S JOURNALS, IN SEPTEMBER OF 2002, YOU DELIBERATELY REVEALED YOURSELF TO A GROUP OF GUN-TOTING REPUBLICAN WIDOWS.

WHY?

THAT WAS A... A COMPLICATED SITUATION. YOU DON'T--

GWUH!

STOP IT!

A FEW DAYS LATER, YOU CONFRONTED A PACK OF AMAZONS, SAYING SOMETHING TO THE EFFECT OF, "IF THIS IS YOUR WORLD, I WANT OUT. JUST GO AHEAD AND KILL ME ALREADY."

THAT'S... THAT'S TAKEN OUT OF CONTEXT.

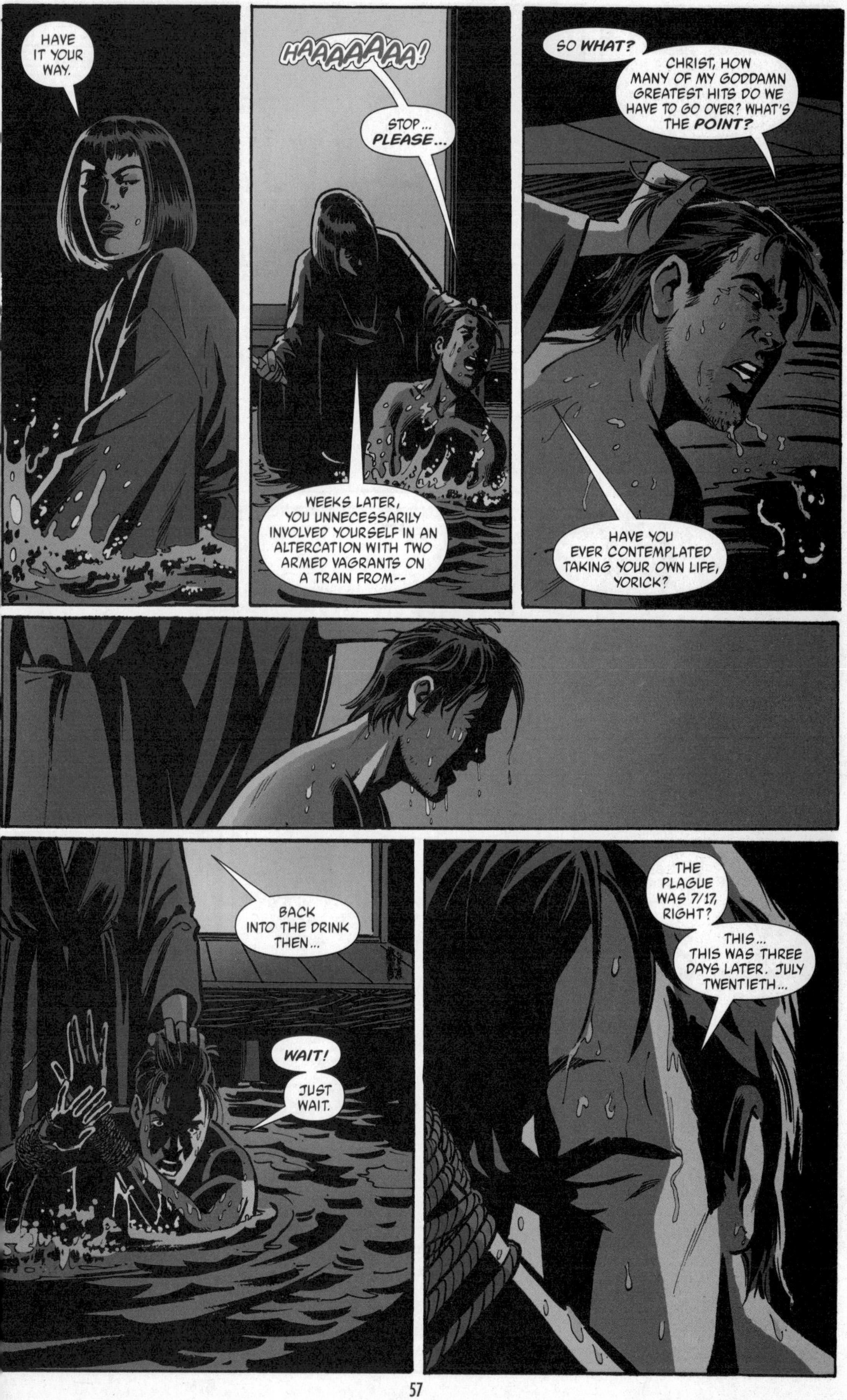
HAVE IT YOUR WAY.
HAAAAAAA!
STOP ... PLEASE...
WEEKS LATER, YOU UNNECESSARILY INVOLVED YOURSELF IN AN ALTERCATION WITH TWO ARMED VAGRANTS ON A TRAIN FROM--
SO WHAT?
CHRIST, HOW MANY OF MY GODDAMN GREATEST HITS DO WE HAVE TO GO OVER? WHAT'S THE POINT?
HAVE YOU EVER CONTEMPLATED TAKING YOUR OWN LIFE, YORICK?
BACK INTO THE DRINK THEN...
WAIT!
JUST WAIT.
THE PLAGUE WAS 7/17, RIGHT?
THIS... THIS WAS THREE DAYS LATER. JULY TWENTIETH...

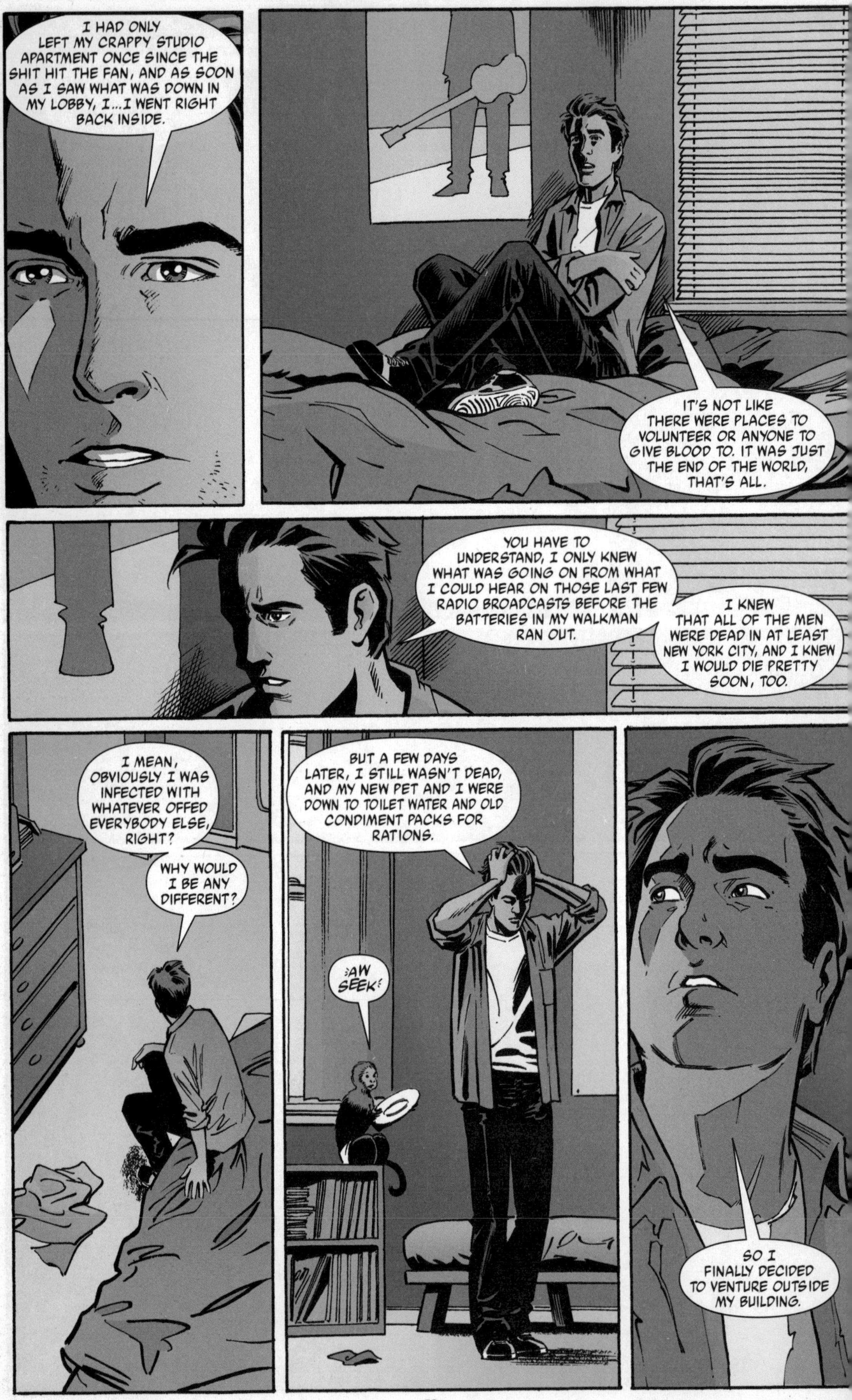
I HAD ONLY LEFT MY CRAPPY STUDIO APARTMENT ONCE SINCE THE SHIT HIT THE FAN, AND AS SOON AS I SAW WHAT WAS DOWN IN MY LOBBY, I...I WENT RIGHT BACK INSIDE.
IT'S NOT LIKE THERE WERE PLACES TO VOLUNTEER OR ANYONE TO GIVE BLOOD TO. IT WAS JUST THE END OF THE WORLD, THAT'S ALL.
YOU HAVE TO UNDERSTAND, I ONLY KNEW WHAT WAS GOING ON FROM WHAT I COULD HEAR ON THOSE LAST FEW RADIO BROADCASTS BEFORE THE BATTERIES IN MY WALKMAN RAN OUT.
I KNEW THAT ALL OF THE MEN WERE DEAD IN AT LEAST NEW YORK CITY, AND I KNEW I WOULD DIE PRETTY SOON, TOO.
I MEAN, OBVIOUSLY I WAS INFECTED WITH WHATEVER OFFED EVERYBODY ELSE, RIGHT?
WHY WOULD I BE ANY DIFFERENT?
BUT A FEW DAYS LATER, I STILL WASN'T DEAD, AND MY NEW PET AND I WERE DOWN TO TOILET WATER AND OLD CONDIMENT PACKS FOR RATIONS.
AW SEEK
SO I FINALLY DECIDED TO VENTURE OUTSIDE MY BUILDING.

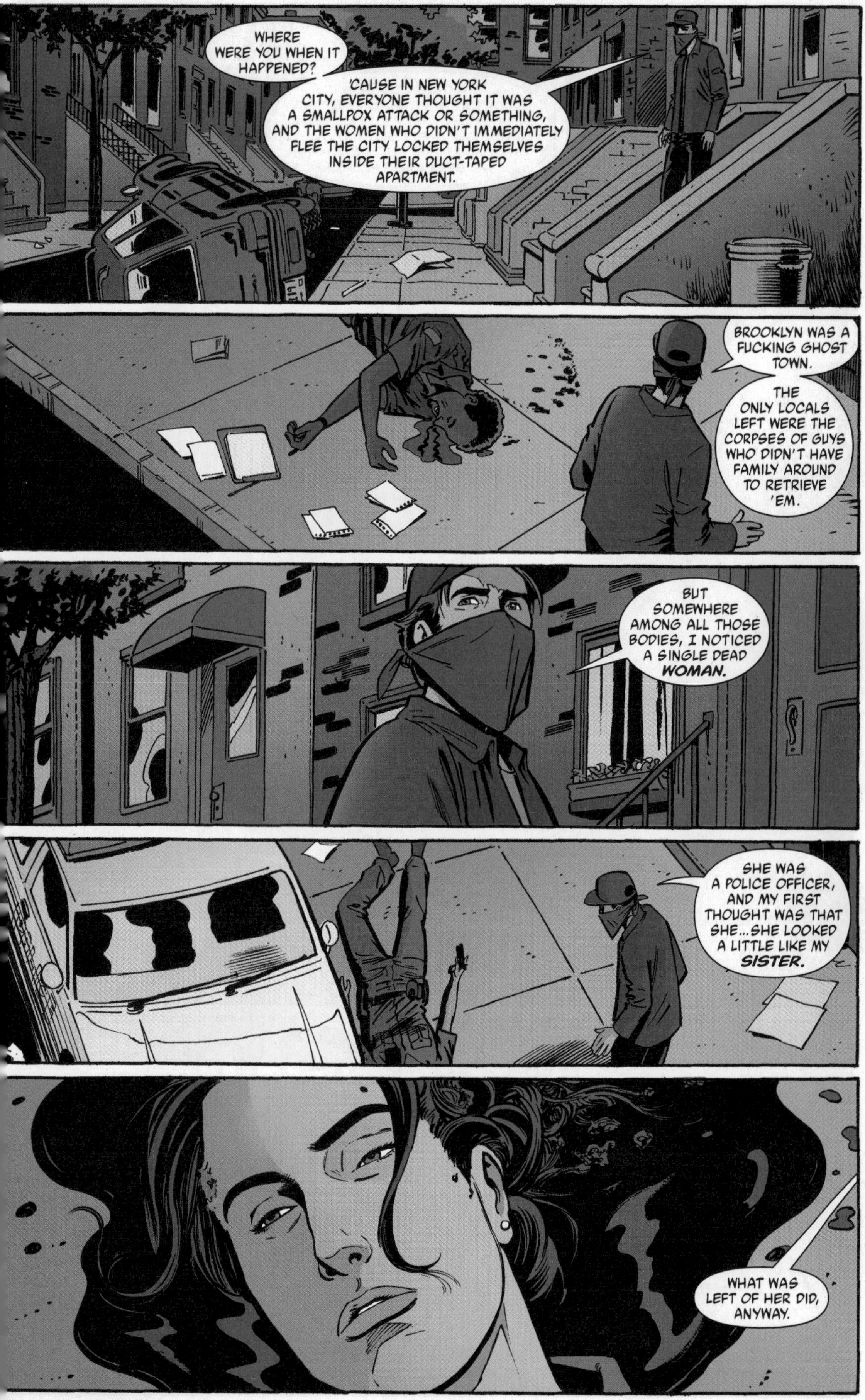
WHERE WERE YOU WHEN IT HAPPENED?
'CAUSE IN NEW YORK CITY, EVERYONE THOUGHT IT WAS A SMALLPOX ATTACK OR SOMETHING, AND THE WOMEN WHO DIDN'T IMMEDIATELY FLEE THE CITY LOCKED THEMSELVES INSIDE THEIR DUCT-TAPED APARTMENT.
BROOKLYN WAS A FUCKING GHOST TOWN.
THE ONLY LOCALS LEFT WERE THE CORPSES OF GUYS WHO DIDN'T HAVE FAMILY AROUND TO RETRIEVE 'EM.
BUT SOMEWHERE AMONG ALL THOSE BODIES, I NOTICED A SINGLE DEAD ***WOMAN.***
SHE WAS A POLICE OFFICER, AND MY FIRST THOUGHT WAS THAT SHE...SHE LOOKED A LITTLE LIKE MY ***SISTER.***
WHAT WAS LEFT OF HER DID, ANYWAY.

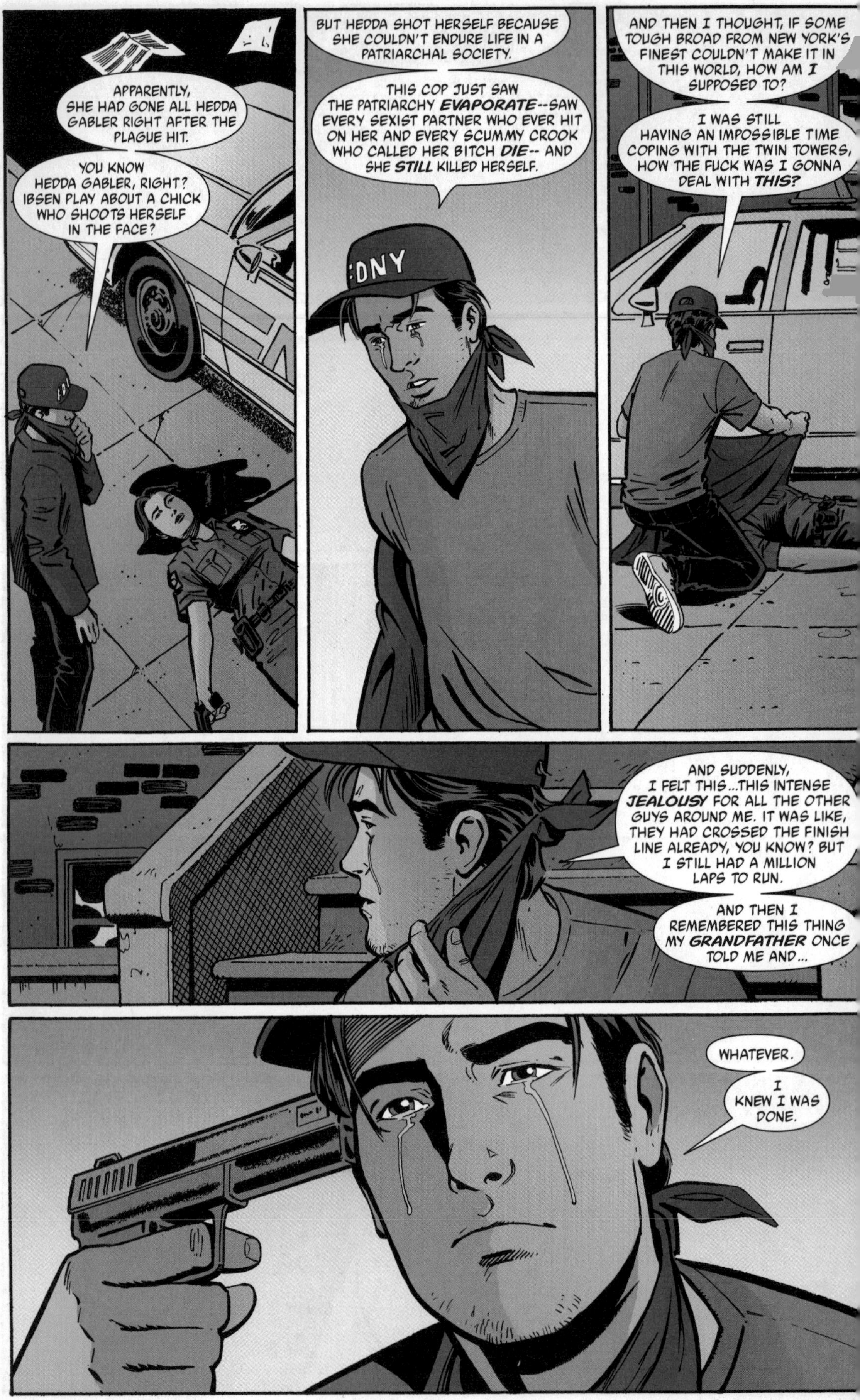

APPARENTLY, SHE HAD GONE ALL HEDDA GABLER RIGHT AFTER THE PLAGUE HIT.
YOU KNOW HEDDA GABLER, RIGHT? IBSEN PLAY ABOUT A CHICK WHO SHOOTS HERSELF IN THE FACE?
BUT HEDDA SHOT HERSELF BECAUSE SHE COULDN'T ENDURE LIFE IN A PATRIARCHAL SOCIETY.
THIS COP JUST SAW THE PATRIARCHY ***EVAPORATE***--SAW EVERY SEXIST PARTNER WHO EVER HIT ON HER AND EVERY SCUMMY CROOK WHO CALLED HER BITCH ***DIE***-- AND SHE ***STILL*** KILLED HERSELF.
FDNY
AND THEN I THOUGHT, IF SOME TOUGH BROAD FROM NEW YORK'S FINEST COULDN'T MAKE IT IN THIS WORLD, HOW AM ***I*** SUPPOSED TO?
I WAS STILL HAVING AN IMPOSSIBLE TIME COPING WITH THE TWIN TOWERS, HOW THE FUCK WAS I GONNA DEAL WITH ***THIS?***
AND SUDDENLY, I FELT THIS...THIS INTENSE ***JEALOUSY*** FOR ALL THE OTHER GUYS AROUND ME. IT WAS LIKE, THEY HAD CROSSED THE FINISH LINE ALREADY, YOU KNOW? BUT I STILL HAD A MILLION LAPS TO RUN.
AND THEN I REMEMBERED THIS THING MY ***GRANDFATHER*** ONCE TOLD ME AND...
WHATEVER.
I KNEW I WAS DONE.

BUT YOU WEREN'T DONE.

NOT UNLESS I'M IN HELL NOW.

YOU REALIZED THAT YOU WERE STRONGER THAN SOME PATHETIC LITTLE METER MAID.

I... I GUESS SO.

BULLSHIT!

AHN!

KRACK!

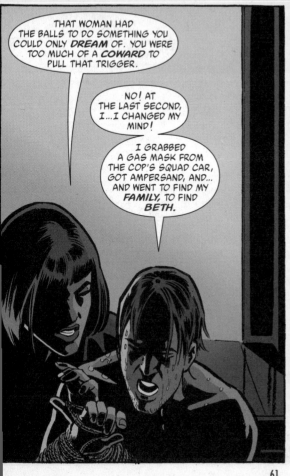

THAT WOMAN HAD THE BALLS TO DO SOMETHING YOU COULD ONLY *DREAM* OF. YOU WERE TOO MUCH OF A *COWARD* TO PULL THAT TRIGGER.

NO! AT THE LAST SECOND, I...I CHANGED MY MIND!

I GRABBED A GAS MASK FROM THE COP'S SQUAD CAR, GOT AMPERSAND, AND... AND WENT TO FIND MY *FAMILY*, TO FIND *BETH*.

IS THAT WHY YOU LEFT?

OR DEEP DOWN, DID YOU KNOW THAT IF YOU THREW YOURSELF INTO ENOUGH DANGEROUS SITUATIONS, SOONER OR LATER...

SOMEONE WOULD PUT A HOLE IN YOUR HEAD *FOR* YOU?

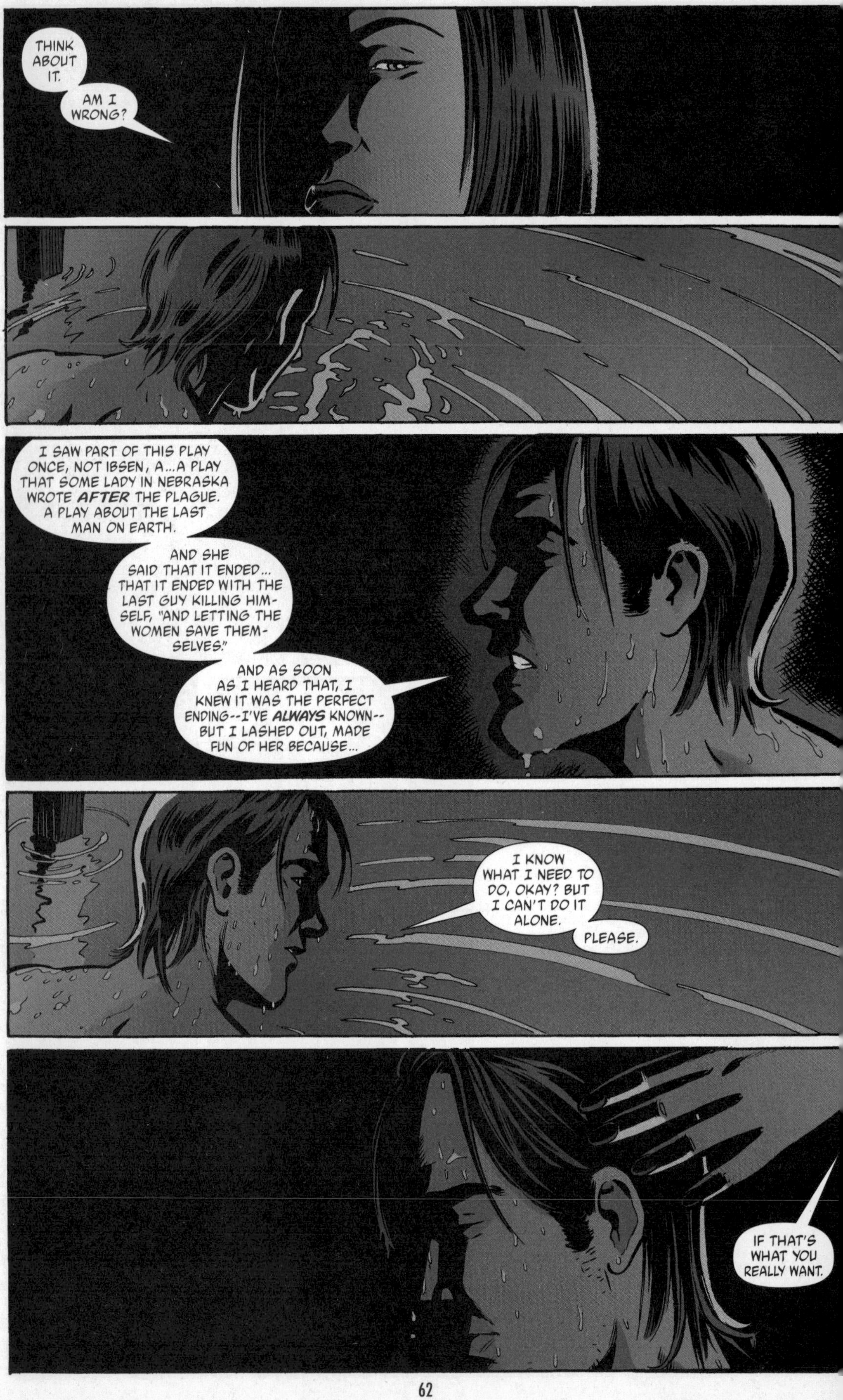
THINK ABOUT IT.
AM I WRONG?
I SAW PART OF THIS PLAY ONCE, NOT IBSEN, A...A PLAY THAT SOME LADY IN NEBRASKA WROTE AFTER THE PLAGUE. A PLAY ABOUT THE LAST MAN ON EARTH.
AND SHE SAID THAT IT ENDED... THAT IT ENDED WITH THE LAST GUY KILLING HIM-SELF, "AND LETTING THE WOMEN SAVE THEM-SELVES."
AND AS SOON AS I HEARD THAT, I KNEW IT WAS THE PERFECT ENDING--I'VE ALWAYS KNOWN--BUT I LASHED OUT, MADE FUN OF HER BECAUSE...
I KNOW WHAT I NEED TO DO, OKAY? BUT I CAN'T DO IT ALONE.
PLEASE.
IF THAT'S WHAT YOU REALLY WANT.

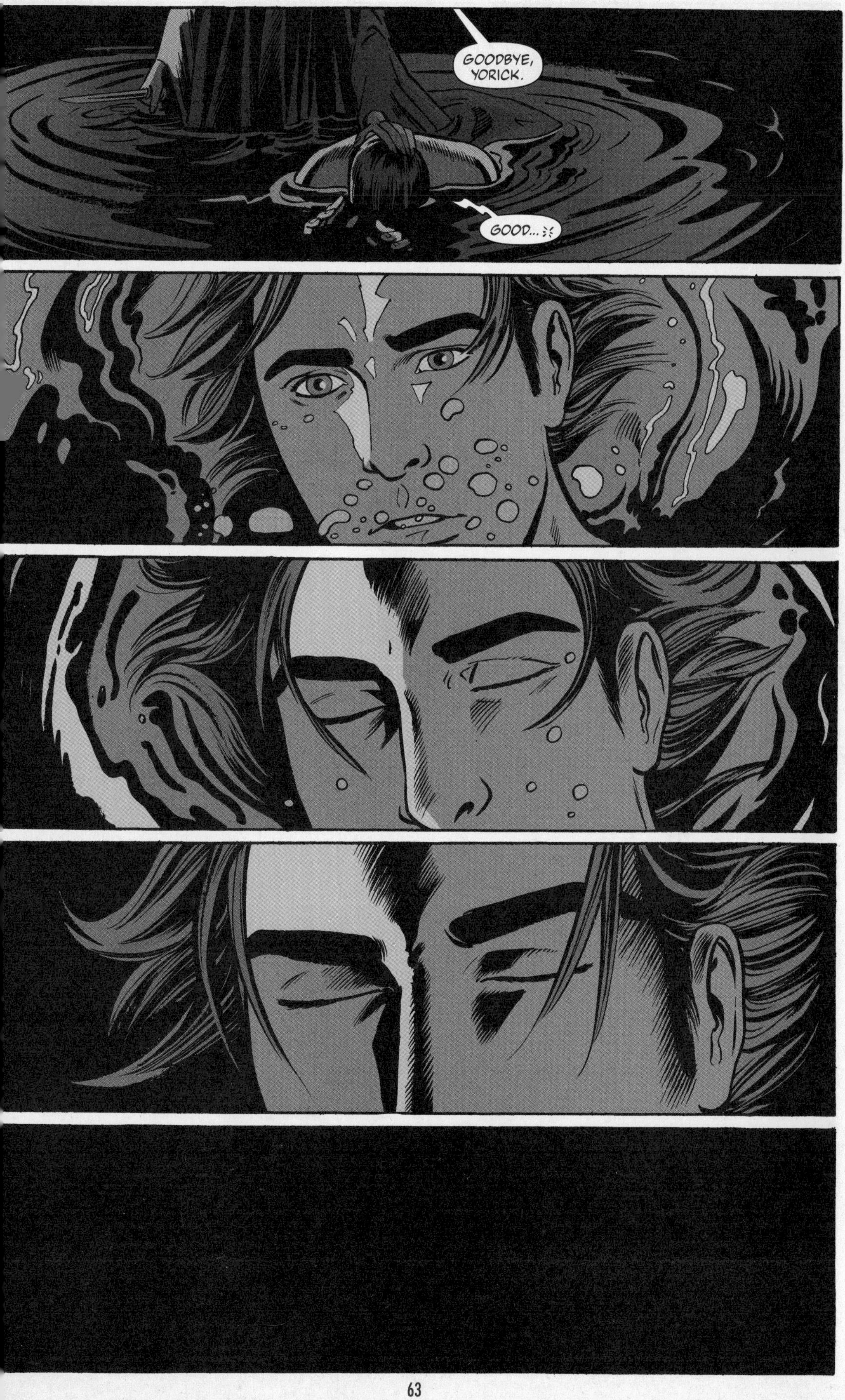
GOODBYE, YORICK.
GOOD...

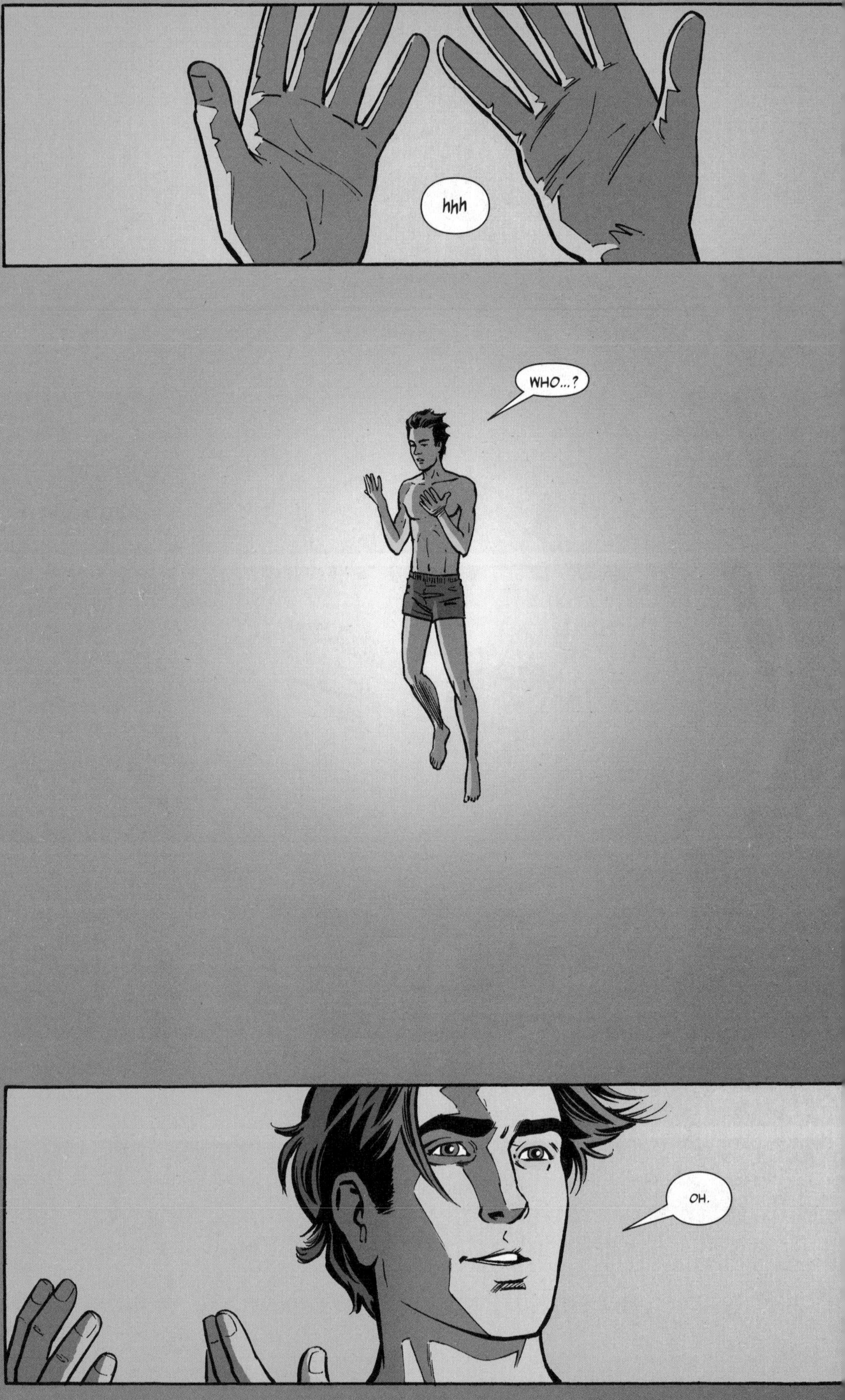
hhh
WHO...?
OH.

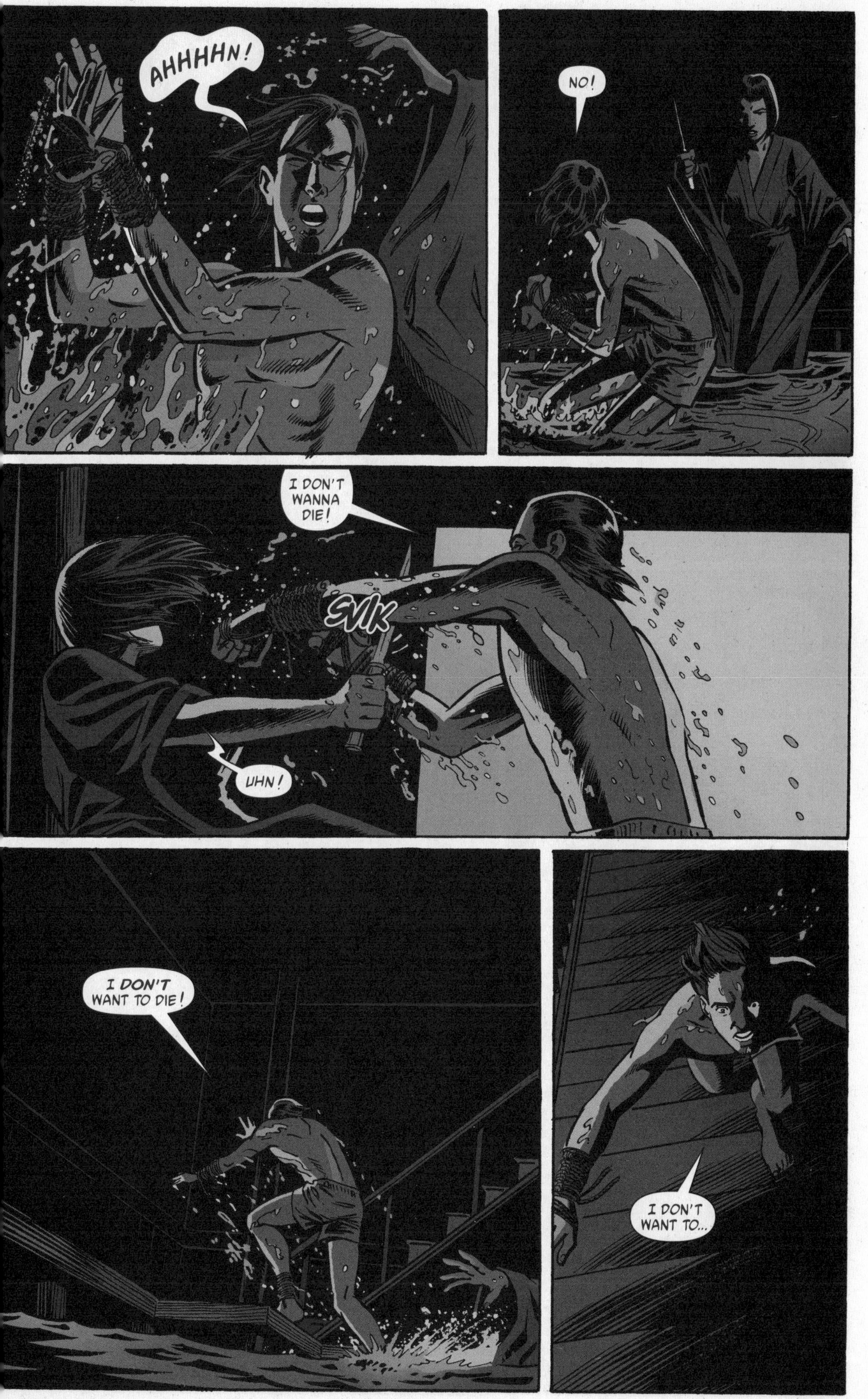
AHHHHN!
NO!
I DON'T WANNA DIE!
SVIK
UHN!
I DON'T WANT TO DIE!
I DON'T WANT TO...

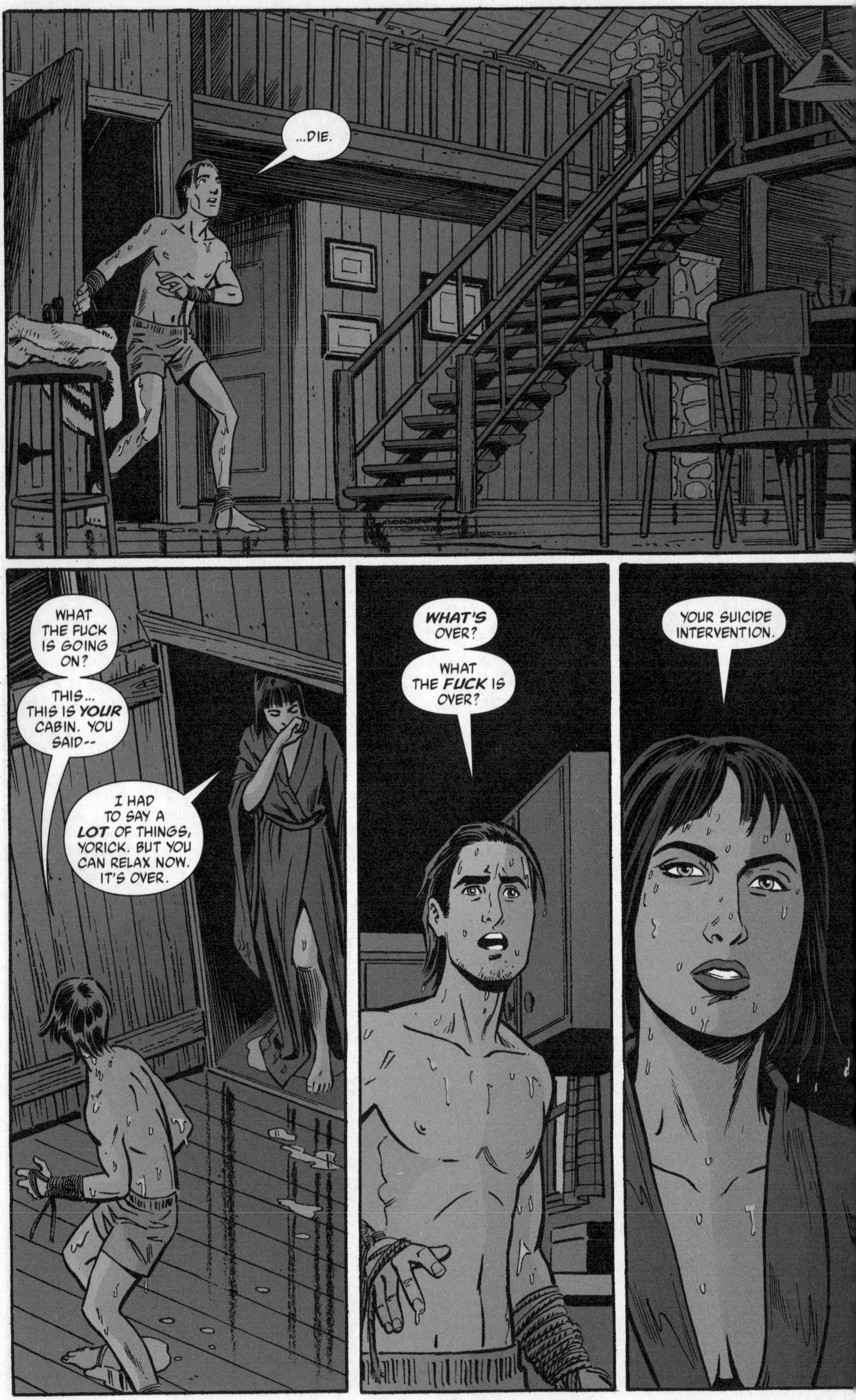
...DIE.
WHAT THE FUCK IS GOING ON?
THIS... THIS IS YOUR CABIN. YOU SAID--
I HAD TO SAY A LOT OF THINGS, YORICK. BUT YOU CAN RELAX NOW. IT'S OVER.
WHAT'S OVER?
WHAT THE FUCK IS OVER?
YOUR SUICIDE INTERVENTION.

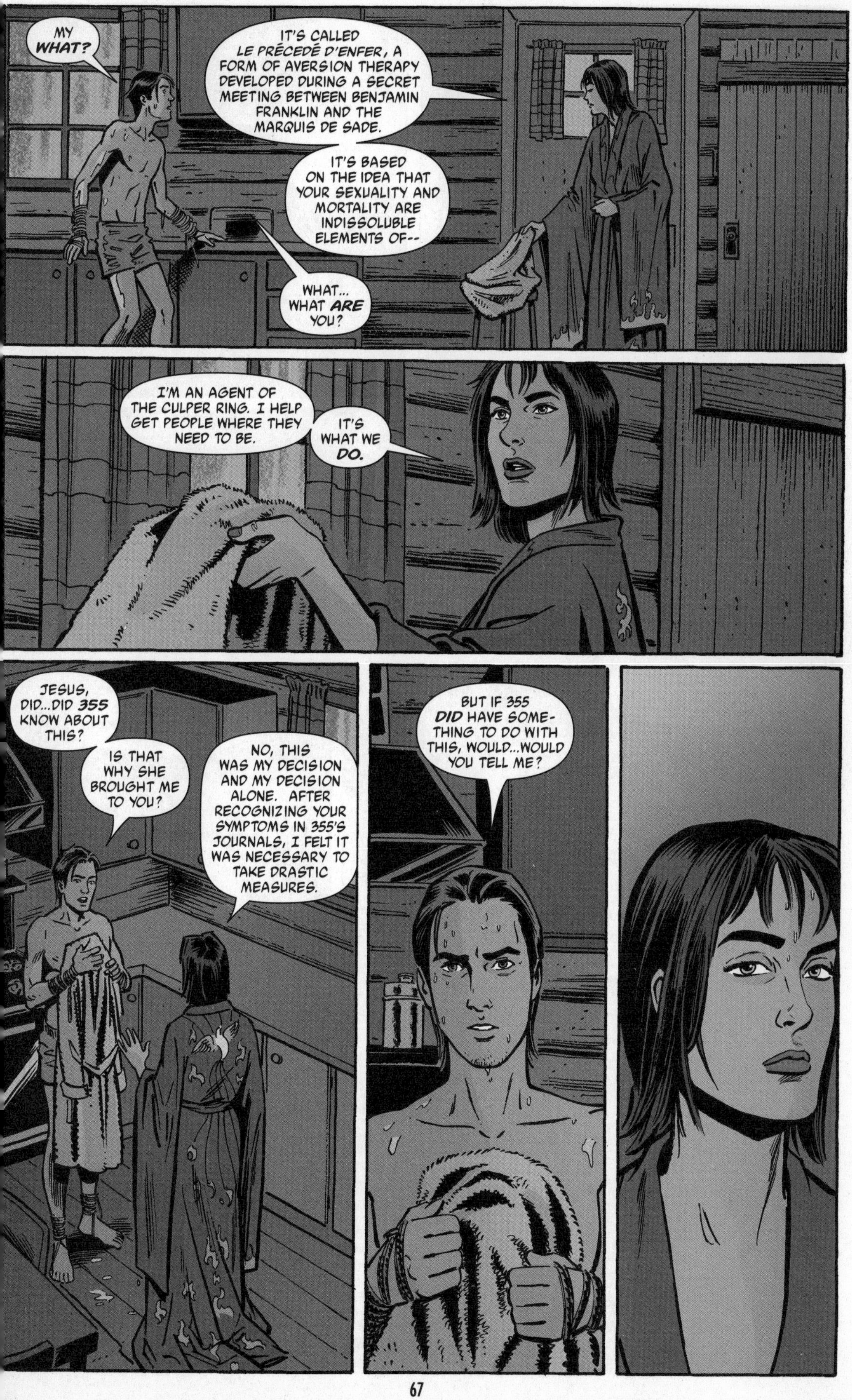
MY WHAT?
IT'S CALLED LE PRÉCEDÉ D'ENFER, A FORM OF AVERSION THERAPY DEVELOPED DURING A SECRET MEETING BETWEEN BENJAMIN FRANKLIN AND THE MARQUIS DE SADE.
IT'S BASED ON THE IDEA THAT YOUR SEXUALITY AND MORTALITY ARE INDISSOLUBLE ELEMENTS OF--
WHAT... WHAT ARE YOU?
I'M AN AGENT OF THE CULPER RING. I HELP GET PEOPLE WHERE THEY NEED TO BE.
IT'S WHAT WE DO.
JESUS, DID...DID 355 KNOW ABOUT THIS?
IS THAT WHY SHE BROUGHT ME TO YOU?
NO, THIS WAS MY DECISION AND MY DECISION ALONE. AFTER RECOGNIZING YOUR SYMPTOMS IN 355'S JOURNALS, I FELT IT WAS NECESSARY TO TAKE DRASTIC MEASURES.
BUT IF 355 DID HAVE SOME-THING TO DO WITH THIS, WOULD...WOULD YOU TELL ME?

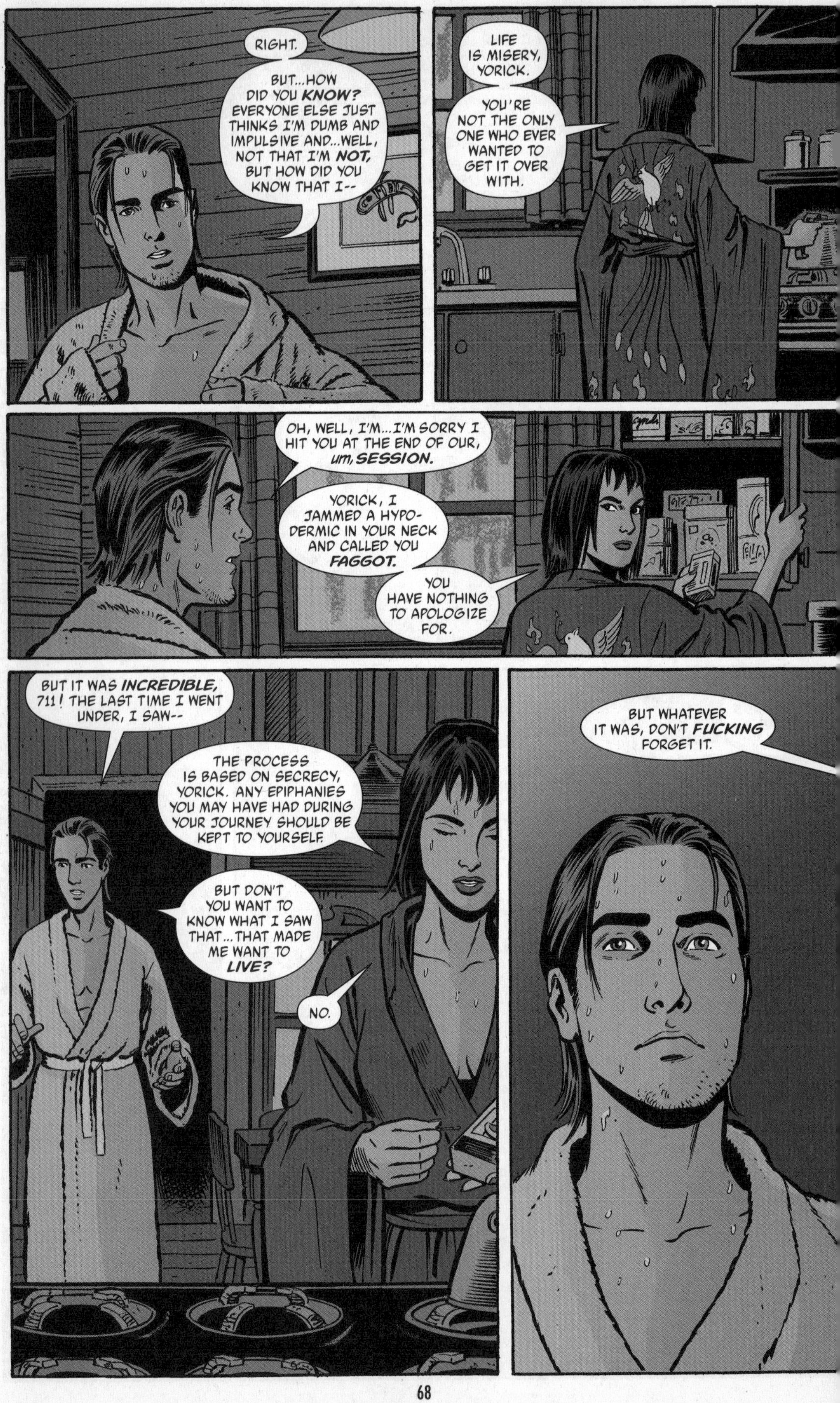
RIGHT.
BUT...HOW DID YOU KNOW? EVERYONE ELSE JUST THINKS I'M DUMB AND IMPULSIVE AND...WELL, NOT THAT I'M NOT, BUT HOW DID YOU KNOW THAT I--
LIFE IS MISERY, YORICK.
YOU'RE NOT THE ONLY ONE WHO EVER WANTED TO GET IT OVER WITH.
OH, WELL, I'M...I'M SORRY I HIT YOU AT THE END OF OUR, um, SESSION.
YORICK, I JAMMED A HYPO-DERMIC IN YOUR NECK AND CALLED YOU FAGGOT.
YOU HAVE NOTHING TO APOLOGIZE FOR.
BUT IT WAS INCREDIBLE, 711! THE LAST TIME I WENT UNDER, I SAW--
THE PROCESS IS BASED ON SECRECY, YORICK. ANY EPIPHANIES YOU MAY HAVE HAD DURING YOUR JOURNEY SHOULD BE KEPT TO YOURSELF.
BUT DON'T YOU WANT TO KNOW WHAT I SAW THAT...THAT MADE ME WANT TO LIVE?
NO.
BUT WHATEVER IT WAS, DON'T FUCKING FORGET IT.

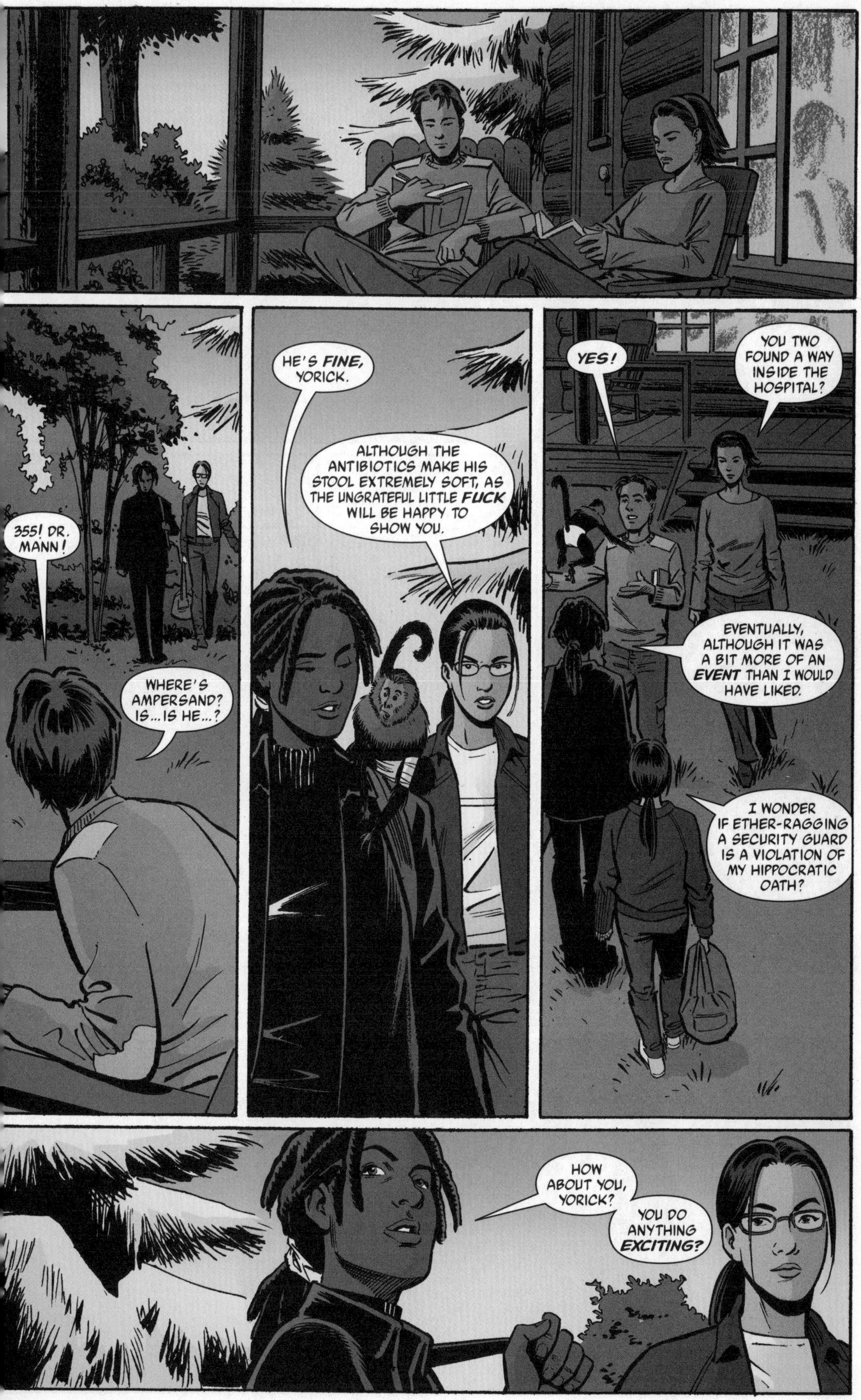
355! DR. MANN!
WHERE'S AMPERSAND? IS...IS HE...?
HE'S FINE, YORICK.
ALTHOUGH THE ANTIBIOTICS MAKE HIS STOOL EXTREMELY SOFT, AS THE UNGRATEFUL LITTLE FUCK WILL BE HAPPY TO SHOW YOU.
YES!
YOU TWO FOUND A WAY INSIDE THE HOSPITAL?
EVENTUALLY, ALTHOUGH IT WAS A BIT MORE OF AN EVENT THAN I WOULD HAVE LIKED.
I WONDER IF ETHER-RAGGING A SECURITY GUARD IS A VIOLATION OF MY HIPPOCRATIC OATH?
HOW ABOUT YOU, YORICK?
YOU DO ANYTHING EXCITING?

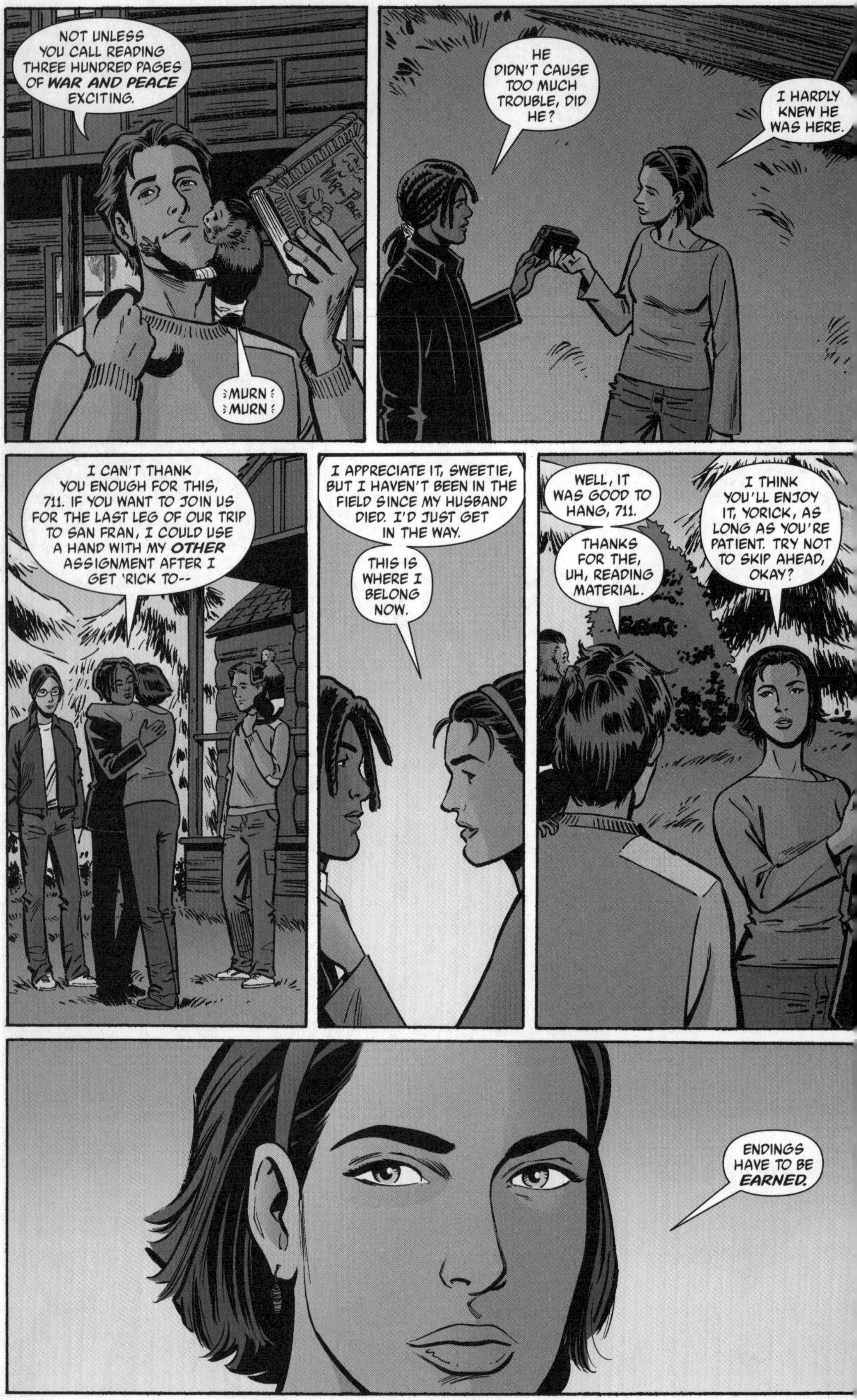

NOT UNLESS YOU CALL READING THREE HUNDRED PAGES OF WAR AND PEACE EXCITING.
MURN MURN
HE DIDN'T CAUSE TOO MUCH TROUBLE, DID HE?
I HARDLY KNEW HE WAS HERE.
I CAN'T THANK YOU ENOUGH FOR THIS, 711. IF YOU WANT TO JOIN US FOR THE LAST LEG OF OUR TRIP TO SAN FRAN, I COULD USE A HAND WITH MY OTHER ASSIGNMENT AFTER I GET 'RICK TO--
I APPRECIATE IT, SWEETIE, BUT I HAVEN'T BEEN IN THE FIELD SINCE MY HUSBAND DIED. I'D JUST GET IN THE WAY.
THIS IS WHERE I BELONG NOW.
WELL, IT WAS GOOD TO HANG, 711.
THANKS FOR THE, UH, READING MATERIAL.
I THINK YOU'LL ENJOY IT, YORICK, AS LONG AS YOU'RE PATIENT. TRY NOT TO SKIP AHEAD, OKAY?
ENDINGS HAVE TO BE EARNED.

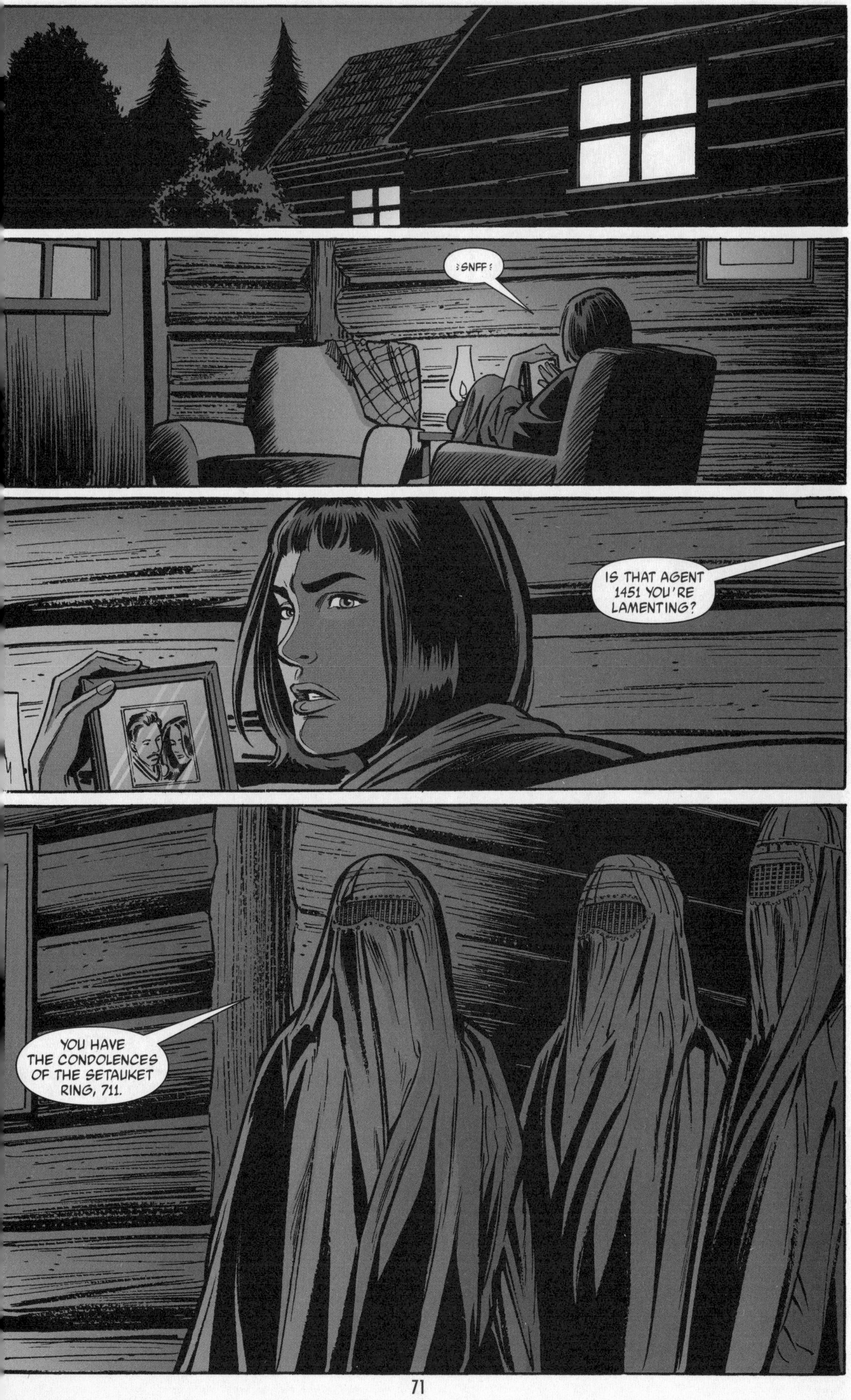
SNFF
IS THAT AGENT 1451 YOU'RE LAMENTING?
YOU HAVE THE CONDOLENCES OF THE SETAUKET RING, 711.

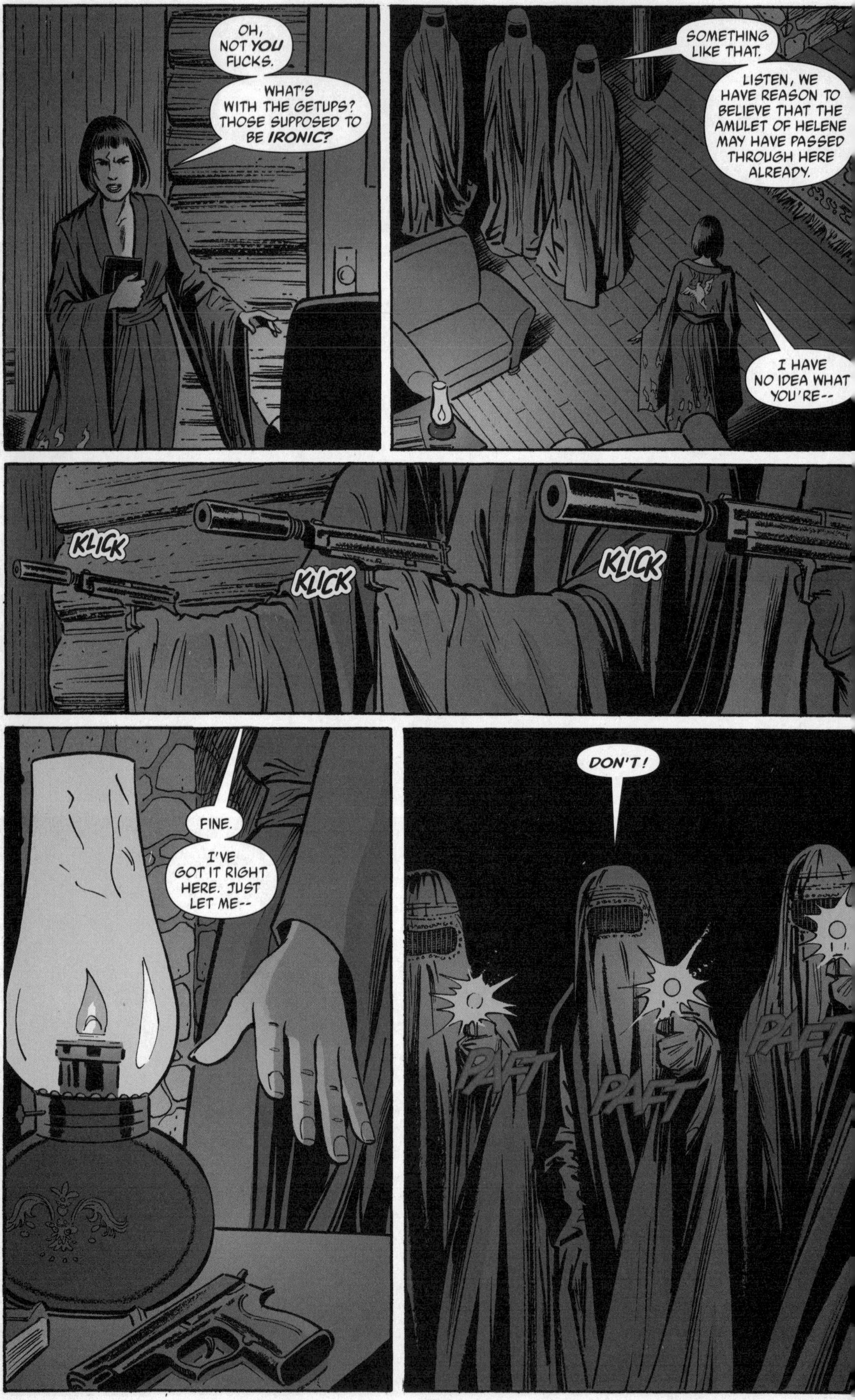
OH, NOT YOU FUCKS.
WHAT'S WITH THE GETUPS? THOSE SUPPOSED TO BE IRONIC?
SOMETHING LIKE THAT.
LISTEN, WE HAVE REASON TO BELIEVE THAT THE AMULET OF HELENE MAY HAVE PASSED THROUGH HERE ALREADY.
I HAVE NO IDEA WHAT YOU'RE--
KLICK
KLICK
KLICK
FINE.
I'VE GOT IT RIGHT HERE. JUST LET ME--
DON'T!
PAFT
PAFT
PAFT

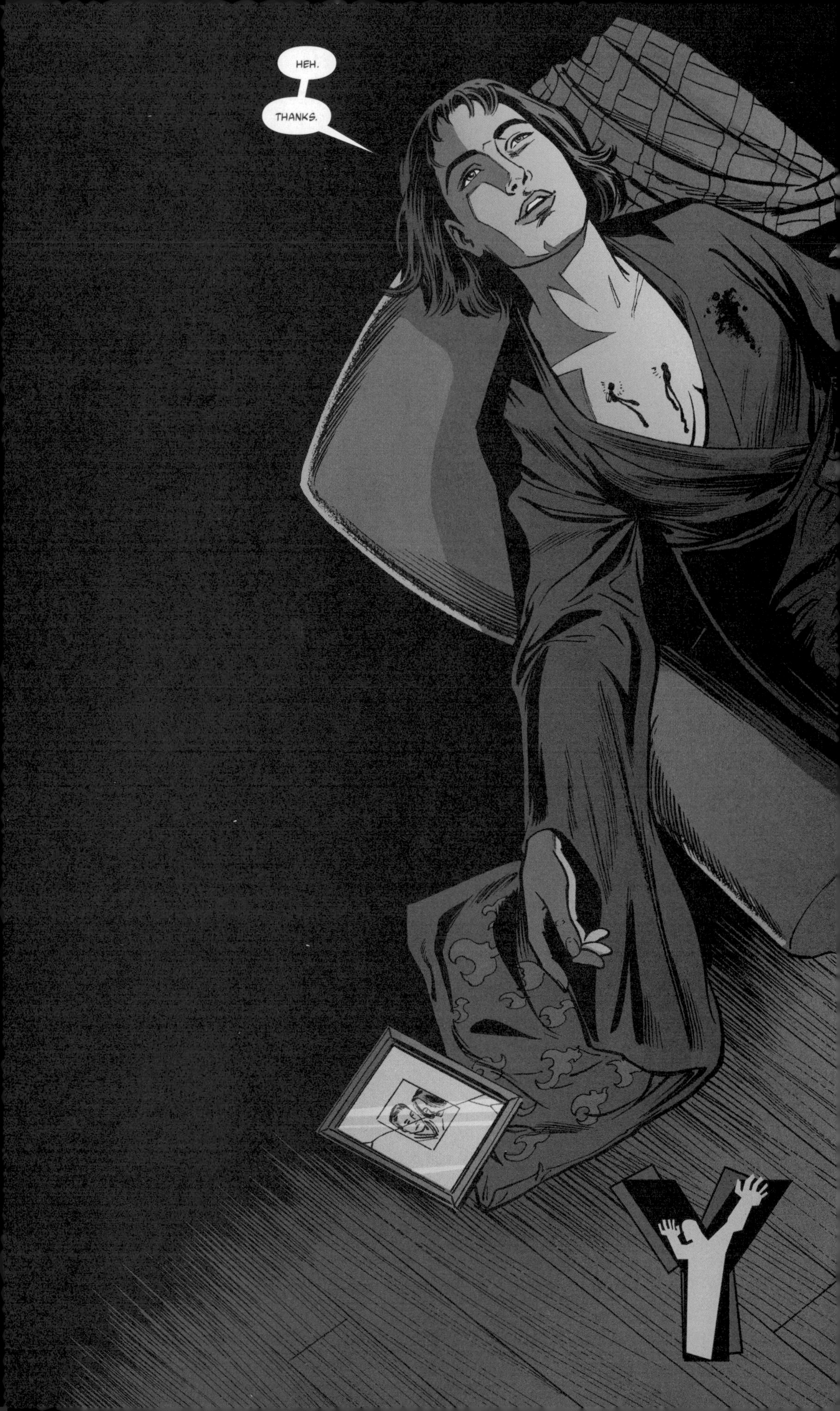
HEH.
THANKS.

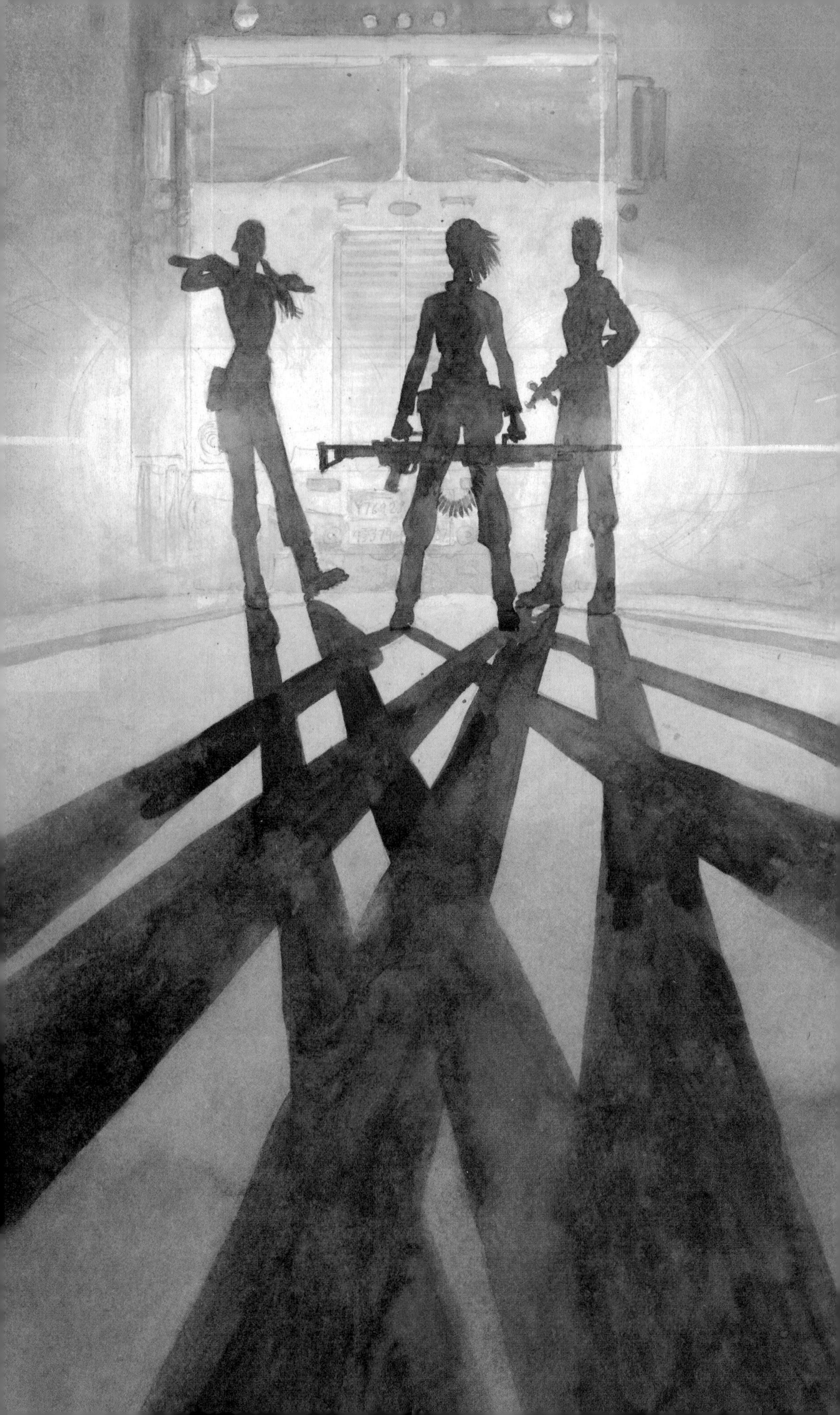

Queensbrook, Arizona
Now

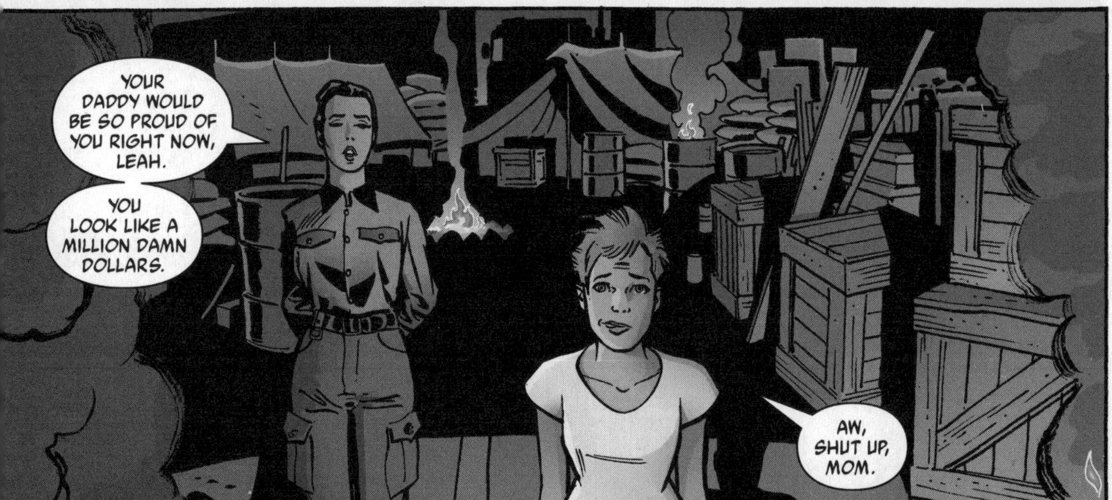
YOUR DADDY WOULD BE SO PROUD OF YOU RIGHT NOW, LEAH.
YOU LOOK LIKE A MILLION DAMN DOLLARS.
AW, SHUT UP, MOM.

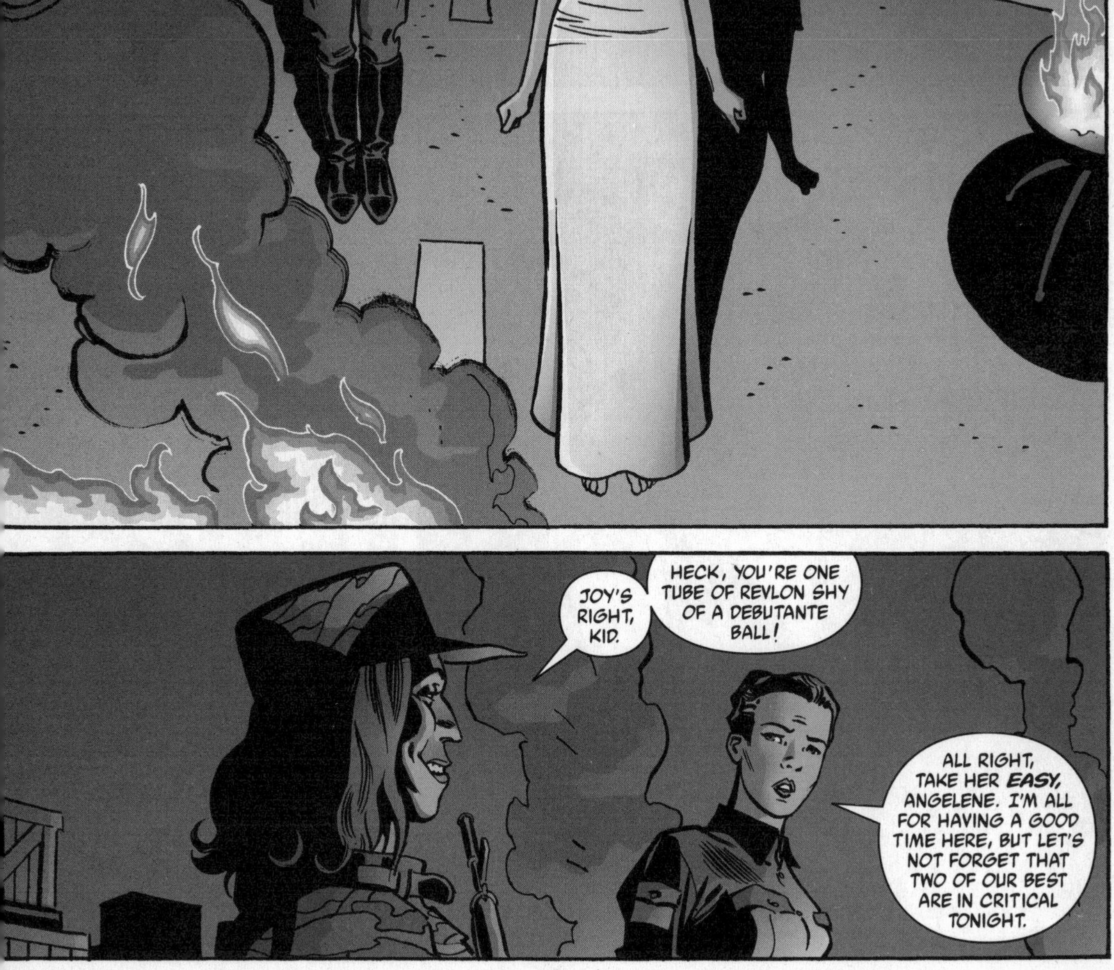
JOY'S RIGHT, KID.
HECK, YOU'RE ONE TUBE OF REVLON SHY OF A DEBUTANTE BALL!
ALL RIGHT, TAKE HER *EASY*, ANGELENE. I'M ALL FOR HAVING A GOOD TIME HERE, BUT LET'S NOT FORGET THAT TWO OF OUR BEST ARE IN CRITICAL TONIGHT.

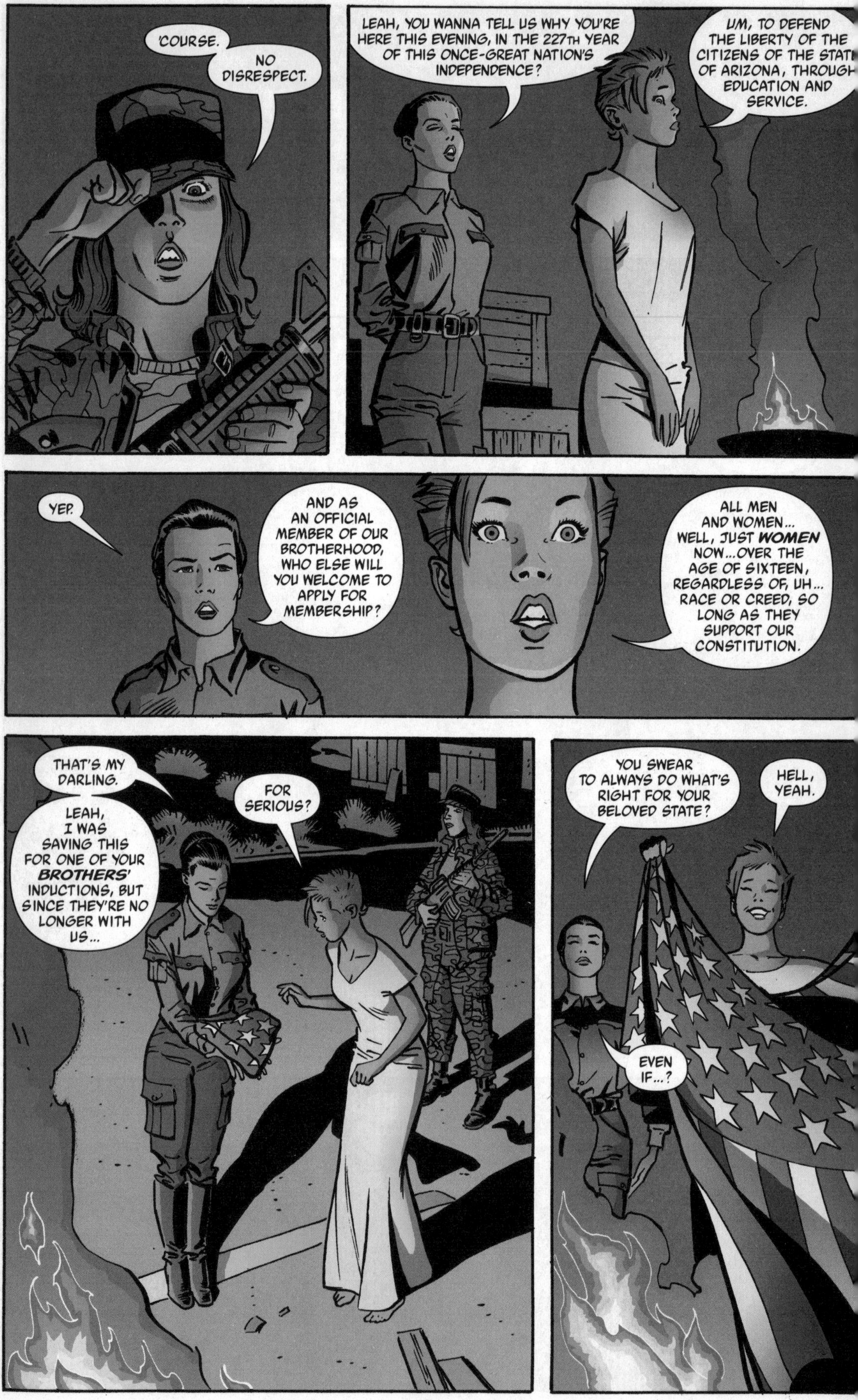

'COURSE.
NO DISRESPECT.
LEAH, YOU WANNA TELL US WHY YOU'RE HERE THIS EVENING, IN THE 227TH YEAR OF THIS ONCE-GREAT NATION'S INDEPENDENCE?
UM, TO DEFEND THE LIBERTY OF THE CITIZENS OF THE STATE OF ARIZONA, THROUGH EDUCATION AND SERVICE.
YEP.
AND AS AN OFFICIAL MEMBER OF OUR BROTHERHOOD, WHO ELSE WILL YOU WELCOME TO APPLY FOR MEMBERSHIP?
ALL MEN AND WOMEN... WELL, JUST ***WOMEN*** NOW...OVER THE AGE OF SIXTEEN, REGARDLESS OF, UH... RACE OR CREED, SO LONG AS THEY SUPPORT OUR CONSTITUTION.
THAT'S MY DARLING.
LEAH, I WAS SAVING THIS FOR ONE OF YOUR ***BROTHERS'*** INDUCTIONS, BUT SINCE THEY'RE NO LONGER WITH US...
FOR SERIOUS?
YOU SWEAR TO ALWAYS DO WHAT'S RIGHT FOR YOUR BELOVED STATE?
HELL, YEAH.
EVEN IF...?

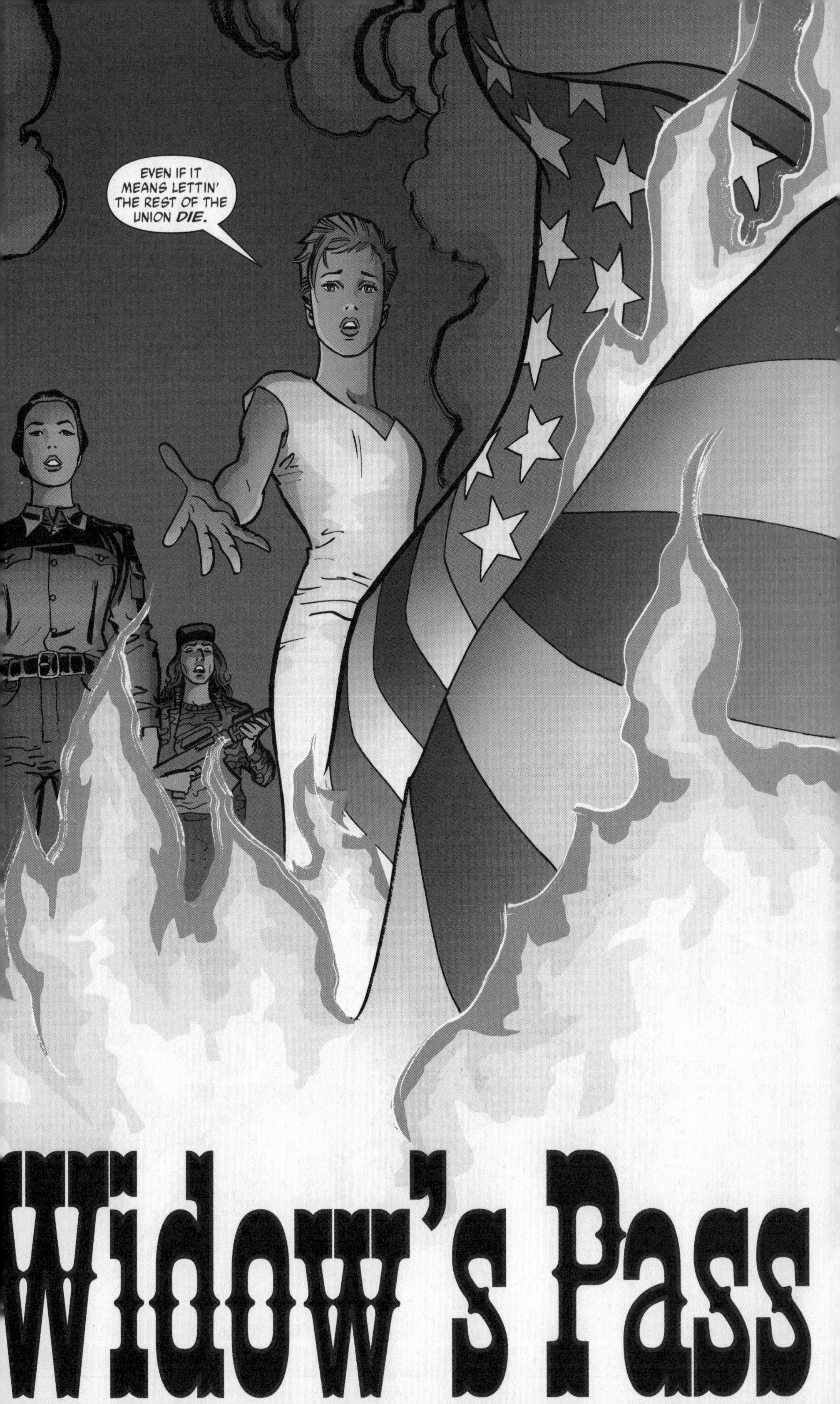
EVEN IF IT MEANS LETTIN' THE REST OF THE UNION DIE.

Widow's Pass

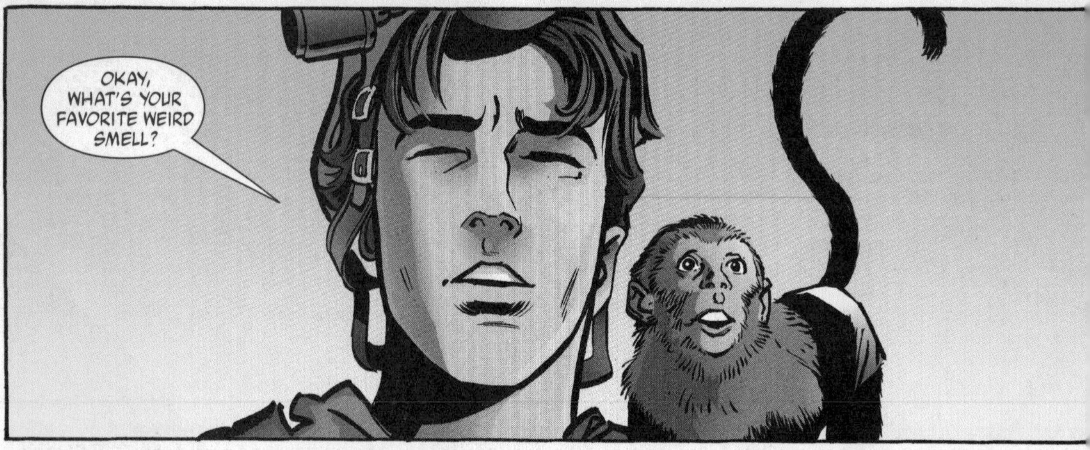
OKAY, WHAT'S YOUR FAVORITE WEIRD SMELL?

Fourteen Miles East
Six Hours Earlier

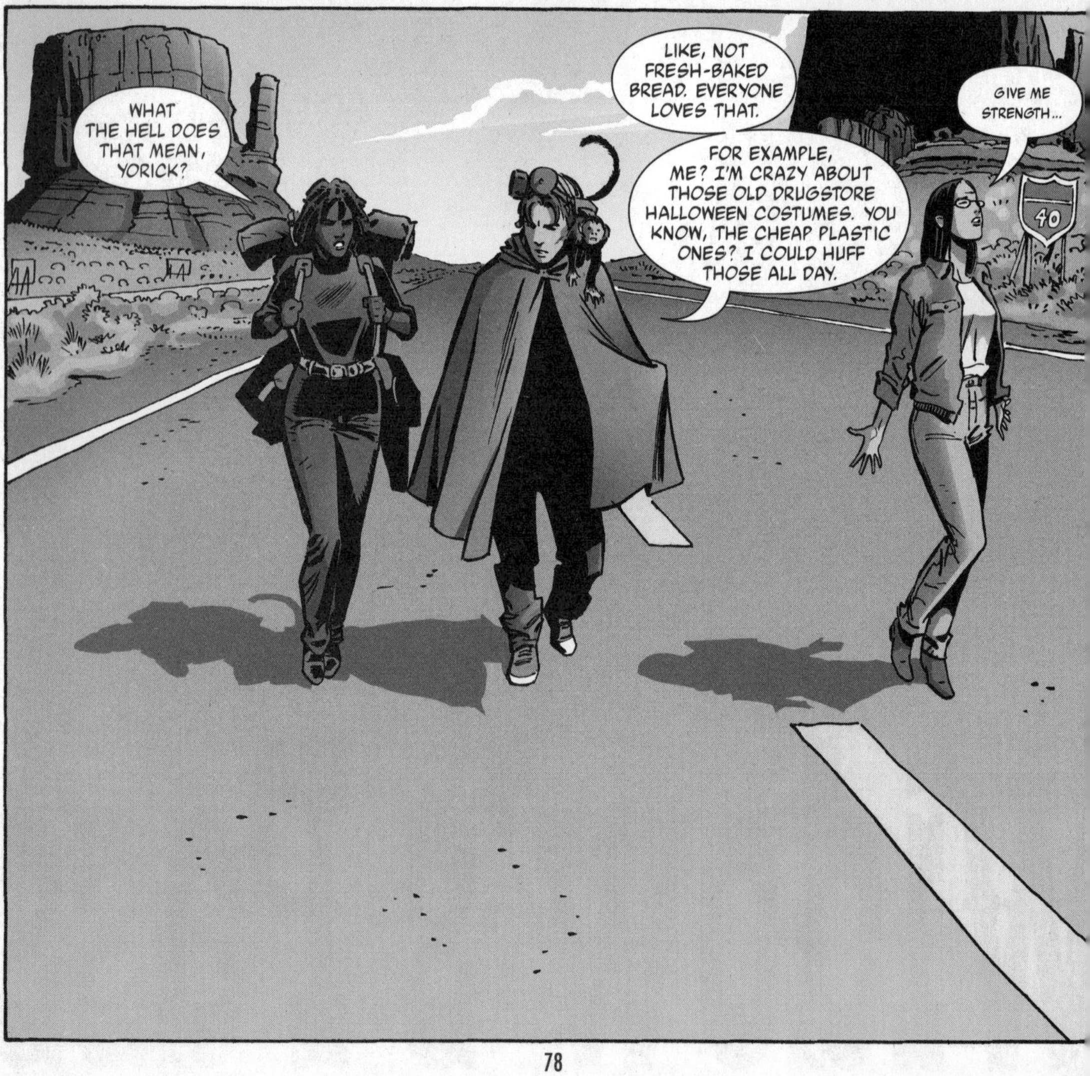
LIKE, NOT FRESH-BAKED BREAD. EVERYONE LOVES THAT.
WHAT THE HELL DOES THAT MEAN, YORICK?
FOR EXAMPLE, ME? I'M CRAZY ABOUT THOSE OLD DRUGSTORE HALLOWEEN COSTUMES. YOU KNOW, THE CHEAP PLASTIC ONES? I COULD HUFF THOSE ALL DAY.
GIVE ME STRENGTH...
40

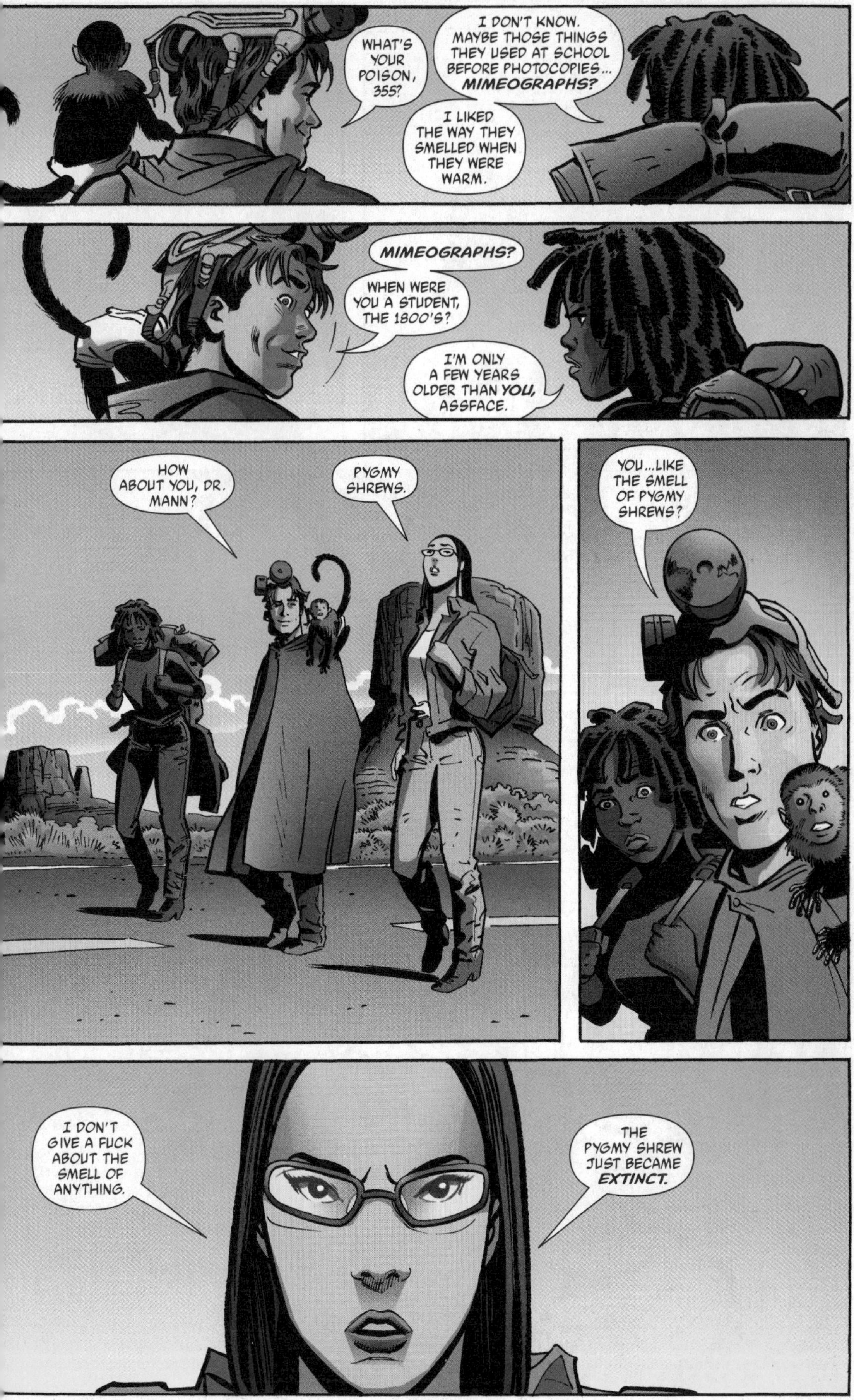
WHAT'S YOUR POISON, 355?
I DON'T KNOW. MAYBE THOSE THINGS THEY USED AT SCHOOL BEFORE PHOTOCOPIES... MIMEOGRAPHS?
I LIKED THE WAY THEY SMELLED WHEN THEY WERE WARM.
MIMEOGRAPHS?
WHEN WERE YOU A STUDENT, THE 1800'S?
I'M ONLY A FEW YEARS OLDER THAN YOU, ASSFACE.
HOW ABOUT YOU, DR. MANN?
PYGMY SHREWS.
YOU...LIKE THE SMELL OF PYGMY SHREWS?
I DON'T GIVE A FUCK ABOUT THE SMELL OF ANYTHING.
THE PYGMY SHREW JUST BECAME EXTINCT.

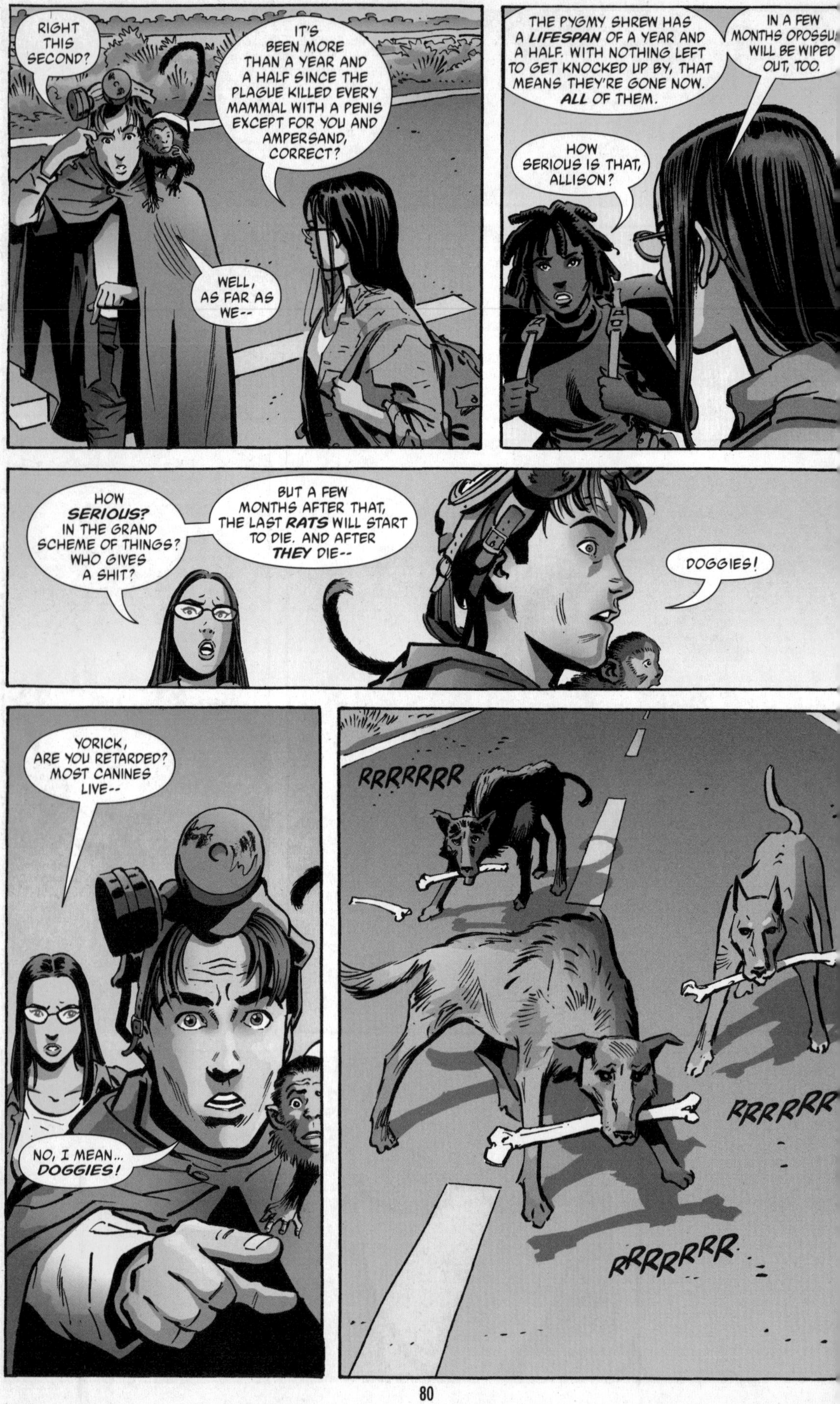
RIGHT THIS SECOND?
IT'S BEEN MORE THAN A YEAR AND A HALF SINCE THE PLAGUE KILLED EVERY MAMMAL WITH A PENIS EXCEPT FOR YOU AND AMPERSAND, CORRECT?
WELL, AS FAR AS WE--
THE PYGMY SHREW HAS A LIFESPAN OF A YEAR AND A HALF. WITH NOTHING LEFT TO GET KNOCKED UP BY, THAT MEANS THEY'RE GONE NOW. ALL OF THEM.
IN A FEW MONTHS OPOSSU WILL BE WIPED OUT, TOO.
HOW SERIOUS IS THAT, ALLISON?
HOW SERIOUS? IN THE GRAND SCHEME OF THINGS? WHO GIVES A SHIT?
BUT A FEW MONTHS AFTER THAT, THE LAST RATS WILL START TO DIE. AND AFTER THEY DIE--
DOGGIES!
YORICK, ARE YOU RETARDED? MOST CANINES LIVE--
NO, I MEAN... DOGGIES!
RRRRRRR
RRRRRR
RRRRRRR

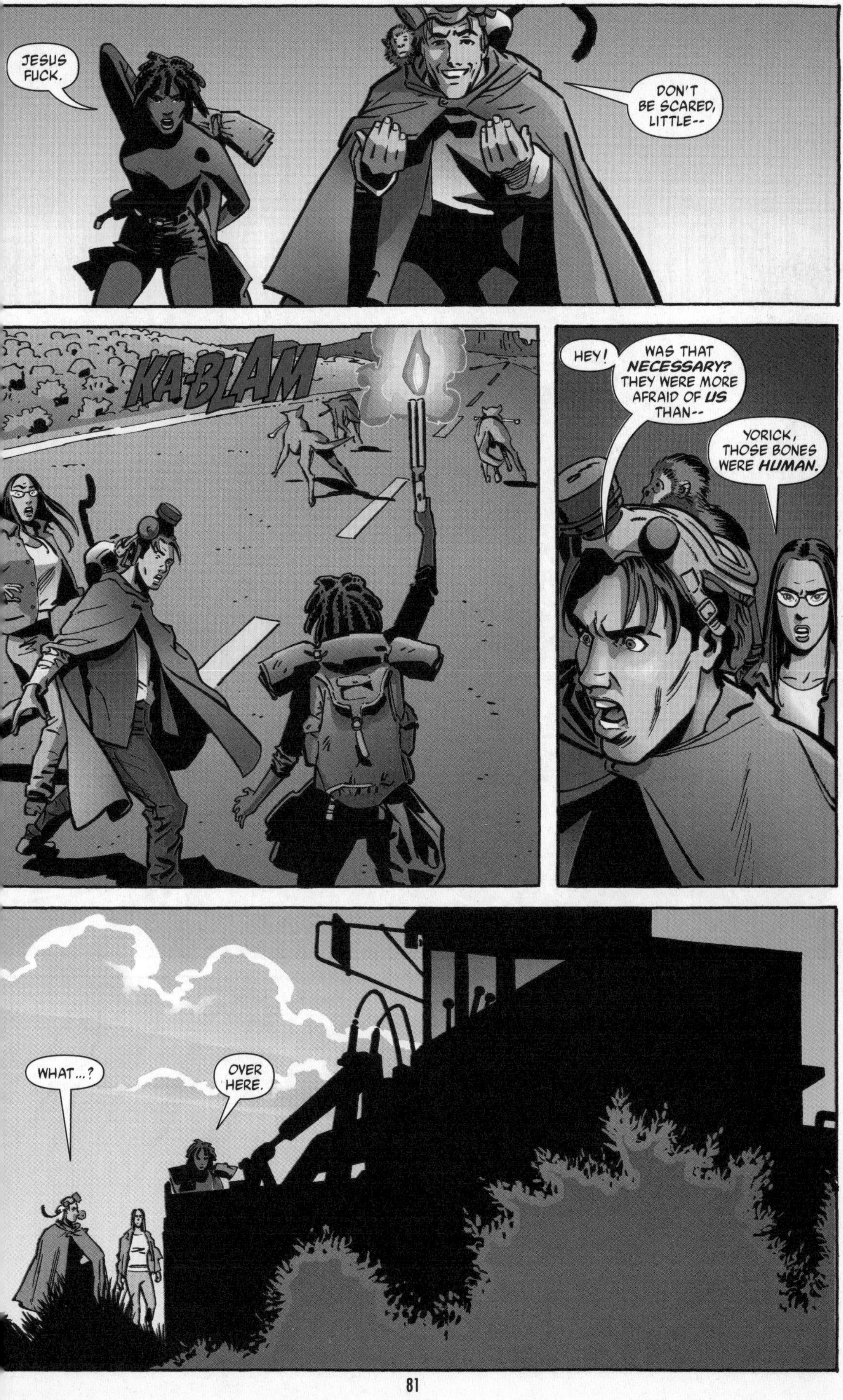
JESUS FUCK.
DON'T BE SCARED, LITTLE--
KA-BLAM
HEY!
WAS THAT NECESSARY? THEY WERE MORE AFRAID OF US THAN--
YORICK, THOSE BONES WERE HUMAN.
WHAT...?
OVER HERE.

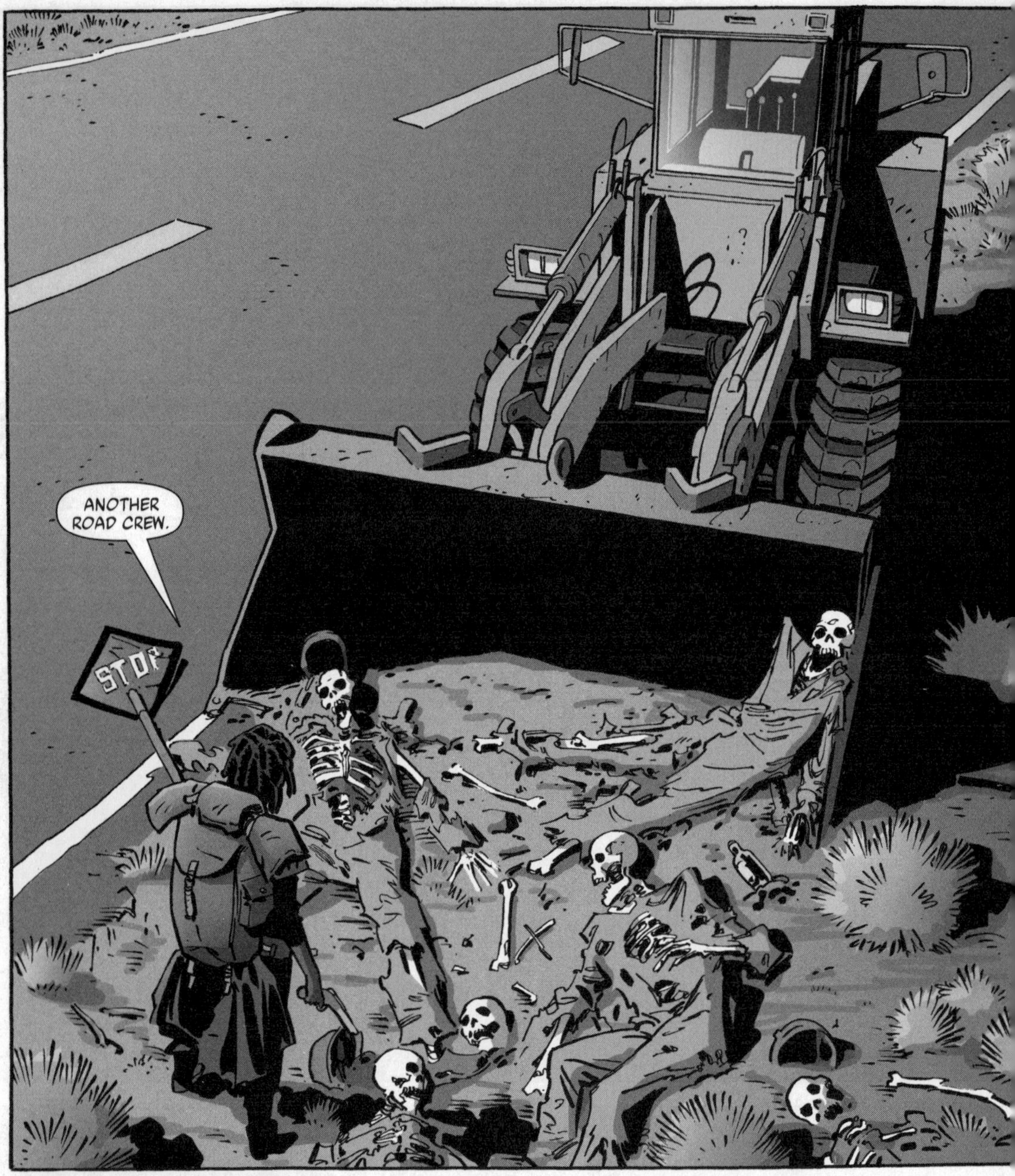
ANOTHER ROAD CREW.
STOP

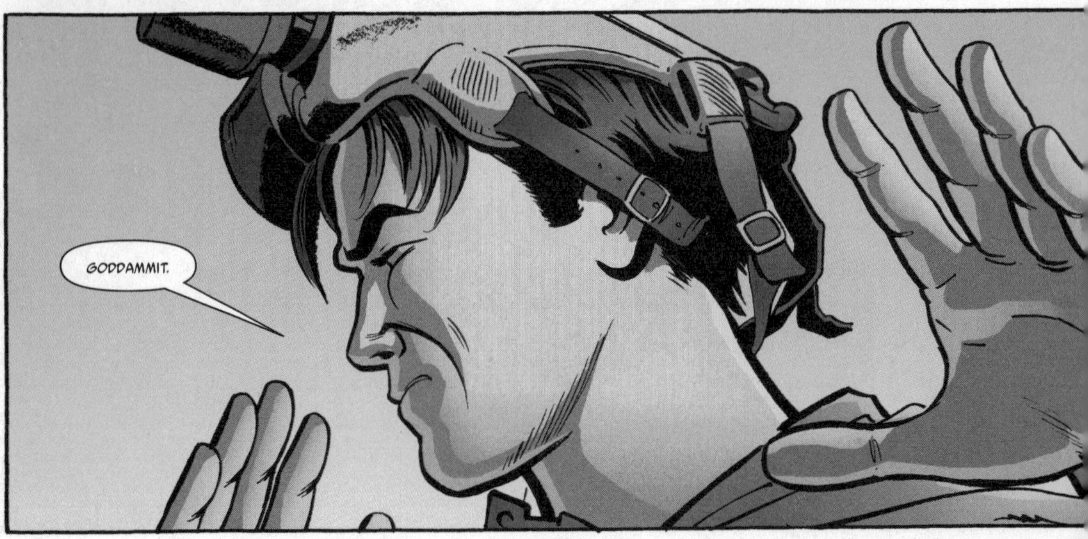
GODDAMMIT.

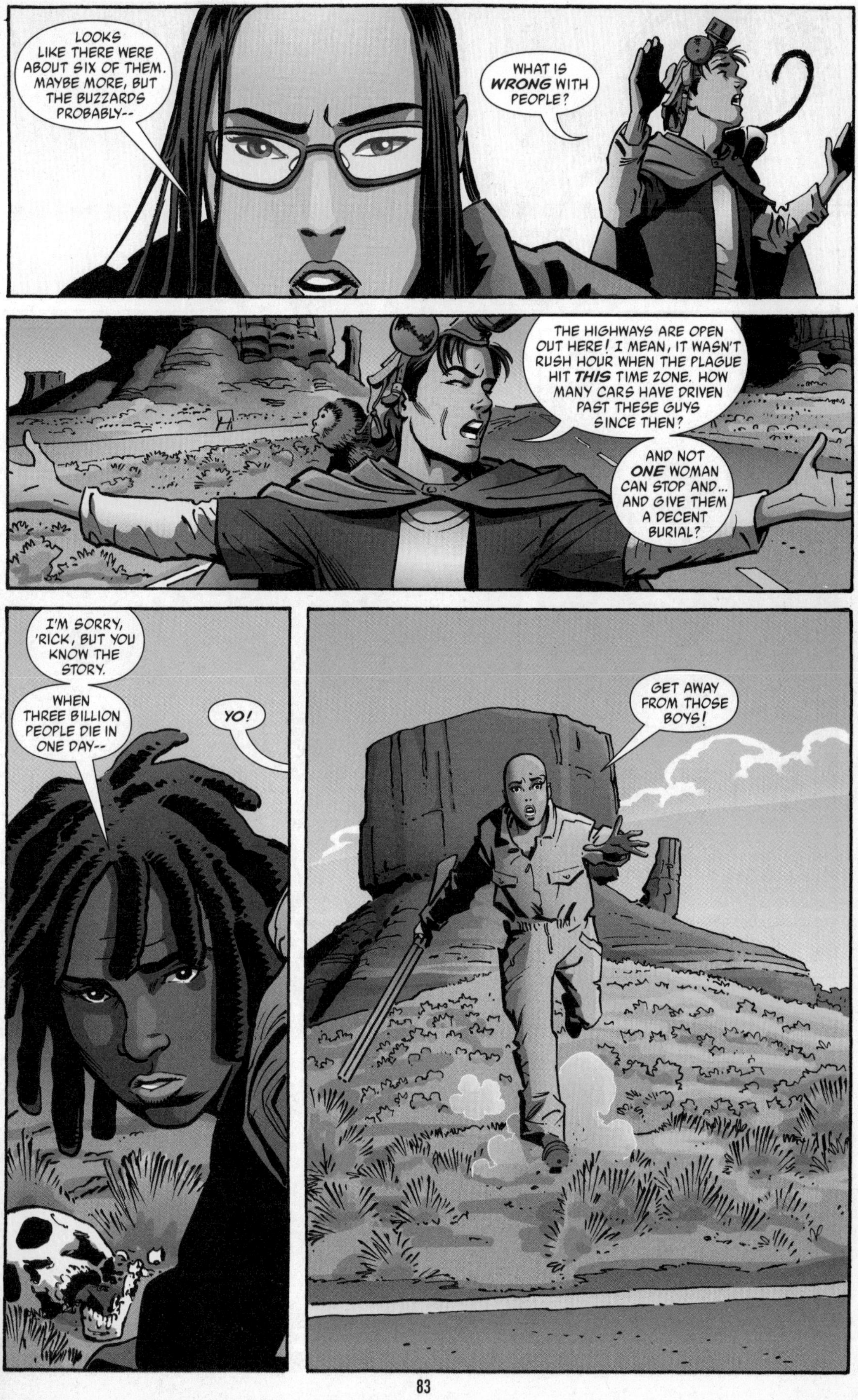
LOOKS LIKE THERE WERE ABOUT SIX OF THEM. MAYBE MORE, BUT THE BUZZARDS PROBABLY--
WHAT IS WRONG WITH PEOPLE?
THE HIGHWAYS ARE OPEN OUT HERE! I MEAN, IT WASN'T RUSH HOUR WHEN THE PLAGUE HIT THIS TIME ZONE. HOW MANY CARS HAVE DRIVEN PAST THESE GUYS SINCE THEN?
AND NOT ONE WOMAN CAN STOP AND... AND GIVE THEM A DECENT BURIAL?
I'M SORRY, 'RICK, BUT YOU KNOW THE STORY.
WHEN THREE BILLION PEOPLE DIE IN ONE DAY--
YO!
GET AWAY FROM THOSE BOYS!

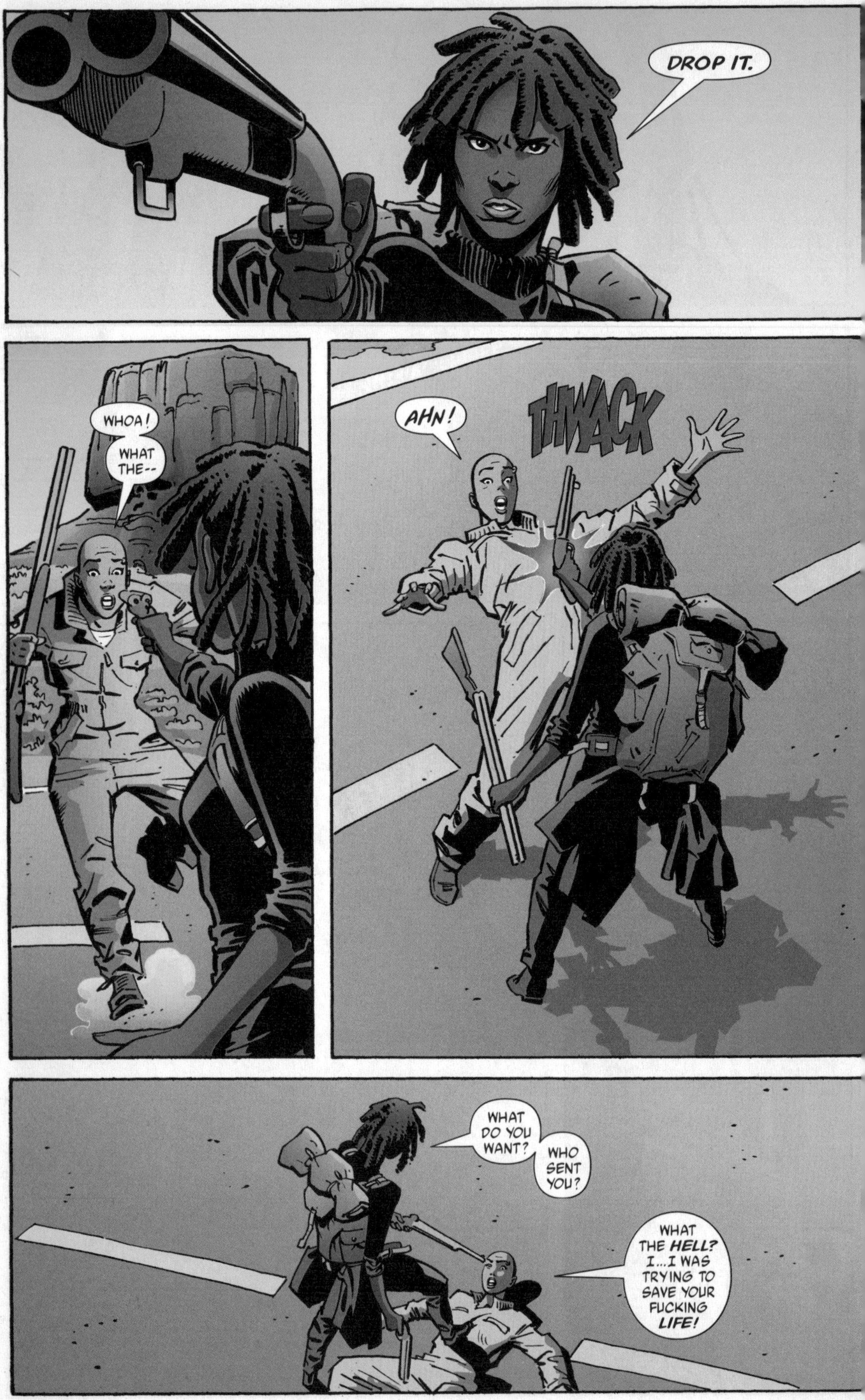
DROP IT.
WHOA!
WHAT THE--
AHN!
THWACK
WHAT DO YOU WANT?
WHO SENT YOU?
WHAT THE HELL? I...I WAS TRYING TO SAVE YOUR FUCKING LIFE!

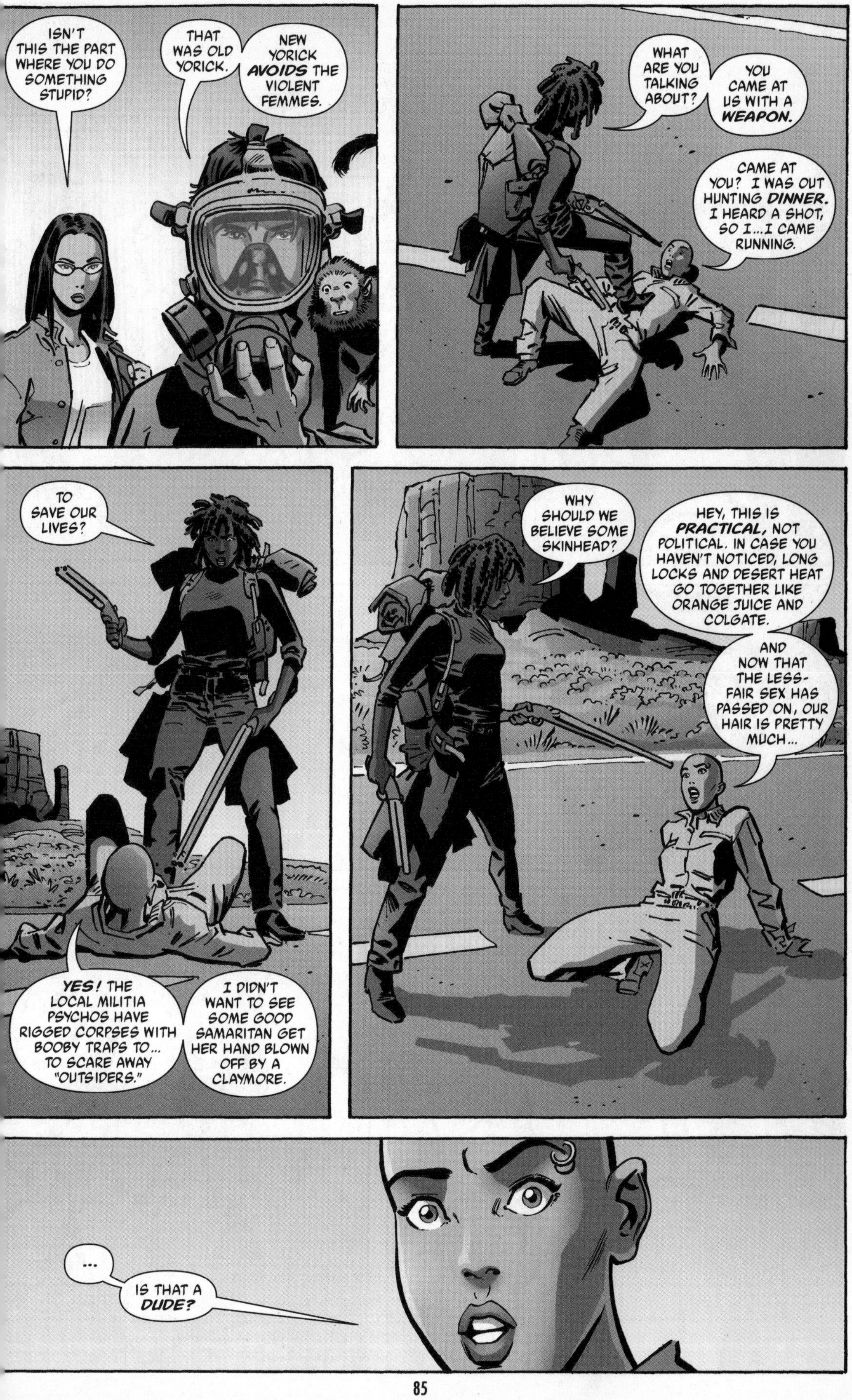
ISN'T THIS THE PART WHERE YOU DO SOMETHING STUPID?
THAT WAS OLD YORICK.
NEW YORICK AVOIDS THE VIOLENT FEMMES.
WHAT ARE YOU TALKING ABOUT?
YOU CAME AT US WITH A WEAPON.
CAME AT YOU? I WAS OUT HUNTING DINNER. I HEARD A SHOT, SO I...I CAME RUNNING.
TO SAVE OUR LIVES?
YES! THE LOCAL MILITIA PSYCHOS HAVE RIGGED CORPSES WITH BOOBY TRAPS TO... TO SCARE AWAY "OUTSIDERS."
I DIDN'T WANT TO SEE SOME GOOD SAMARITAN GET HER HAND BLOWN OFF BY A CLAYMORE.
WHY SHOULD WE BELIEVE SOME SKINHEAD?
HEY, THIS IS PRACTICAL, NOT POLITICAL. IN CASE YOU HAVEN'T NOTICED, LONG LOCKS AND DESERT HEAT GO TOGETHER LIKE ORANGE JUICE AND COLGATE.
AND NOW THAT THE LESS-FAIR SEX HAS PASSED ON, OUR HAIR IS PRETTY MUCH...
...
IS THAT A DUDE?

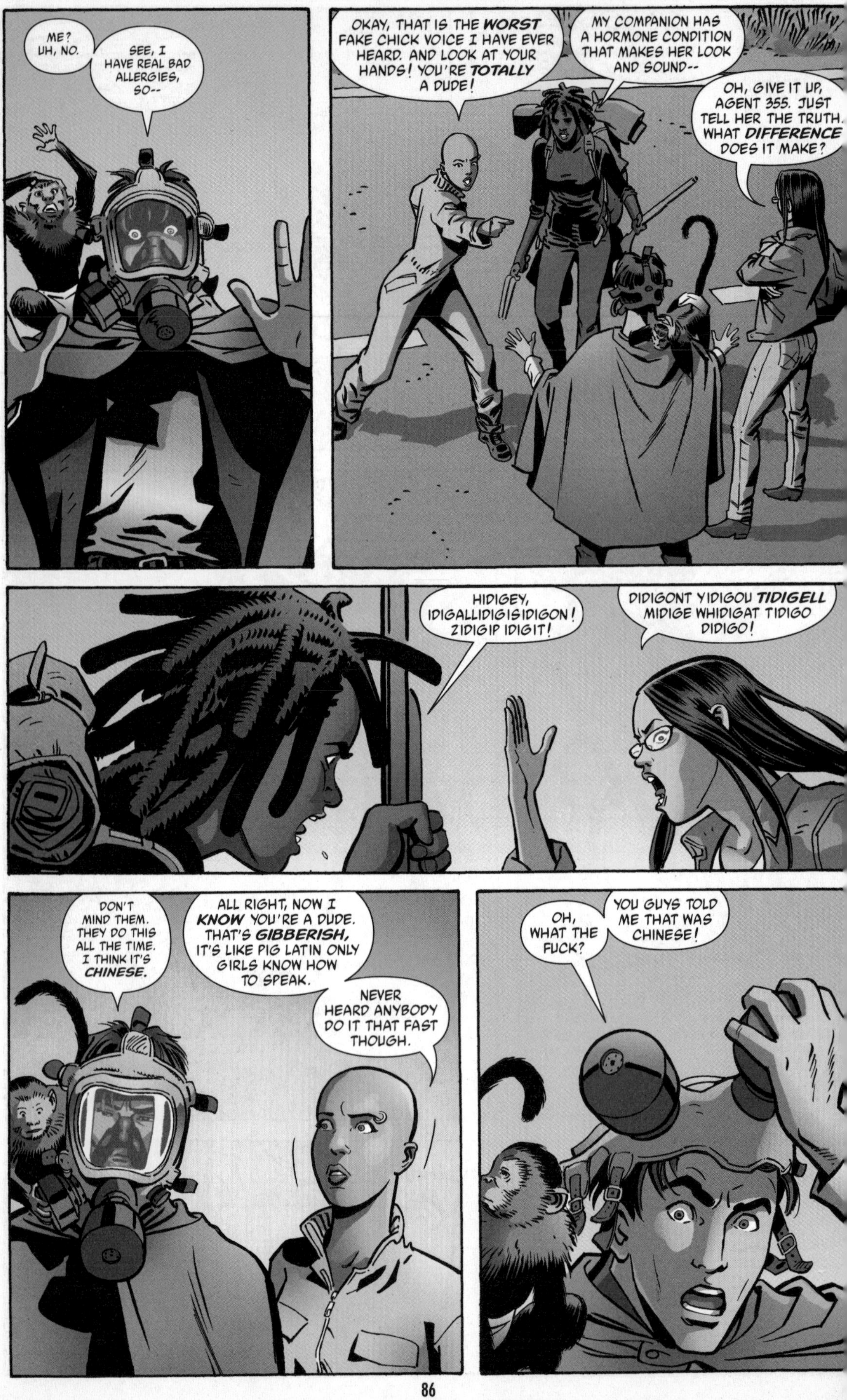

ME? UH, NO.
SEE, I HAVE REAL BAD ALLERGIES, SO--
OKAY, THAT IS THE WORST FAKE CHICK VOICE I HAVE EVER HEARD. AND LOOK AT YOUR HANDS! YOU'RE TOTALLY A DUDE!
MY COMPANION HAS A HORMONE CONDITION THAT MAKES HER LOOK AND SOUND--
OH, GIVE IT UP, AGENT 355. JUST TELL HER THE TRUTH. WHAT DIFFERENCE DOES IT MAKE?
HIDIGEY, IDIGALLIDIGISIDIGON! ZIDIGIP IDIGIT!
DIDIGONT YIDIGOU TIDIGELL MIDIGE WHIDIGAT TIDIGO DIDIGO!
DON'T MIND THEM. THEY DO THIS ALL THE TIME. I THINK IT'S CHINESE.
ALL RIGHT, NOW I KNOW YOU'RE A DUDE. THAT'S GIBBERISH, IT'S LIKE PIG LATIN ONLY GIRLS KNOW HOW TO SPEAK.
NEVER HEARD ANYBODY DO IT THAT FAST THOUGH.
OH, WHAT THE FUCK?
YOU GUYS TOLD ME THAT WAS CHINESE!

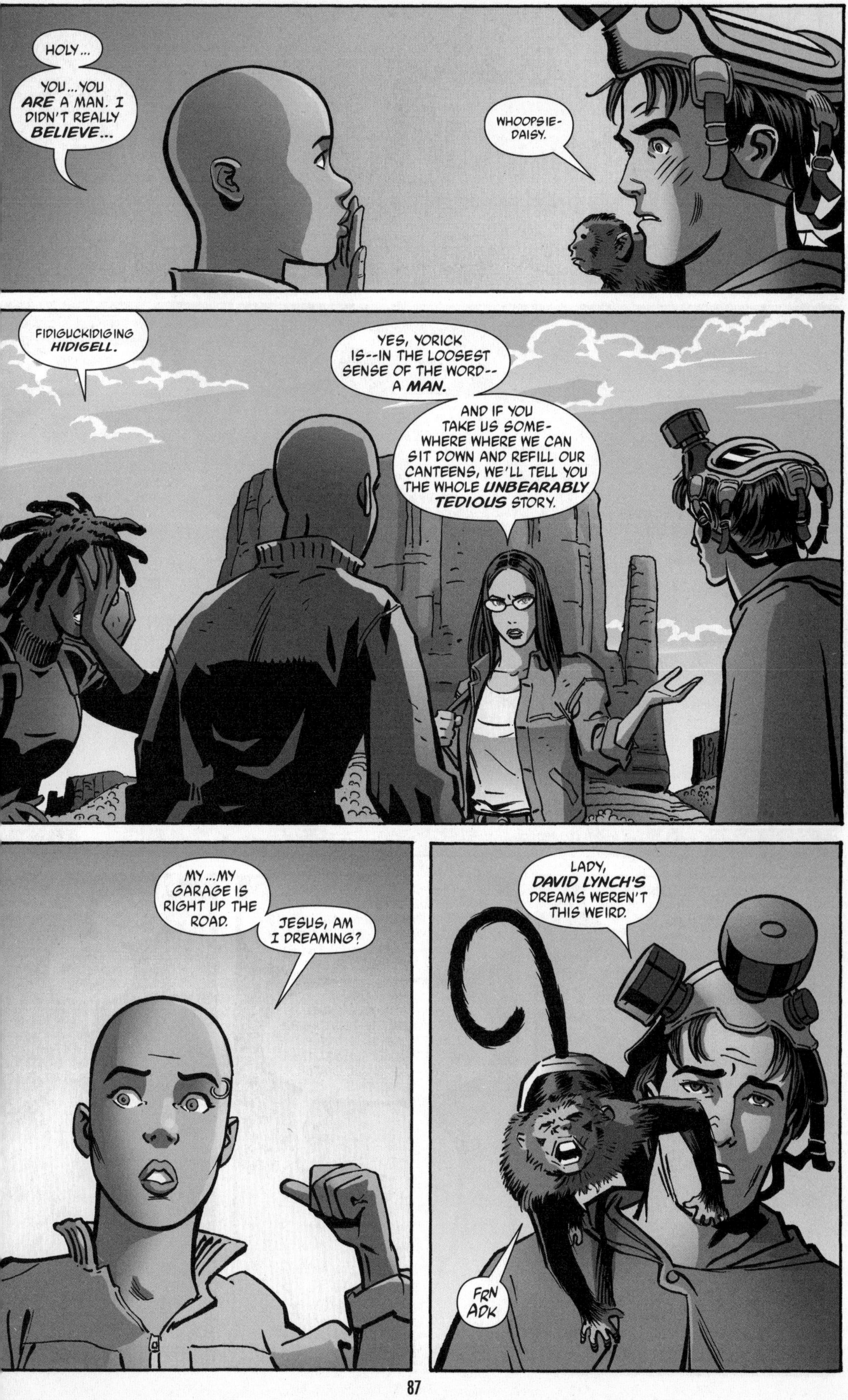
HOLY...
YOU...YOU *ARE* A MAN. I DIDN'T REALLY *BELIEVE...*
WHOOPSIE-DAISY.
FIDIGUCKIDIGING *HIDIGELL.*
YES, YORICK IS--IN THE LOOSEST SENSE OF THE WORD--A *MAN.*
AND IF YOU TAKE US SOME-WHERE WHERE WE CAN SIT DOWN AND REFILL OUR CANTEENS, WE'LL TELL YOU THE WHOLE *UNBEARABLY TEDIOUS* STORY.
MY...MY GARAGE IS RIGHT UP THE ROAD.
JESUS, AM I DREAMING?
LADY, *DAVID LYNCH'S* DREAMS WEREN'T THIS WEIRD.
FRN ADK

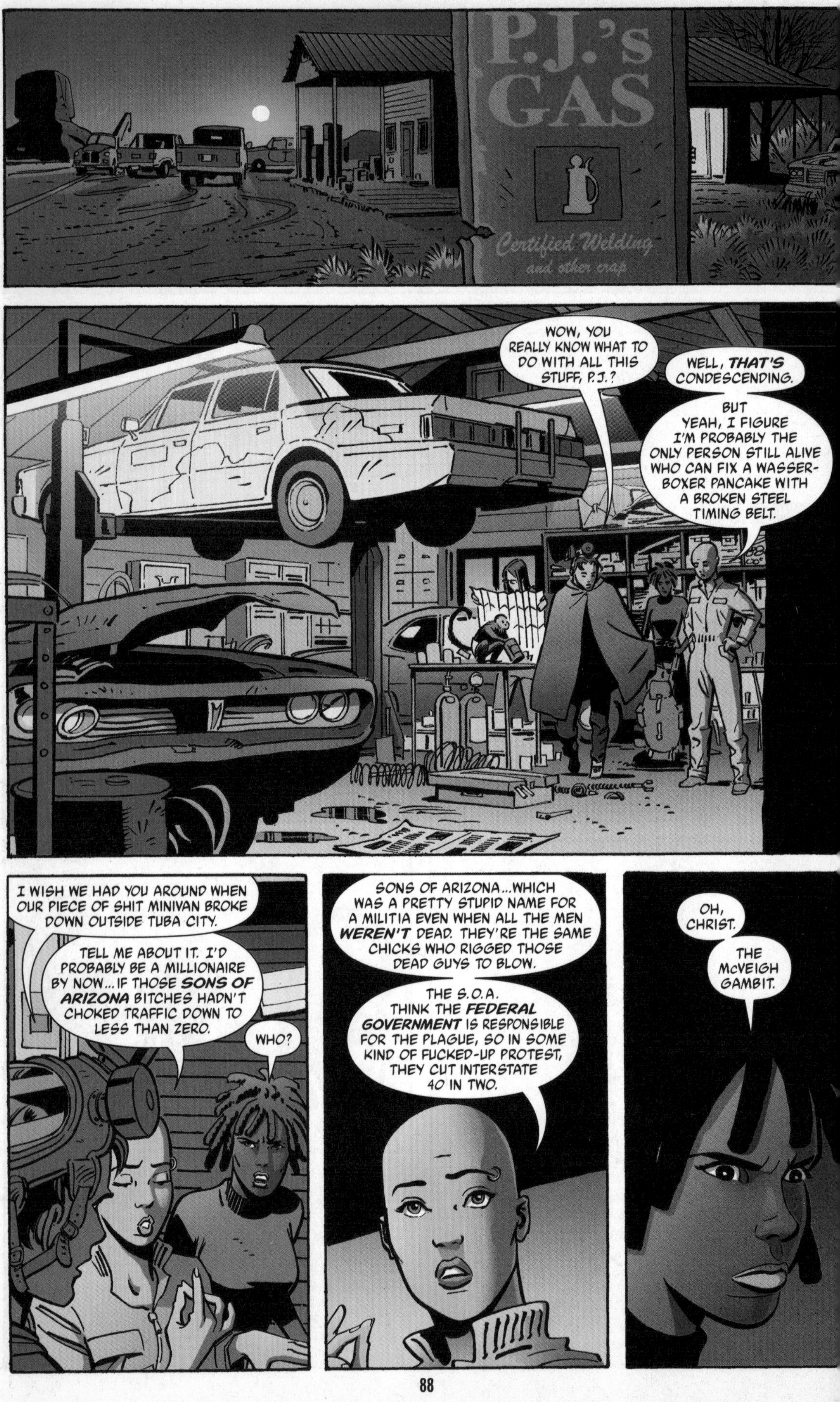
P.J.'s GAS
Certified Welding and other crap
WOW, YOU REALLY KNOW WHAT TO DO WITH ALL THIS STUFF, P.J.?
WELL, THAT'S CONDESCENDING.
BUT YEAH, I FIGURE I'M PROBABLY THE ONLY PERSON STILL ALIVE WHO CAN FIX A WASSER-BOXER PANCAKE WITH A BROKEN STEEL TIMING BELT.
I WISH WE HAD YOU AROUND WHEN OUR PIECE OF SHIT MINIVAN BROKE DOWN OUTSIDE TUBA CITY.
TELL ME ABOUT IT. I'D PROBABLY BE A MILLIONAIRE BY NOW... IF THOSE SONS OF ARIZONA BITCHES HADN'T CHOKED TRAFFIC DOWN TO LESS THAN ZERO.
WHO?
SONS OF ARIZONA... WHICH WAS A PRETTY STUPID NAME FOR A MILITIA EVEN WHEN ALL THE MEN WEREN'T DEAD. THEY'RE THE SAME CHICKS WHO RIGGED THOSE DEAD GUYS TO BLOW.
THE S.O.A. THINK THE FEDERAL GOVERNMENT IS RESPONSIBLE FOR THE PLAGUE, SO IN SOME KIND OF FUCKED-UP PROTEST, THEY CUT INTERSTATE 40 IN TWO.
OH, CHRIST.
THE McVEIGH GAMBIT.

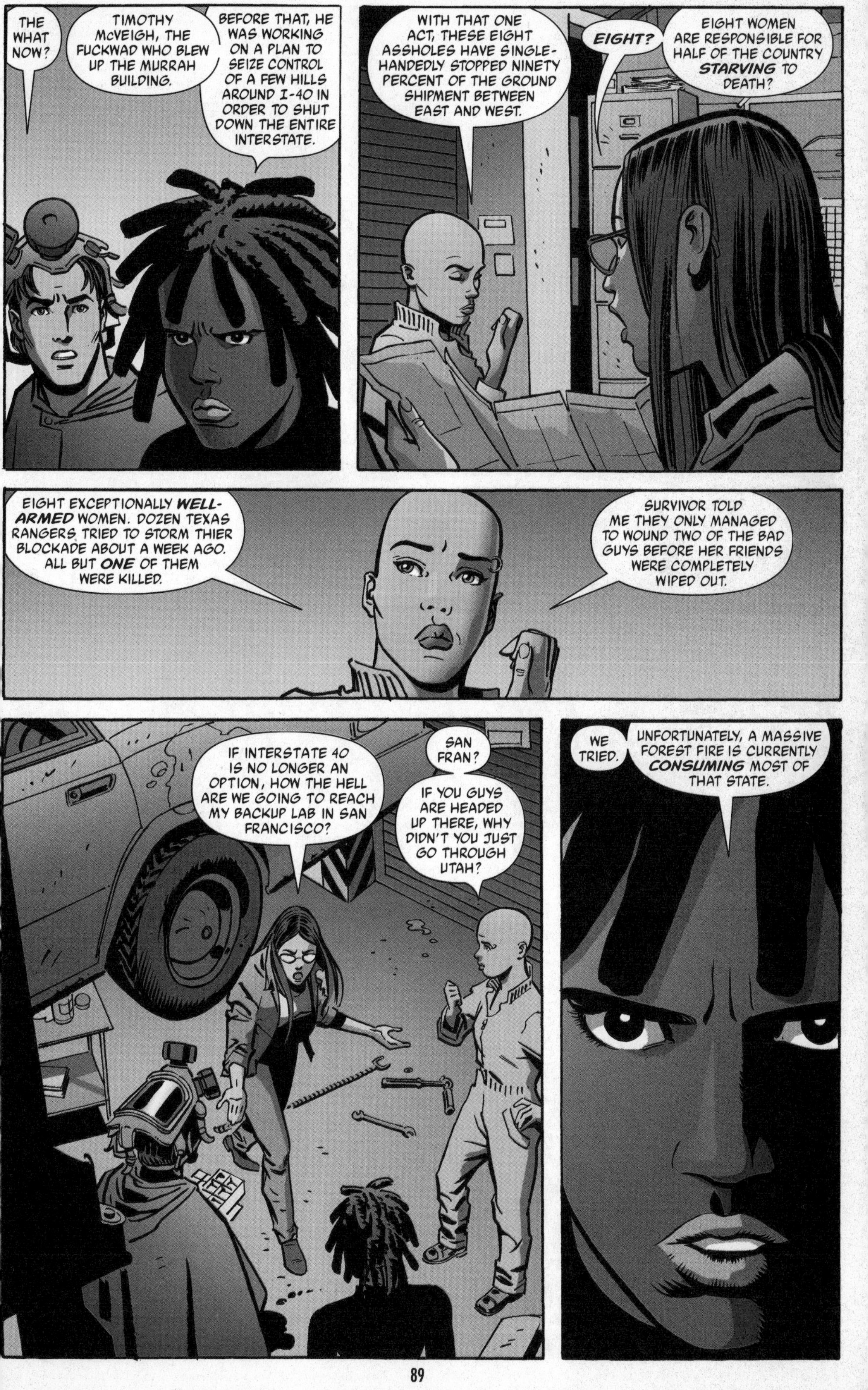
THE WHAT NOW?
TIMOTHY McVEIGH, THE FUCKWAD WHO BLEW UP THE MURRAH BUILDING.
BEFORE THAT, HE WAS WORKING ON A PLAN TO SEIZE CONTROL OF A FEW HILLS AROUND I-40 IN ORDER TO SHUT DOWN THE ENTIRE INTERSTATE.
WITH THAT ONE ACT, THESE EIGHT ASSHOLES HAVE SINGLE-HANDEDLY STOPPED NINETY PERCENT OF THE GROUND SHIPMENT BETWEEN EAST AND WEST.
EIGHT?
EIGHT WOMEN ARE RESPONSIBLE FOR HALF OF THE COUNTRY STARVING TO DEATH?
EIGHT EXCEPTIONALLY WELL-ARMED WOMEN. DOZEN TEXAS RANGERS TRIED TO STORM THIER BLOCKADE ABOUT A WEEK AGO. ALL BUT ONE OF THEM WERE KILLED.
SURVIVOR TOLD ME THEY ONLY MANAGED TO WOUND TWO OF THE BAD GUYS BEFORE HER FRIENDS WERE COMPLETELY WIPED OUT.
IF INTERSTATE 40 IS NO LONGER AN OPTION, HOW THE HELL ARE WE GOING TO REACH MY BACKUP LAB IN SAN FRANCISCO?
SAN FRAN?
IF YOU GUYS ARE HEADED UP THERE, WHY DIDN'T YOU JUST GO THROUGH UTAH?
WE TRIED.
UNFORTUNATELY, A MASSIVE FOREST FIRE IS CURRENTLY CONSUMING MOST OF THAT STATE.

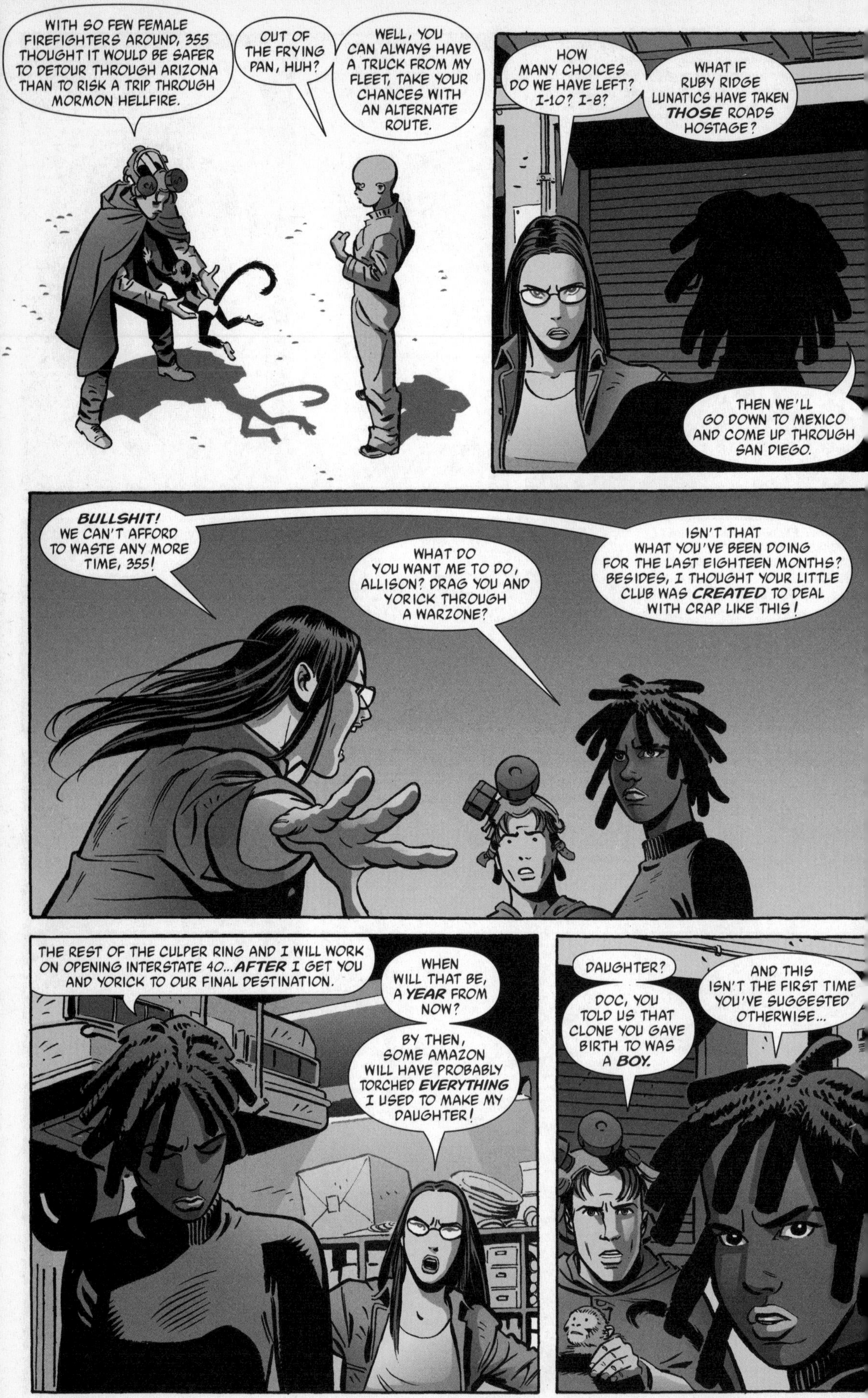
WITH SO FEW FEMALE FIREFIGHTERS AROUND, 355 THOUGHT IT WOULD BE SAFER TO DETOUR THROUGH ARIZONA THAN TO RISK A TRIP THROUGH MORMON HELLFIRE.
OUT OF THE FRYING PAN, HUH?
WELL, YOU CAN ALWAYS HAVE A TRUCK FROM MY FLEET, TAKE YOUR CHANCES WITH AN ALTERNATE ROUTE.
HOW MANY CHOICES DO WE HAVE LEFT? I-10? I-8?
WHAT IF RUBY RIDGE LUNATICS HAVE TAKEN THOSE ROADS HOSTAGE?
THEN WE'LL GO DOWN TO MEXICO AND COME UP THROUGH SAN DIEGO.
BULLSHIT! WE CAN'T AFFORD TO WASTE ANY MORE TIME, 355!
WHAT DO YOU WANT ME TO DO, ALLISON? DRAG YOU AND YORICK THROUGH A WARZONE?
ISN'T THAT WHAT YOU'VE BEEN DOING FOR THE LAST EIGHTEEN MONTHS? BESIDES, I THOUGHT YOUR LITTLE CLUB WAS CREATED TO DEAL WITH CRAP LIKE THIS!
THE REST OF THE CULPER RING AND I WILL WORK ON OPENING INTERSTATE 40...AFTER I GET YOU AND YORICK TO OUR FINAL DESTINATION.
WHEN WILL THAT BE, A YEAR FROM NOW?
BY THEN, SOME AMAZON WILL HAVE PROBABLY TORCHED EVERYTHING I USED TO MAKE MY DAUGHTER!
DAUGHTER?
DOC, YOU TOLD US THAT CLONE YOU GAVE BIRTH TO WAS A BOY.
AND THIS ISN'T THE FIRST TIME YOU'VE SUGGESTED OTHERWISE...

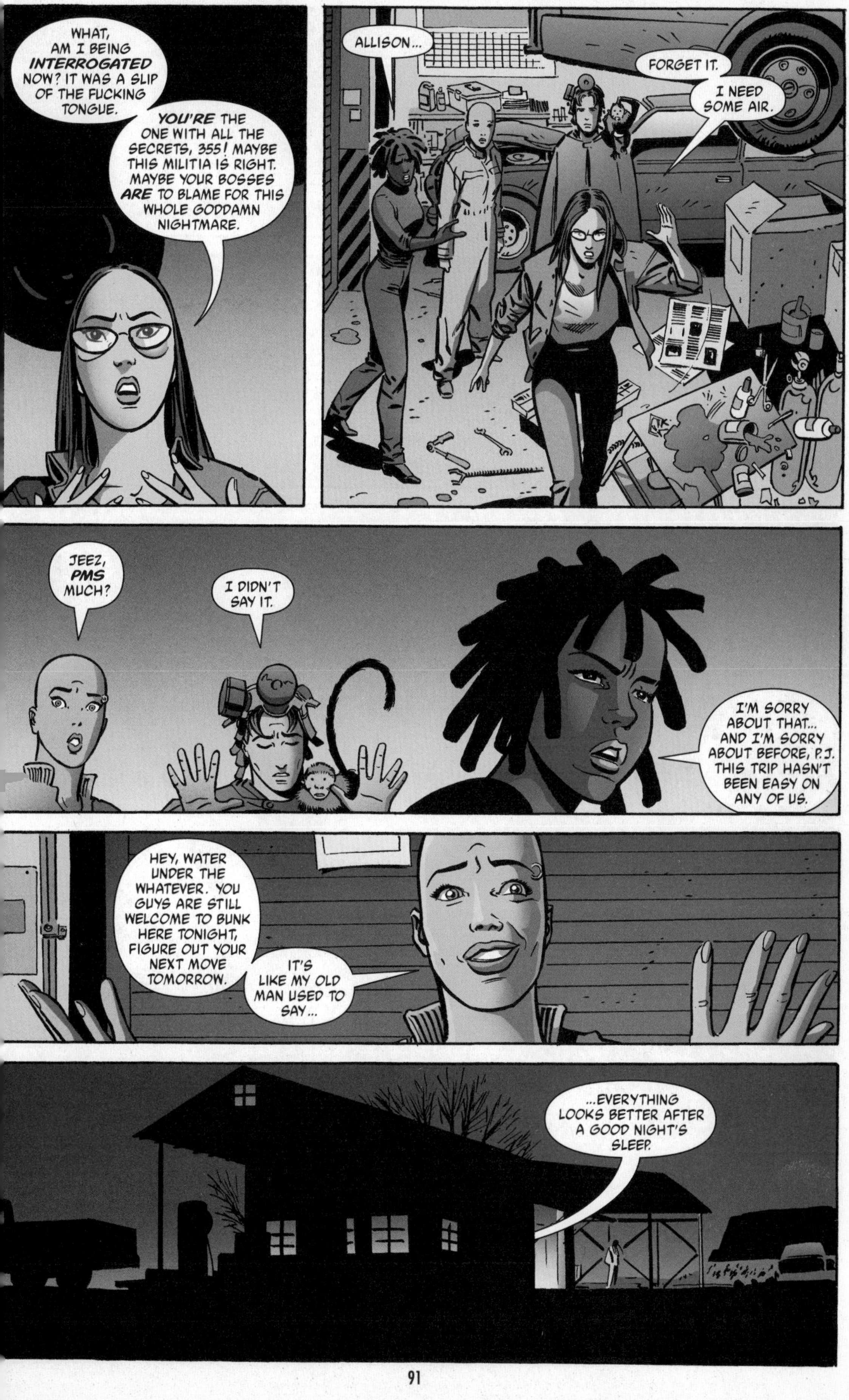
WHAT, AM I BEING INTERROGATED NOW? IT WAS A SLIP OF THE FUCKING TONGUE.
YOU'RE THE ONE WITH ALL THE SECRETS, 355! MAYBE THIS MILITIA IS RIGHT. MAYBE YOUR BOSSES ARE TO BLAME FOR THIS WHOLE GODDAMN NIGHTMARE.
ALLISON...
FORGET IT.
I NEED SOME AIR.
JEEZ, PMS MUCH?
I DIDN'T SAY IT.
I'M SORRY ABOUT THAT... AND I'M SORRY ABOUT BEFORE, P.J. THIS TRIP HASN'T BEEN EASY ON ANY OF US.
HEY, WATER UNDER THE WHATEVER. YOU GUYS ARE STILL WELCOME TO BUNK HERE TONIGHT, FIGURE OUT YOUR NEXT MOVE TOMORROW.
IT'S LIKE MY OLD MAN USED TO SAY...
...EVERYTHING LOOKS BETTER AFTER A GOOD NIGHT'S SLEEP.

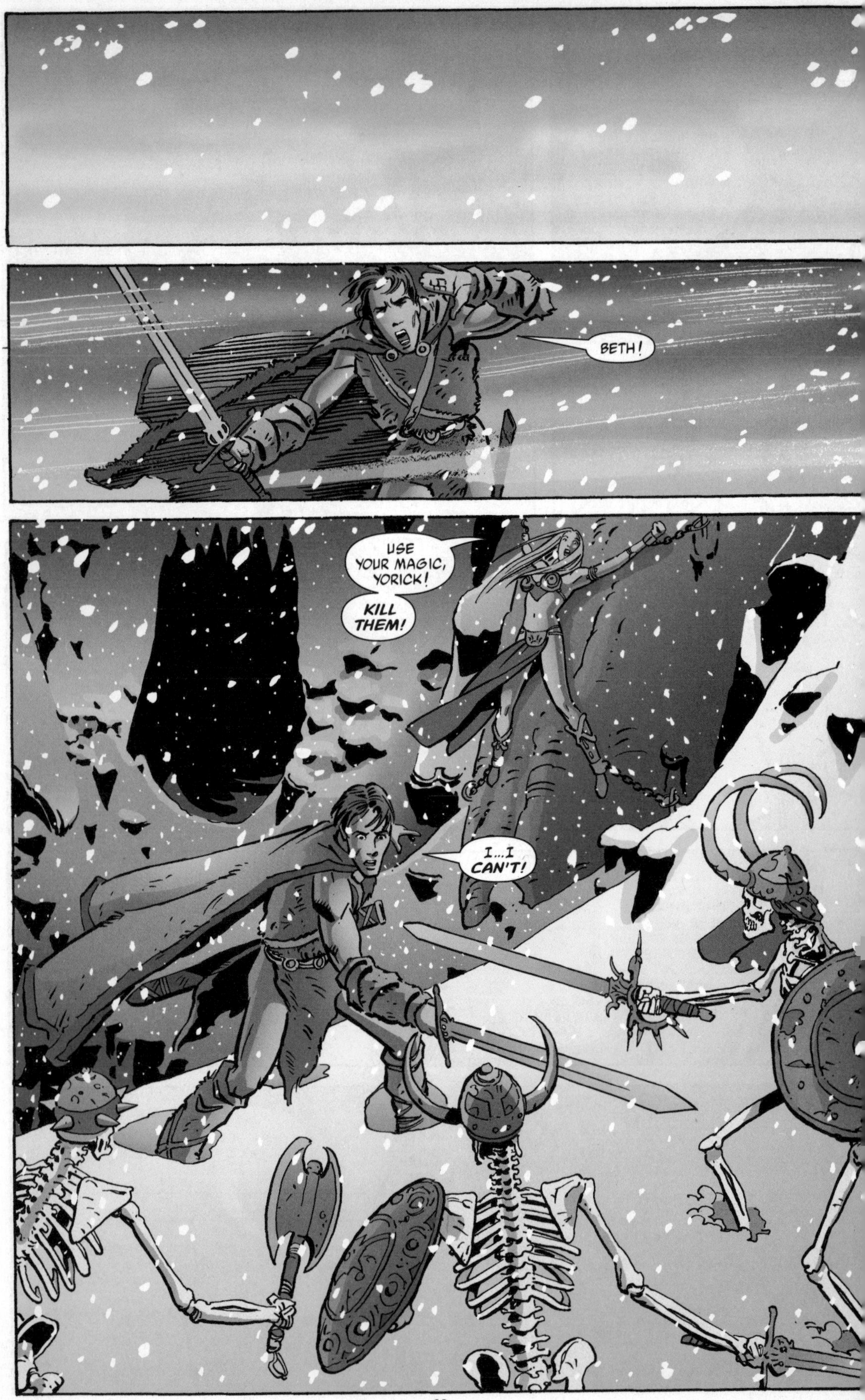

BETH!
USE YOUR MAGIC, YORICK!
KILL THEM!
I...I CAN'T!

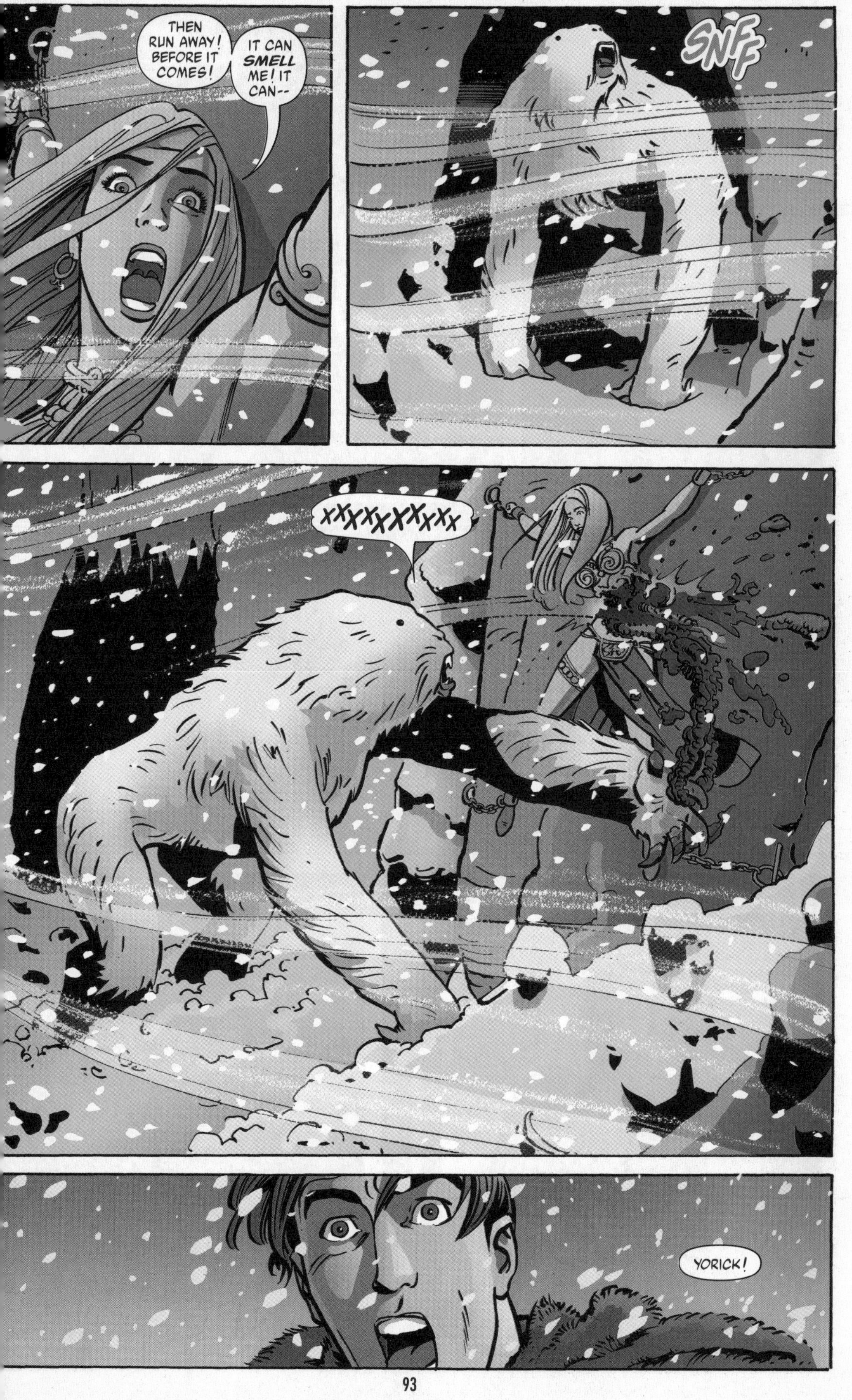
THEN RUN AWAY! BEFORE IT COMES!
IT CAN SMELL ME! IT CAN--
SNFF
XXXXXXXXXX
YORICK!

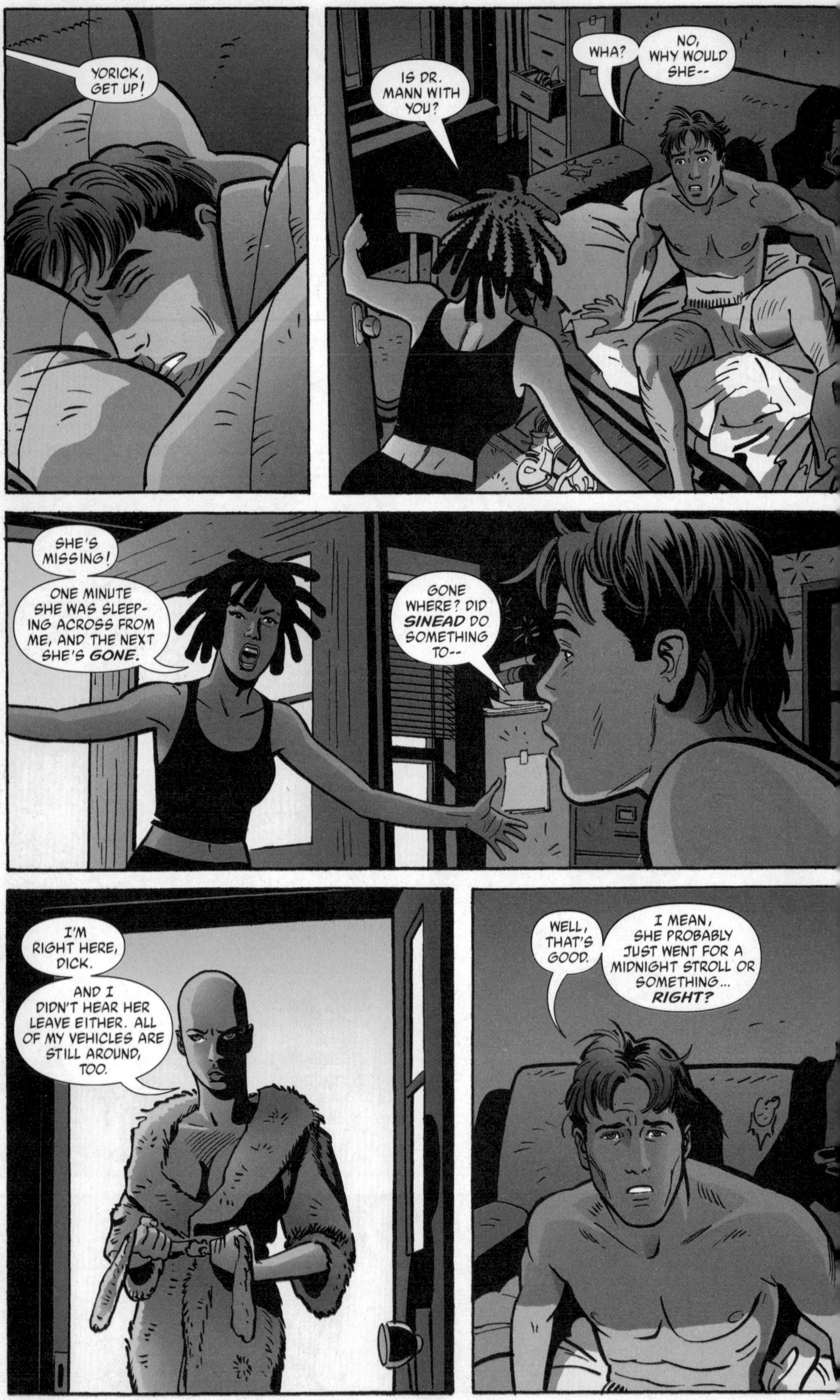

YORICK, GET UP!
IS DR. MANN WITH YOU?
WHA?
NO, WHY WOULD SHE--
SHE'S MISSING!
ONE MINUTE SHE WAS SLEEPING ACROSS FROM ME, AND THE NEXT SHE'S *GONE.*
GONE WHERE? DID ***SINEAD*** DO SOMETHING TO--
I'M RIGHT HERE, DICK.
AND I DIDN'T HEAR HER LEAVE EITHER. ALL OF MY VEHICLES ARE STILL AROUND, TOO.
WELL, THAT'S GOOD.
I MEAN, SHE PROBABLY JUST WENT FOR A MIDNIGHT STROLL OR SOMETHING... ***RIGHT?***

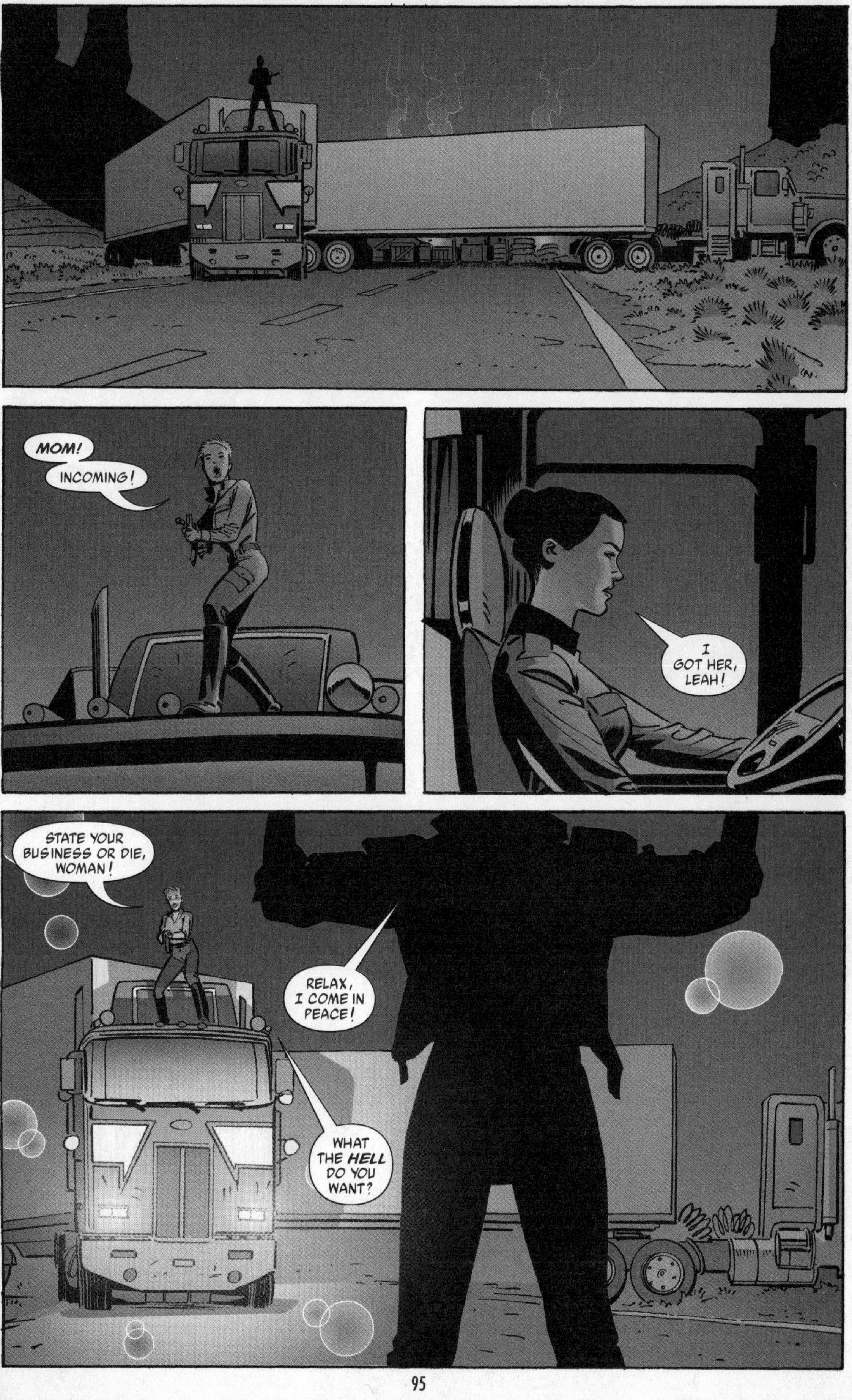
MOM!
INCOMING!
I GOT HER, LEAH!
STATE YOUR BUSINESS OR DIE, WOMAN!
RELAX, I COME IN PEACE!
WHAT THE HELL DO YOU WANT?

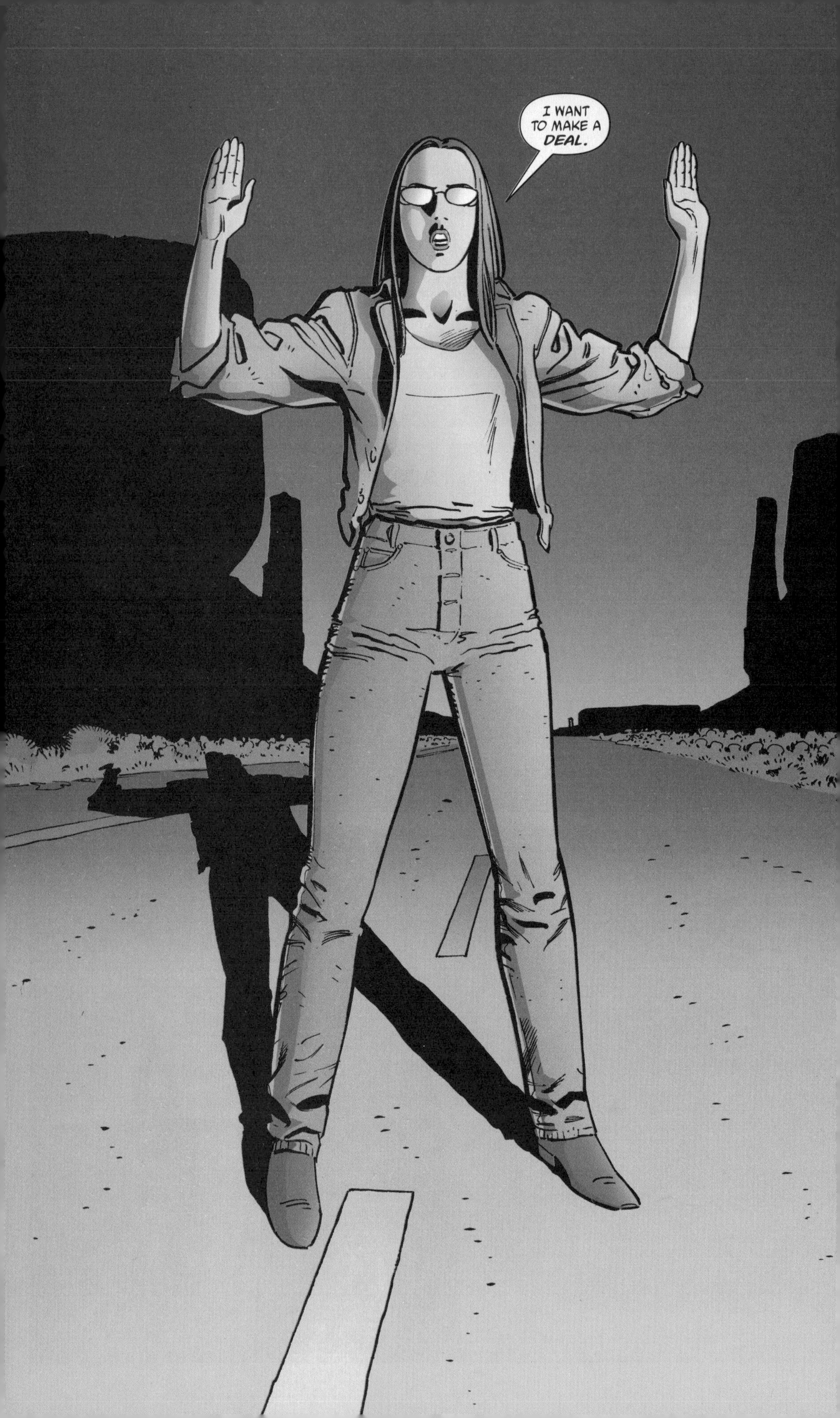
I WANT TO MAKE A DEAL.

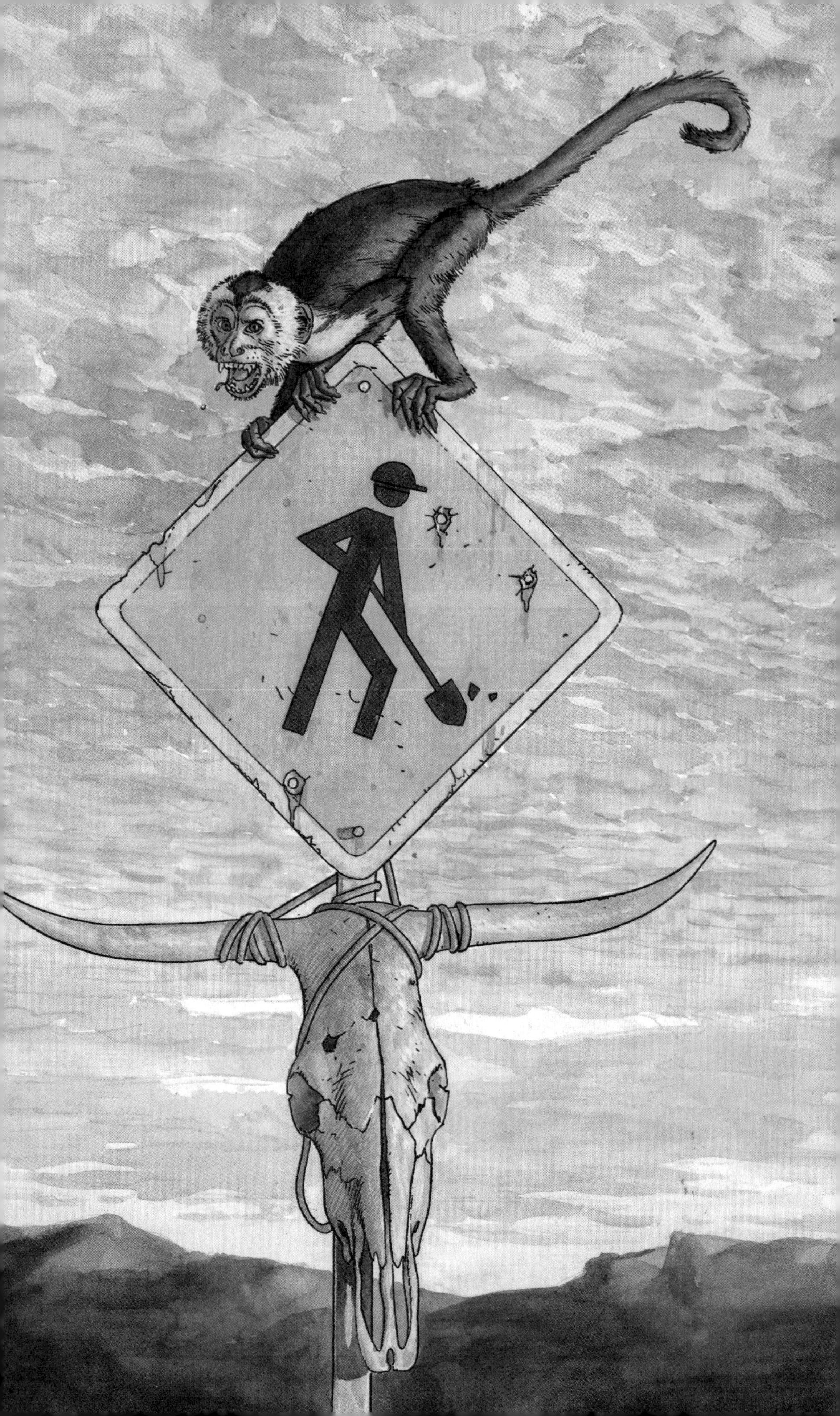

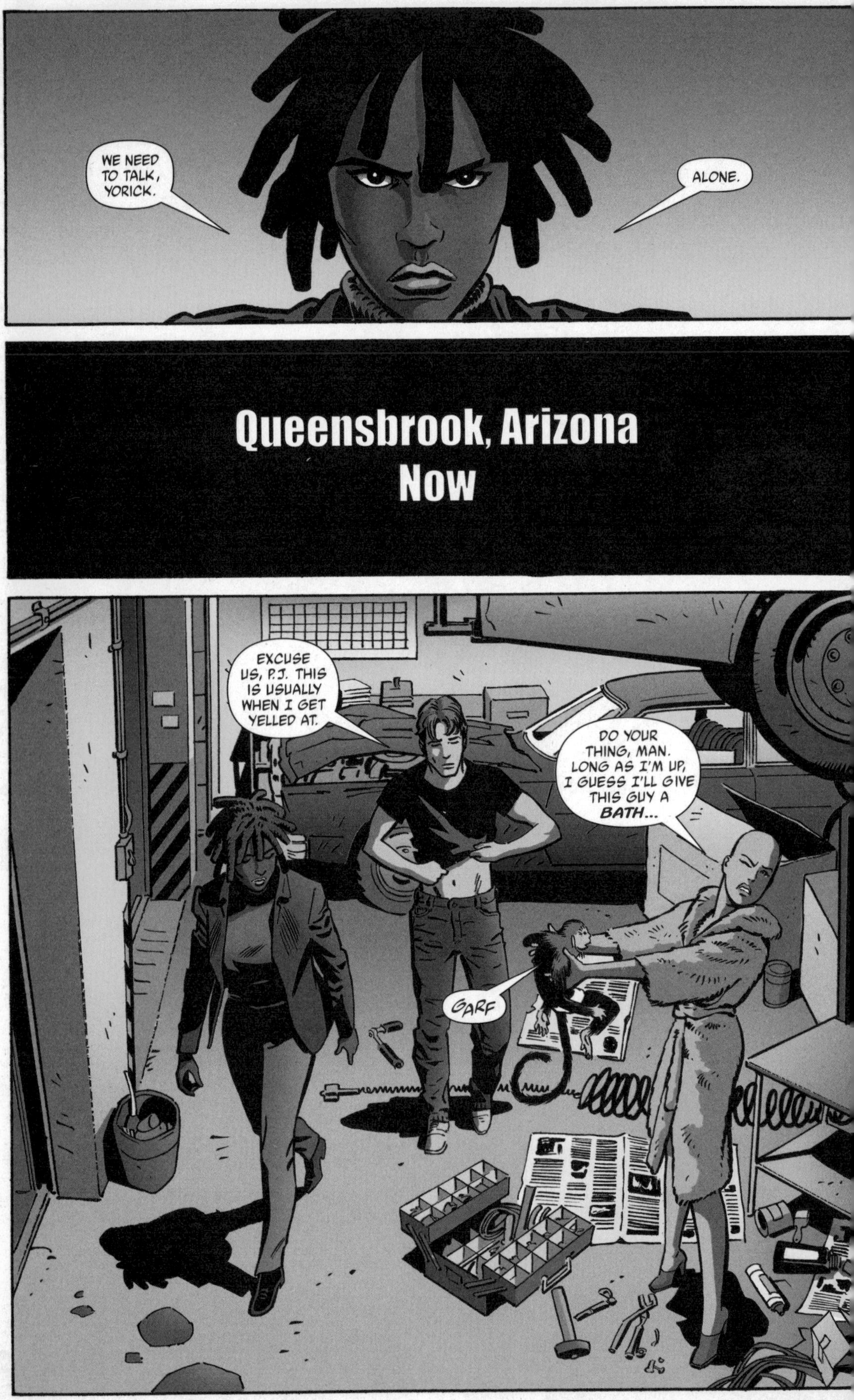
WE NEED TO TALK, YORICK.
ALONE.
Queensbrook, Arizona
Now
EXCUSE US, P.J. THIS IS USUALLY WHEN I GET YELLED AT.
DO YOUR THING, MAN. LONG AS I'M UP, I GUESS I'LL GIVE THIS GUY A BATH...
GARF

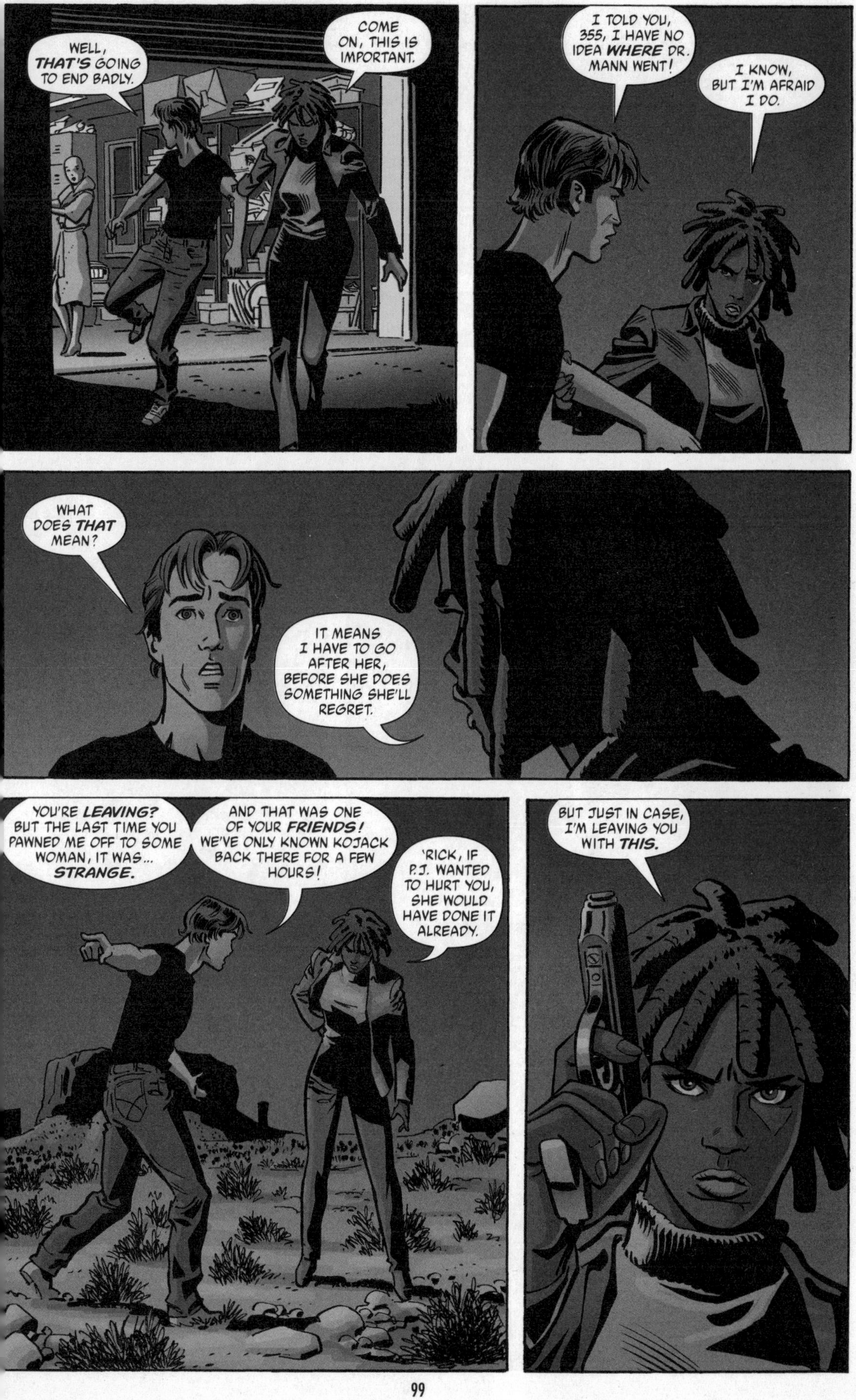
WELL, THAT'S GOING TO END BADLY.
COME ON, THIS IS IMPORTANT.
I TOLD YOU, 355, I HAVE NO IDEA WHERE DR. MANN WENT!
I KNOW, BUT I'M AFRAID I DO.
WHAT DOES THAT MEAN?
IT MEANS I HAVE TO GO AFTER HER, BEFORE SHE DOES SOMETHING SHE'LL REGRET.
YOU'RE LEAVING? BUT THE LAST TIME YOU PAWNED ME OFF TO SOME WOMAN, IT WAS... STRANGE.
AND THAT WAS ONE OF YOUR FRIENDS! WE'VE ONLY KNOWN KOJACK BACK THERE FOR A FEW HOURS!
'RICK, IF P.J. WANTED TO HURT YOU, SHE WOULD HAVE DONE IT ALREADY.
BUT JUST IN CASE, I'M LEAVING YOU WITH THIS.

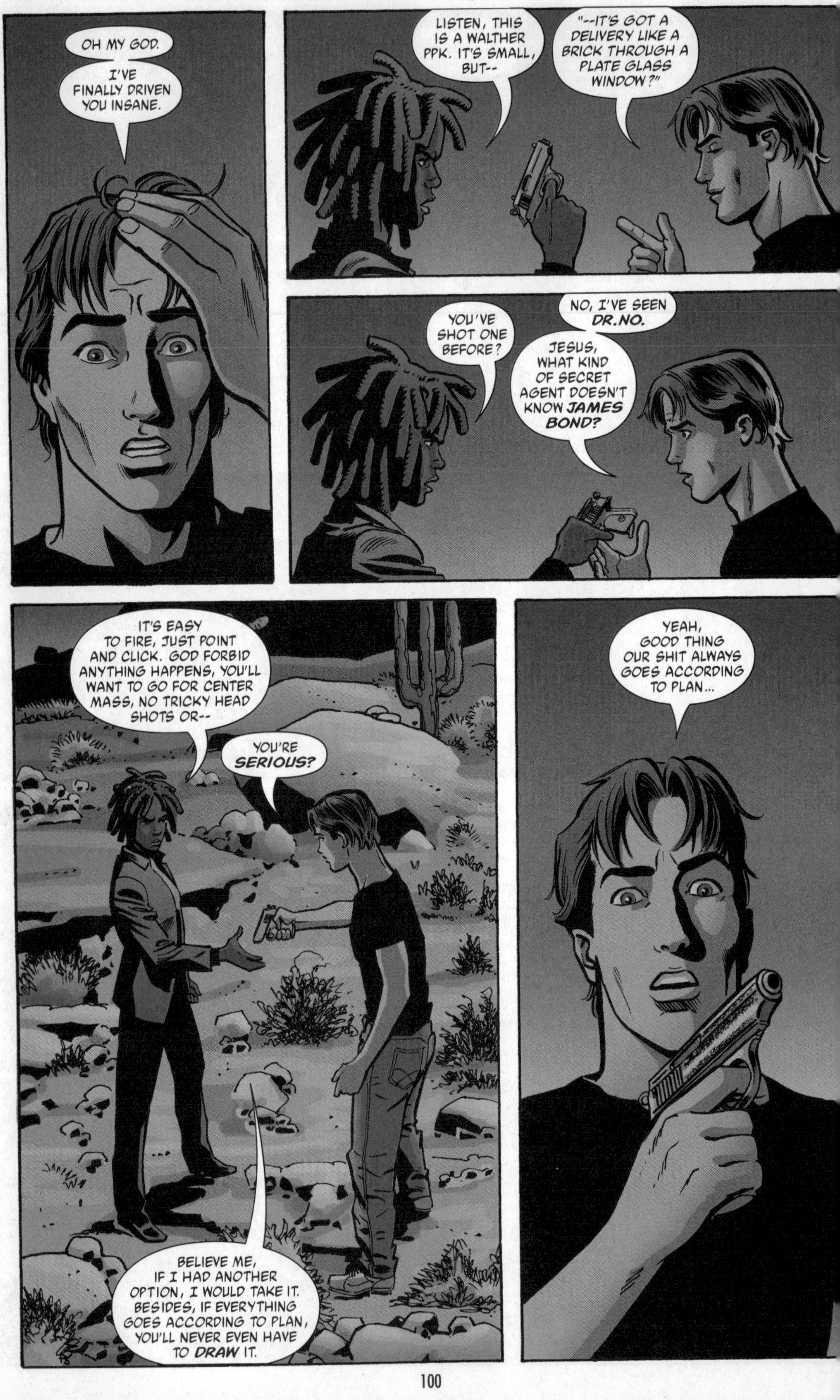
OH MY GOD.
I'VE FINALLY DRIVEN YOU INSANE.
LISTEN, THIS IS A WALTHER PPK. IT'S SMALL, BUT--
"--IT'S GOT A DELIVERY LIKE A BRICK THROUGH A PLATE GLASS WINDOW?"
YOU'VE SHOT ONE BEFORE?
NO, I'VE SEEN DR. NO.
JESUS, WHAT KIND OF SECRET AGENT DOESN'T KNOW JAMES BOND?
IT'S EASY TO FIRE, JUST POINT AND CLICK. GOD FORBID ANYTHING HAPPENS, YOU'LL WANT TO GO FOR CENTER MASS, NO TRICKY HEAD SHOTS OR--
YOU'RE SERIOUS?
BELIEVE ME, IF I HAD ANOTHER OPTION, I WOULD TAKE IT. BESIDES, IF EVERYTHING GOES ACCORDING TO PLAN, YOU'LL NEVER EVEN HAVE TO DRAW IT.
YEAH, GOOD THING OUR SHIT ALWAYS GOES ACCORDING TO PLAN...

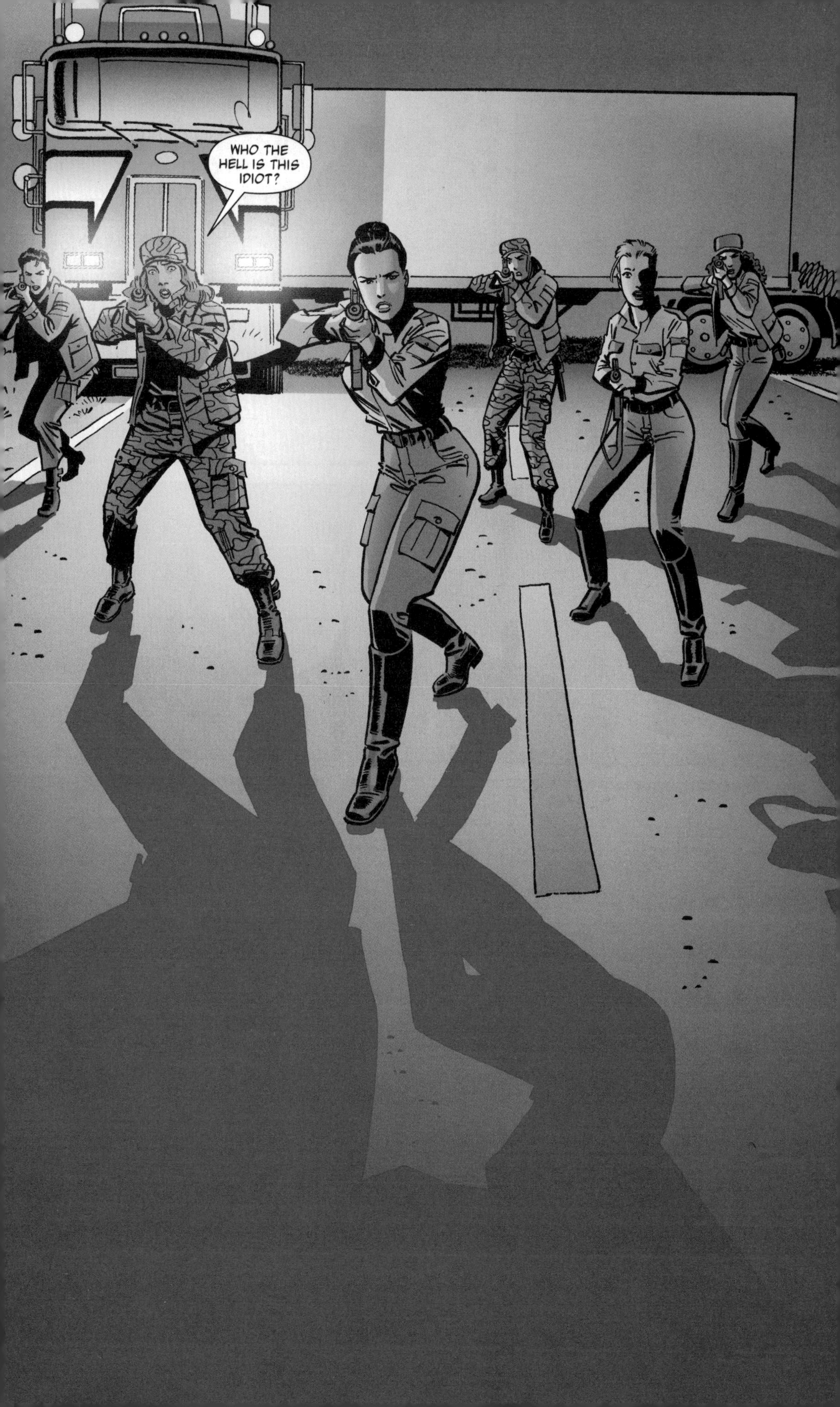
WHO THE HELL IS THIS IDIOT?

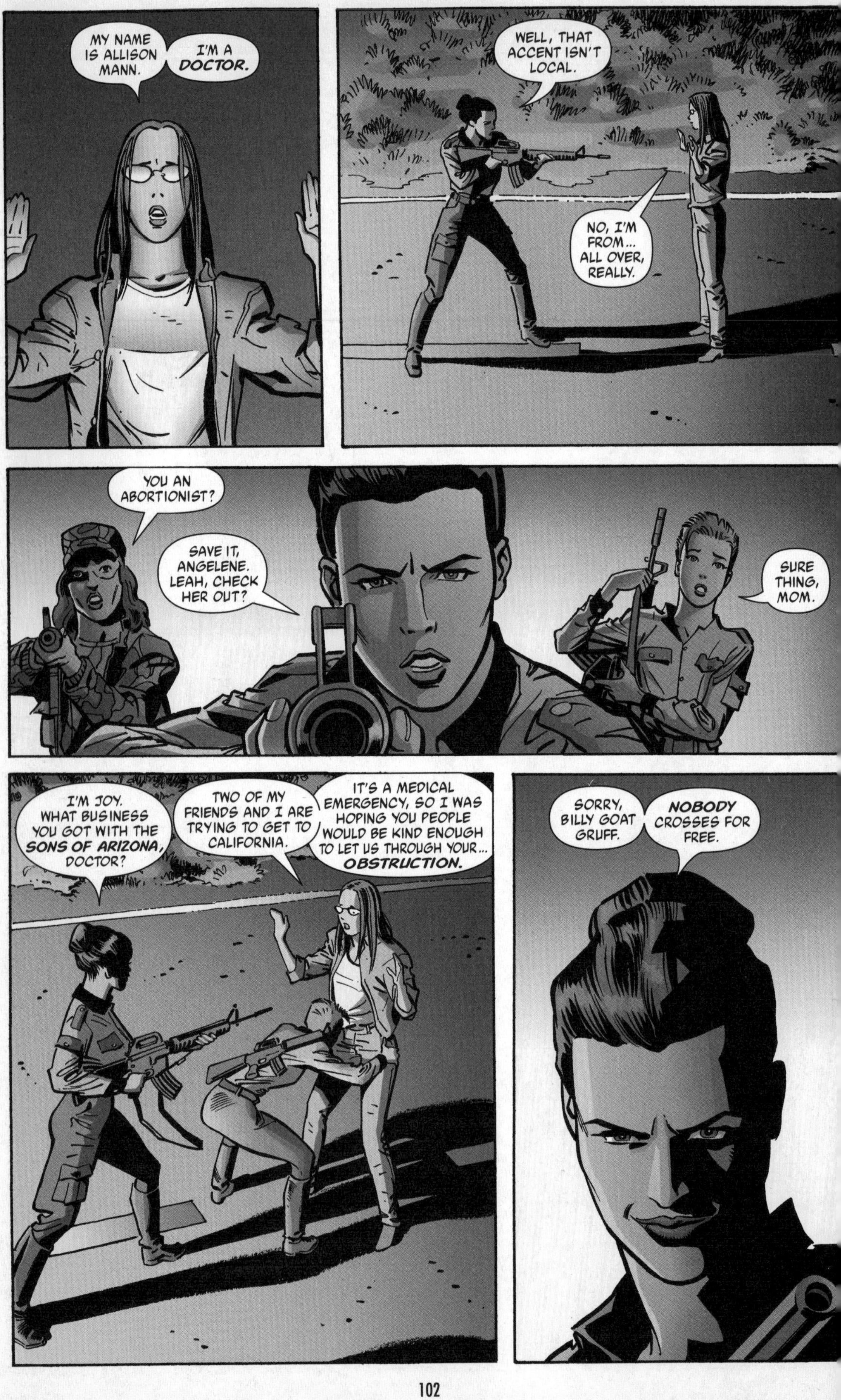
MY NAME IS ALLISON MANN.
I'M A **DOCTOR.**
WELL, THAT ACCENT ISN'T LOCAL.
NO, I'M FROM... ALL OVER, REALLY.
YOU AN ABORTIONIST?
SAVE IT, ANGELENE. LEAH, CHECK HER OUT?
SURE THING, MOM.
I'M JOY. WHAT BUSINESS YOU GOT WITH THE **SONS OF ARIZONA,** DOCTOR?
TWO OF MY FRIENDS AND I ARE TRYING TO GET TO CALIFORNIA.
IT'S A MEDICAL EMERGENCY, SO I WAS HOPING YOU PEOPLE WOULD BE KIND ENOUGH TO LET US THROUGH YOUR... **OBSTRUCTION.**
SORRY, BILLY GOAT GRUFF.
NOBODY CROSSES FOR FREE.

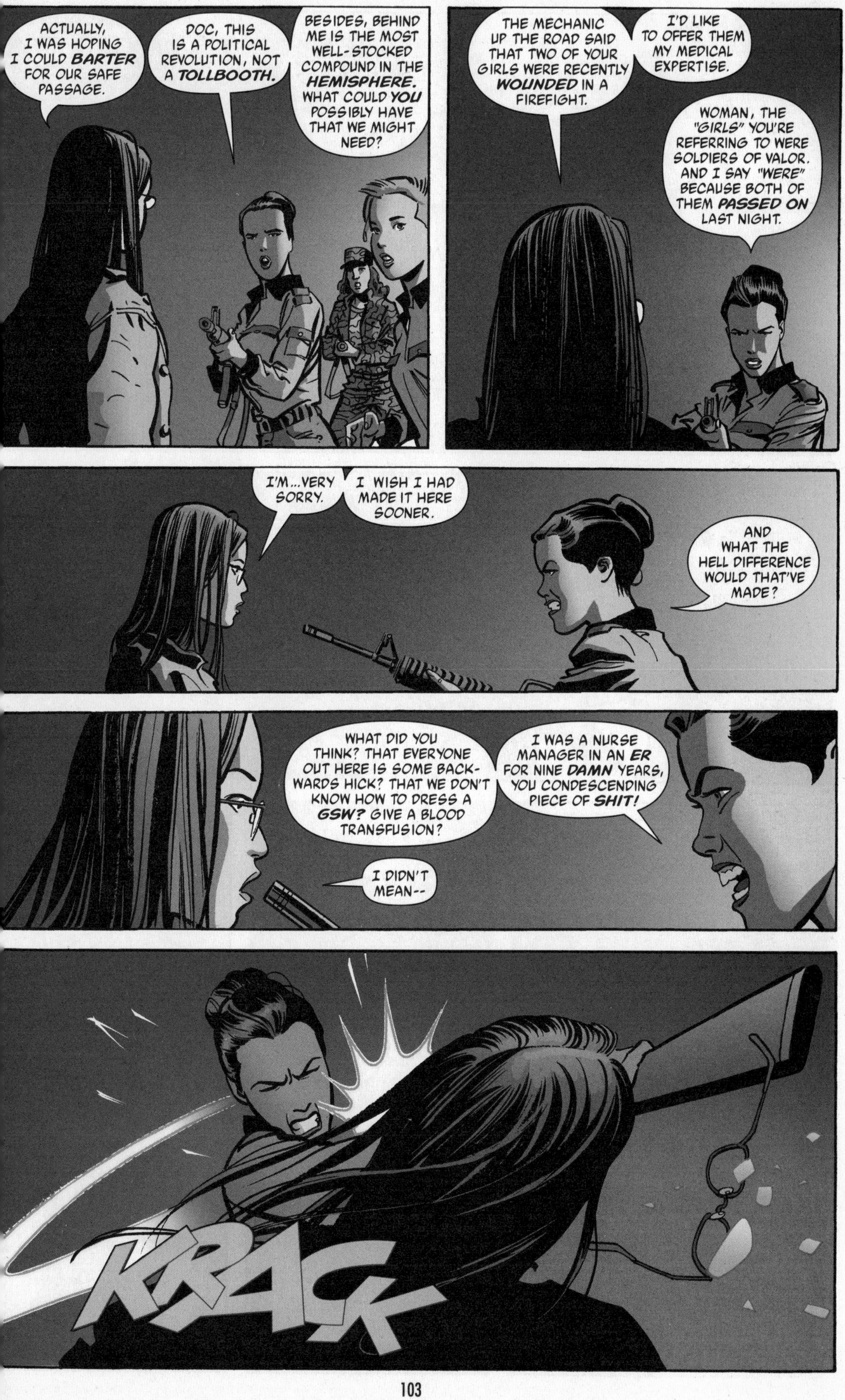
ACTUALLY, I WAS HOPING I COULD BARTER FOR OUR SAFE PASSAGE.
DOC, THIS IS A POLITICAL REVOLUTION, NOT A TOLLBOOTH.
BESIDES, BEHIND ME IS THE MOST WELL-STOCKED COMPOUND IN THE HEMISPHERE. WHAT COULD YOU POSSIBLY HAVE THAT WE MIGHT NEED?
THE MECHANIC UP THE ROAD SAID THAT TWO OF YOUR GIRLS WERE RECENTLY WOUNDED IN A FIREFIGHT.
I'D LIKE TO OFFER THEM MY MEDICAL EXPERTISE.
WOMAN, THE "GIRLS" YOU'RE REFERRING TO WERE SOLDIERS OF VALOR. AND I SAY "WERE" BECAUSE BOTH OF THEM PASSED ON LAST NIGHT.
I'M...VERY SORRY.
I WISH I HAD MADE IT HERE SOONER.
AND WHAT THE HELL DIFFERENCE WOULD THAT'VE MADE?
WHAT DID YOU THINK? THAT EVERYONE OUT HERE IS SOME BACK-WARDS HICK? THAT WE DON'T KNOW HOW TO DRESS A GSW? GIVE A BLOOD TRANSFUSION?
I DIDN'T MEAN--
I WAS A NURSE MANAGER IN AN ER FOR NINE DAMN YEARS, YOU CONDESCENDING PIECE OF SHIT!
KRACK

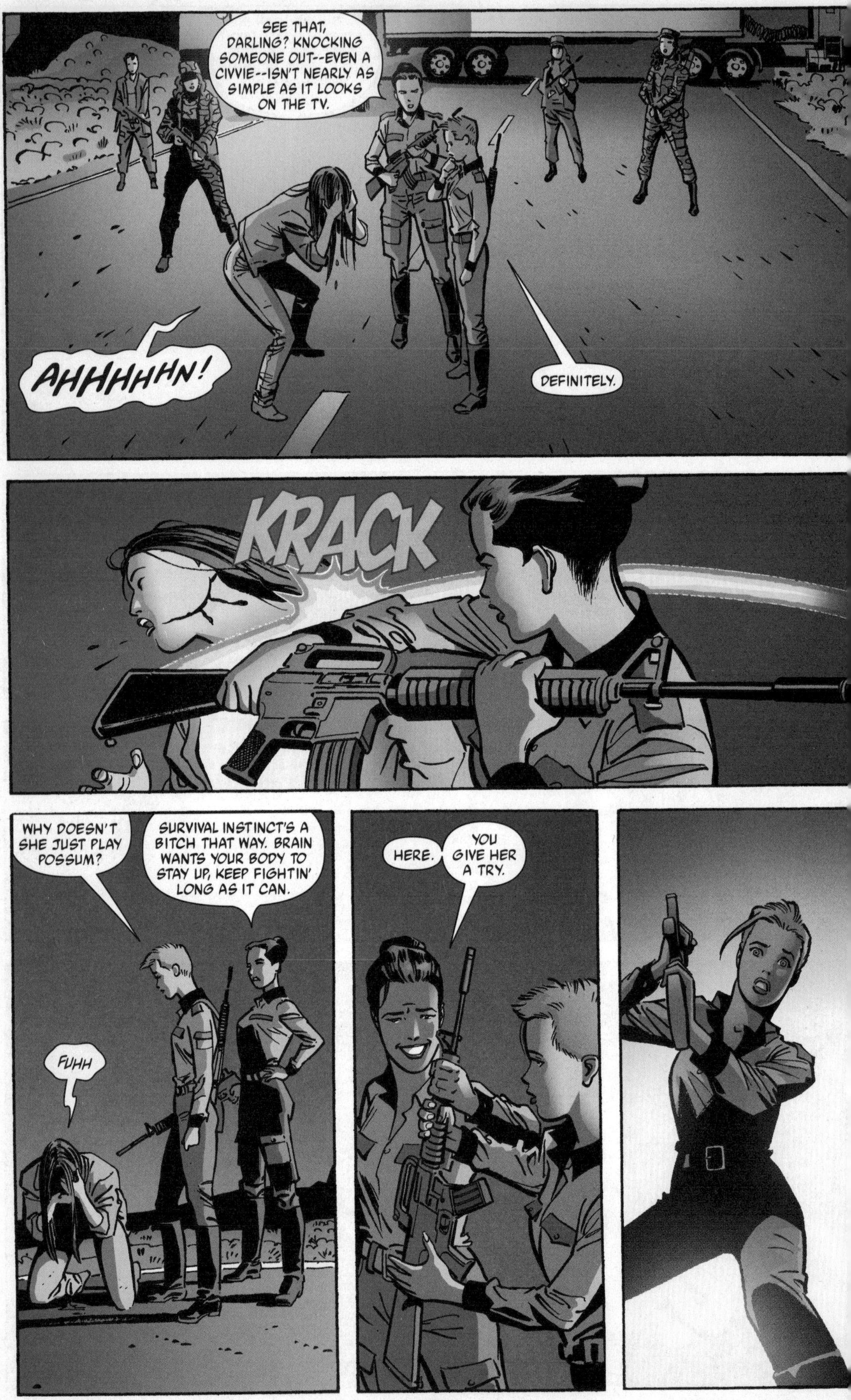
SEE THAT, DARLING? KNOCKING SOMEONE OUT--EVEN A CIVVIE--ISN'T NEARLY AS SIMPLE AS IT LOOKS ON THE TV.
AHHHHHN!
DEFINITELY.
KRACK
WHY DOESN'T SHE JUST PLAY POSSUM?
SURVIVAL INSTINCT'S A BITCH THAT WAY. BRAIN WANTS YOUR BODY TO STAY UP, KEEP FIGHTIN' LONG AS IT CAN.
FUHH
HERE.
YOU GIVE HER A TRY.

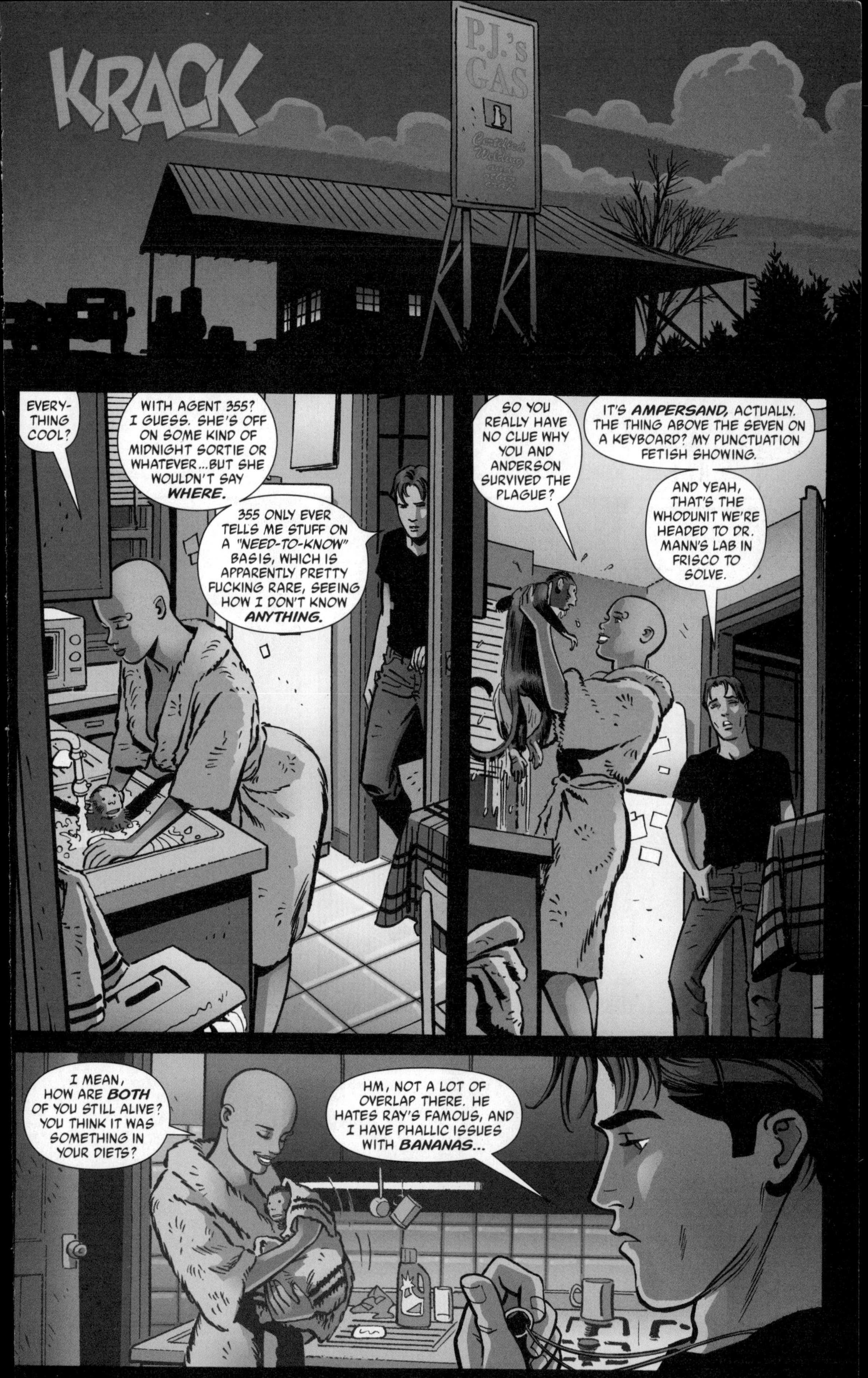
KRACK
P.J.'s GAS
EVERY-THING COOL?
WITH AGENT 355? I GUESS. SHE'S OFF ON SOME KIND OF MIDNIGHT SORTIE OR WHATEVER...BUT SHE WOULDN'T SAY WHERE.
355 ONLY EVER TELLS ME STUFF ON A "NEED-TO-KNOW" BASIS, WHICH IS APPARENTLY PRETTY FUCKING RARE, SEEING HOW I DON'T KNOW ANYTHING.
SO YOU REALLY HAVE NO CLUE WHY YOU AND ANDERSON SURVIVED THE PLAGUE?
IT'S AMPERSAND, ACTUALLY. THE THING ABOVE THE SEVEN ON A KEYBOARD? MY PUNCTUATION FETISH SHOWING.
AND YEAH, THAT'S THE WHODUNIT WE'RE HEADED TO DR. MANN'S LAB IN FRISCO TO SOLVE.
I MEAN, HOW ARE BOTH OF YOU STILL ALIVE? YOU THINK IT WAS SOMETHING IN YOUR DIETS?
HM, NOT A LOT OF OVERLAP THERE. HE HATES RAY'S FAMOUS, AND I HAVE PHALLIC ISSUES WITH BANANAS...

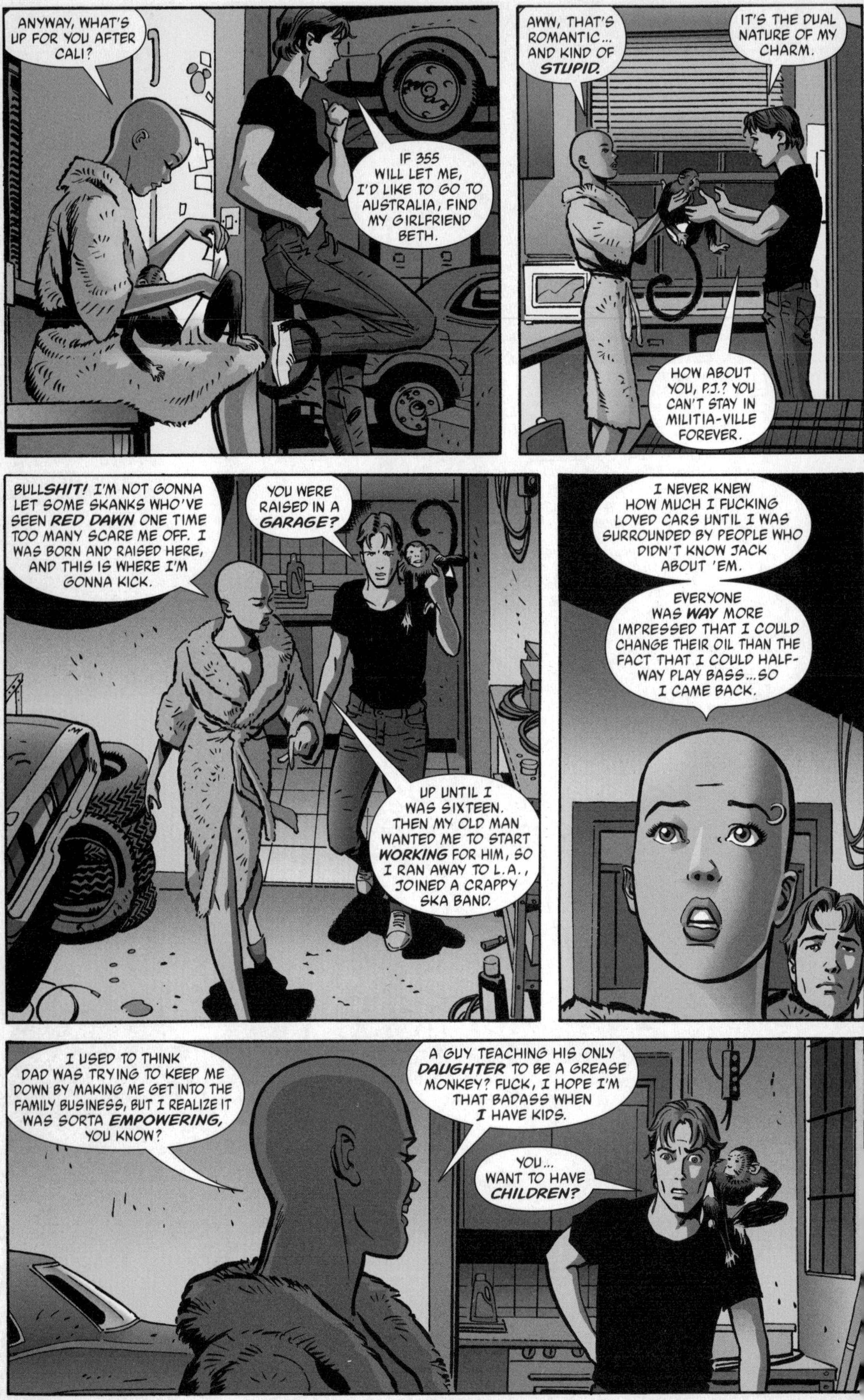
ANYWAY, WHAT'S UP FOR YOU AFTER CALI?
IF 355 WILL LET ME, I'D LIKE TO GO TO AUSTRALIA, FIND MY GIRLFRIEND BETH.
AWW, THAT'S ROMANTIC... AND KIND OF STUPID.
IT'S THE DUAL NATURE OF MY CHARM.
HOW ABOUT YOU, P.J.? YOU CAN'T STAY IN MILITIA-VILLE FOREVER.
BULLSHIT! I'M NOT GONNA LET SOME SKANKS WHO'VE SEEN RED DAWN ONE TIME TOO MANY SCARE ME OFF. I WAS BORN AND RAISED HERE, AND THIS IS WHERE I'M GONNA KICK.
YOU WERE RAISED IN A GARAGE?
UP UNTIL I WAS SIXTEEN. THEN MY OLD MAN WANTED ME TO START WORKING FOR HIM, SO I RAN AWAY TO L.A., JOINED A CRAPPY SKA BAND.
I NEVER KNEW HOW MUCH I FUCKING LOVED CARS UNTIL I WAS SURROUNDED BY PEOPLE WHO DIDN'T KNOW JACK ABOUT 'EM.
EVERYONE WAS WAY MORE IMPRESSED THAT I COULD CHANGE THEIR OIL THAN THE FACT THAT I COULD HALF-WAY PLAY BASS...SO I CAME BACK.
I USED TO THINK DAD WAS TRYING TO KEEP ME DOWN BY MAKING ME GET INTO THE FAMILY BUSINESS, BUT I REALIZE IT WAS SORTA EMPOWERING, YOU KNOW?
A GUY TEACHING HIS ONLY DAUGHTER TO BE A GREASE MONKEY? FUCK, I HOPE I'M THAT BADASS WHEN I HAVE KIDS.
YOU... WANT TO HAVE CHILDREN?

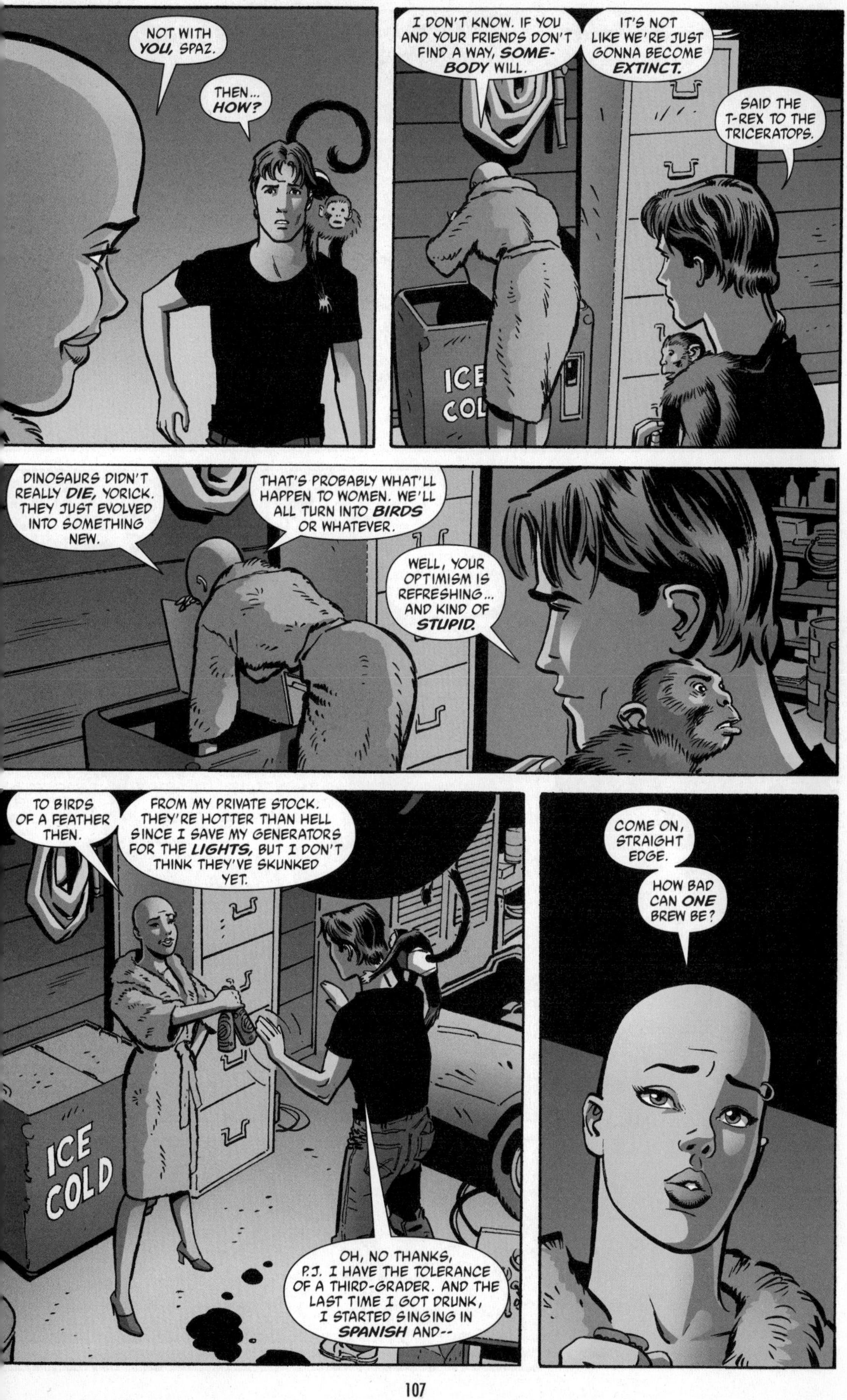
NOT WITH YOU, SPAZ.
THEN... HOW?
I DON'T KNOW. IF YOU AND YOUR FRIENDS DON'T FIND A WAY, SOMEBODY WILL.
IT'S NOT LIKE WE'RE JUST GONNA BECOME EXTINCT.
SAID THE T-REX TO THE TRICERATOPS.
ICE COL
DINOSAURS DIDN'T REALLY DIE, YORICK. THEY JUST EVOLVED INTO SOMETHING NEW.
THAT'S PROBABLY WHAT'LL HAPPEN TO WOMEN. WE'LL ALL TURN INTO BIRDS OR WHATEVER.
WELL, YOUR OPTIMISM IS REFRESHING... AND KIND OF STUPID.
TO BIRDS OF A FEATHER THEN.
FROM MY PRIVATE STOCK. THEY'RE HOTTER THAN HELL SINCE I SAVE MY GENERATORS FOR THE LIGHTS, BUT I DON'T THINK THEY'VE SKUNKED YET.
ICE COLD
OH, NO THANKS, P.J. I HAVE THE TOLERANCE OF A THIRD-GRADER. AND THE LAST TIME I GOT DRUNK, I STARTED SINGING IN SPANISH AND--
COME ON, STRAIGHT EDGE.
HOW BAD CAN ONE BREW BE?

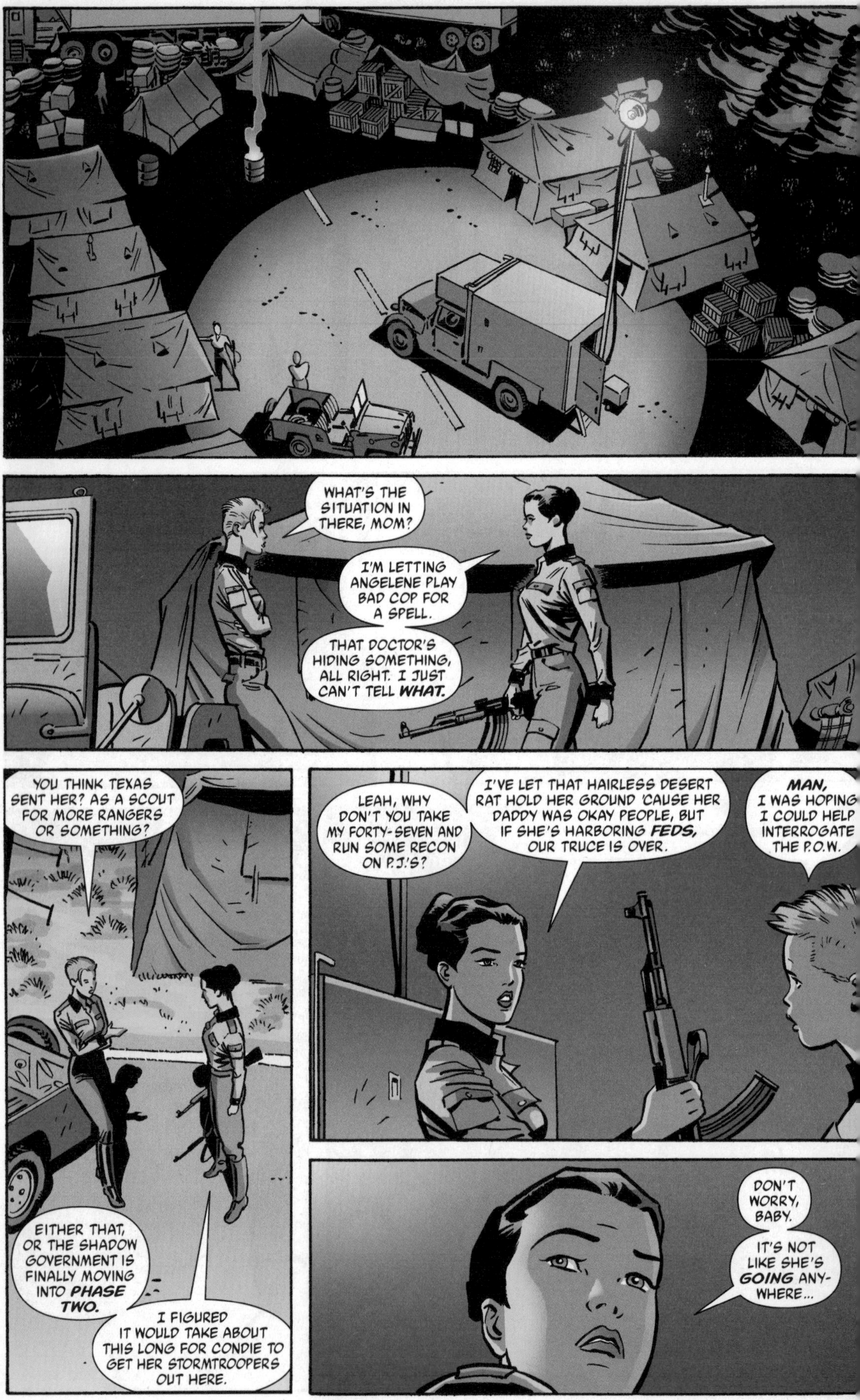
WHAT'S THE SITUATION IN THERE, MOM?
I'M LETTING ANGELENE PLAY BAD COP FOR A SPELL.
THAT DOCTOR'S HIDING SOMETHING, ALL RIGHT. I JUST CAN'T TELL WHAT.
YOU THINK TEXAS SENT HER? AS A SCOUT FOR MORE RANGERS OR SOMETHING?
EITHER THAT, OR THE SHADOW GOVERNMENT IS FINALLY MOVING INTO PHASE TWO.
I FIGURED IT WOULD TAKE ABOUT THIS LONG FOR CONDIE TO GET HER STORMTROOPERS OUT HERE.
LEAH, WHY DON'T YOU TAKE MY FORTY-SEVEN AND RUN SOME RECON ON P.J.'S?
I'VE LET THAT HAIRLESS DESERT RAT HOLD HER GROUND 'CAUSE HER DADDY WAS OKAY PEOPLE, BUT IF SHE'S HARBORING FEDS, OUR TRUCE IS OVER.
MAN, I WAS HOPING I COULD HELP INTERROGATE THE P.O.W.
DON'T WORRY, BABY.
IT'S NOT LIKE SHE'S GOING ANYWHERE...

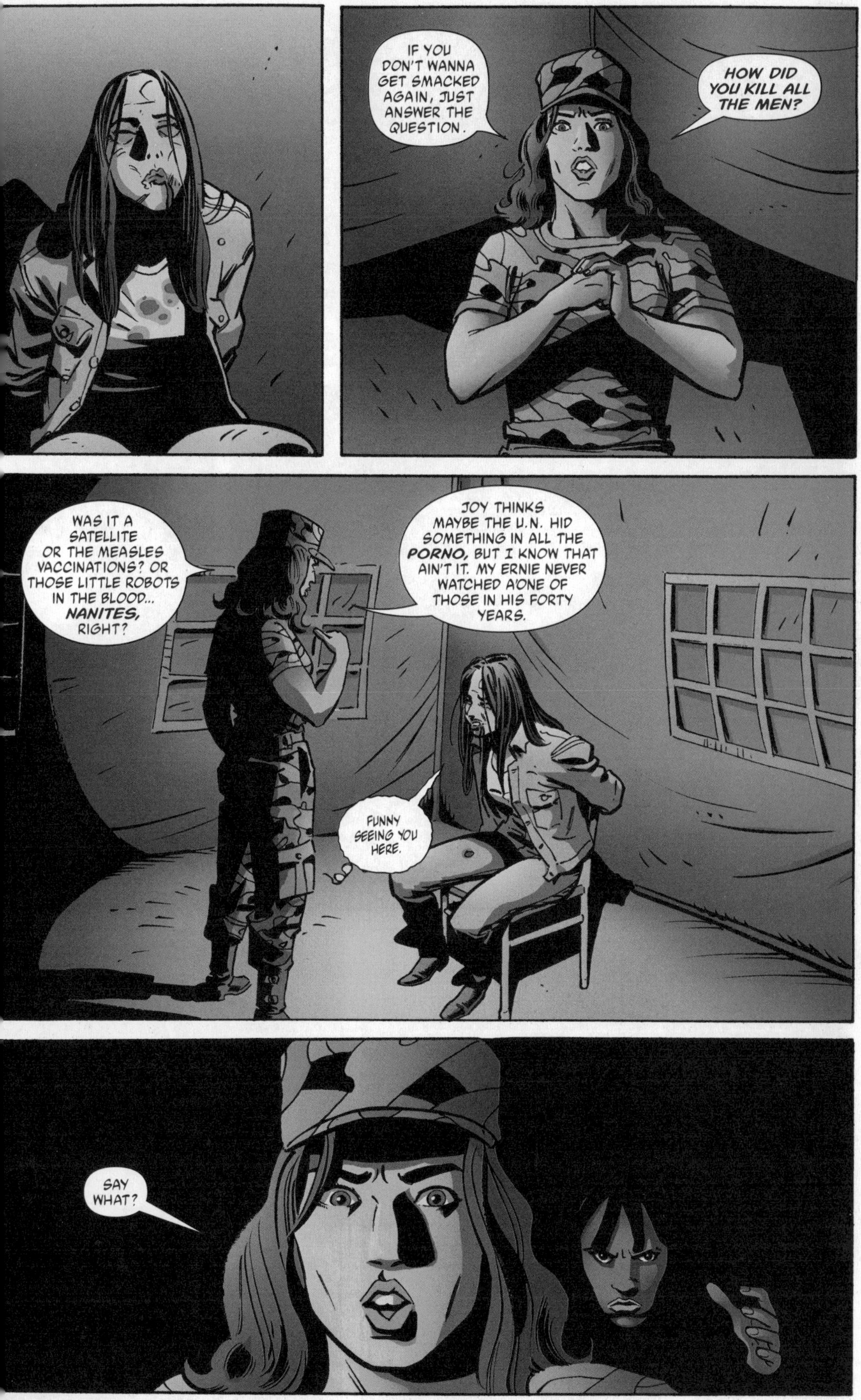
IF YOU DON'T WANNA GET SMACKED AGAIN, JUST ANSWER THE QUESTION.
HOW DID YOU KILL ALL THE MEN?
WAS IT A SATELLITE OR THE MEASLES VACCINATIONS? OR THOSE LITTLE ROBOTS IN THE BLOOD... NANITES, RIGHT?
JOY THINKS MAYBE THE U.N. HID SOMETHING IN ALL THE PORNO, BUT I KNOW THAT AIN'T IT. MY ERNIE NEVER WATCHED A'ONE OF THOSE IN HIS FORTY YEARS.
FUNNY SEEING YOU HERE.
SAY WHAT?

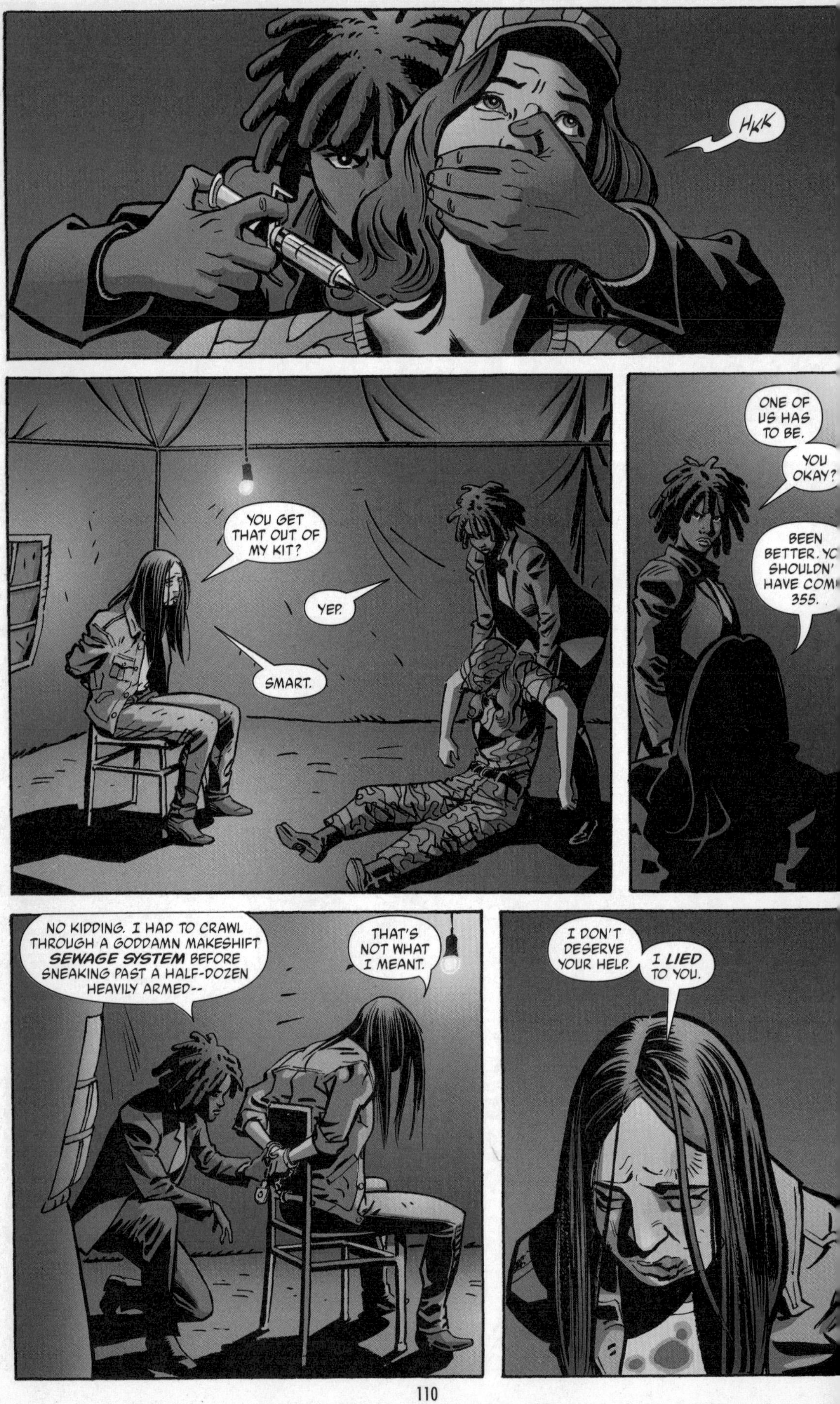
HKK
YOU GET THAT OUT OF MY KIT?
YEP.
SMART.
ONE OF US HAS TO BE.
YOU OKAY?
BEEN BETTER. YO SHOULDN' HAVE COM 355.
NO KIDDING. I HAD TO CRAWL THROUGH A GODDAMN MAKESHIFT SEWAGE SYSTEM BEFORE SNEAKING PAST A HALF-DOZEN HEAVILY ARMED--
THAT'S NOT WHAT I MEANT.
I DON'T DESERVE YOUR HELP.
I LIED TO YOU.

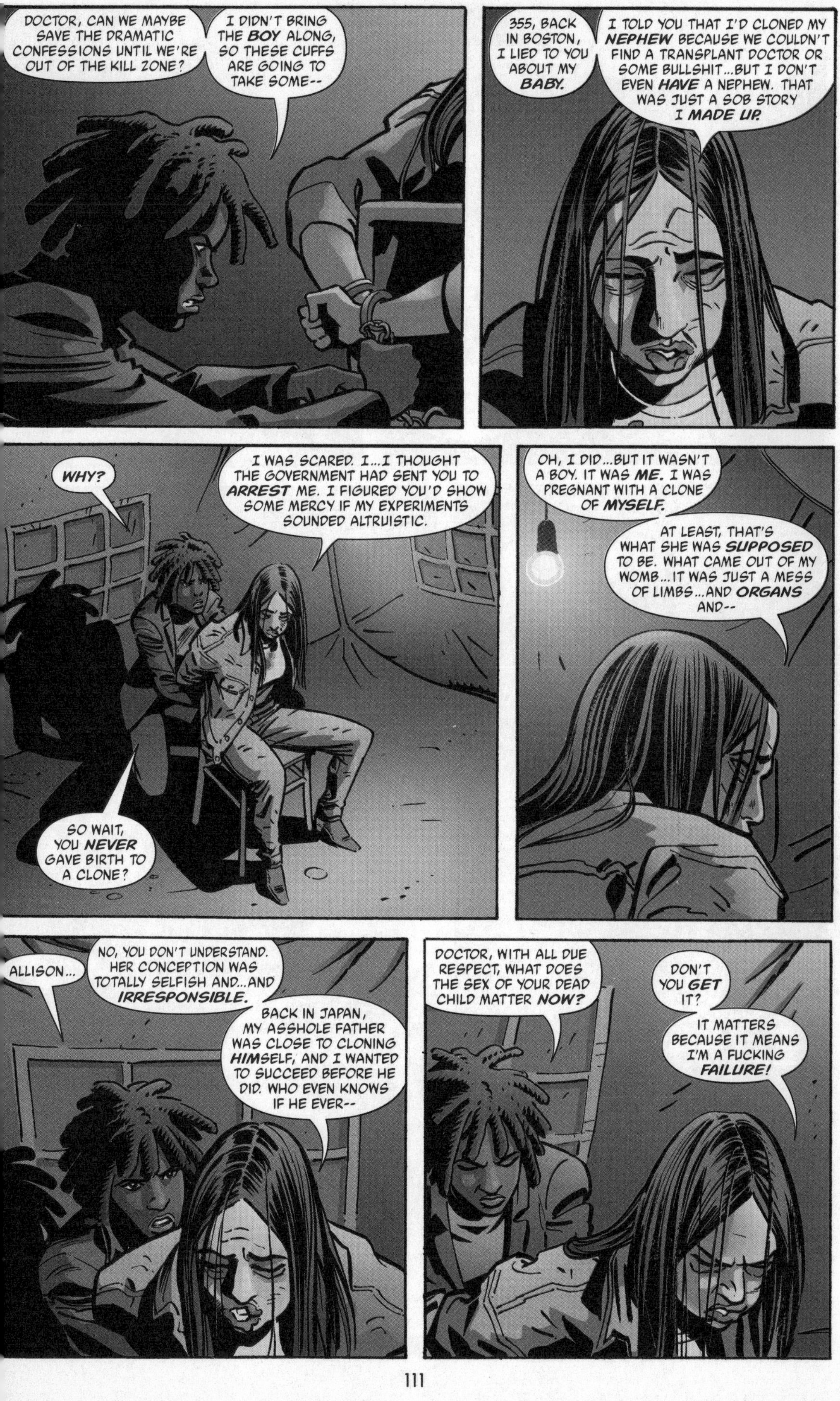
DOCTOR, CAN WE MAYBE SAVE THE DRAMATIC CONFESSIONS UNTIL WE'RE OUT OF THE KILL ZONE?
I DIDN'T BRING THE BOY ALONG, SO THESE CUFFS ARE GOING TO TAKE SOME--
355, BACK IN BOSTON, I LIED TO YOU ABOUT MY BABY.
I TOLD YOU THAT I'D CLONED MY NEPHEW BECAUSE WE COULDN'T FIND A TRANSPLANT DOCTOR OR SOME BULLSHIT...BUT I DON'T EVEN HAVE A NEPHEW. THAT WAS JUST A SOB STORY I MADE UP.
WHY?
I WAS SCARED. I...I THOUGHT THE GOVERNMENT HAD SENT YOU TO ARREST ME. I FIGURED YOU'D SHOW SOME MERCY IF MY EXPERIMENTS SOUNDED ALTRUISTIC.
SO WAIT, YOU NEVER GAVE BIRTH TO A CLONE?
OH, I DID...BUT IT WASN'T A BOY. IT WAS ME. I WAS PREGNANT WITH A CLONE OF MYSELF.
AT LEAST, THAT'S WHAT SHE WAS SUPPOSED TO BE. WHAT CAME OUT OF MY WOMB...IT WAS JUST A MESS OF LIMBS...AND ORGANS AND--
ALLISON...
NO, YOU DON'T UNDERSTAND. HER CONCEPTION WAS TOTALLY SELFISH AND...AND IRRESPONSIBLE.
BACK IN JAPAN, MY ASSHOLE FATHER WAS CLOSE TO CLONING HIMSELF, AND I WANTED TO SUCCEED BEFORE HE DID. WHO EVEN KNOWS IF HE EVER--
DOCTOR, WITH ALL DUE RESPECT, WHAT DOES THE SEX OF YOUR DEAD CHILD MATTER NOW?
DON'T YOU GET IT?
IT MATTERS BECAUSE IT MEANS I'M A FUCKING FAILURE!

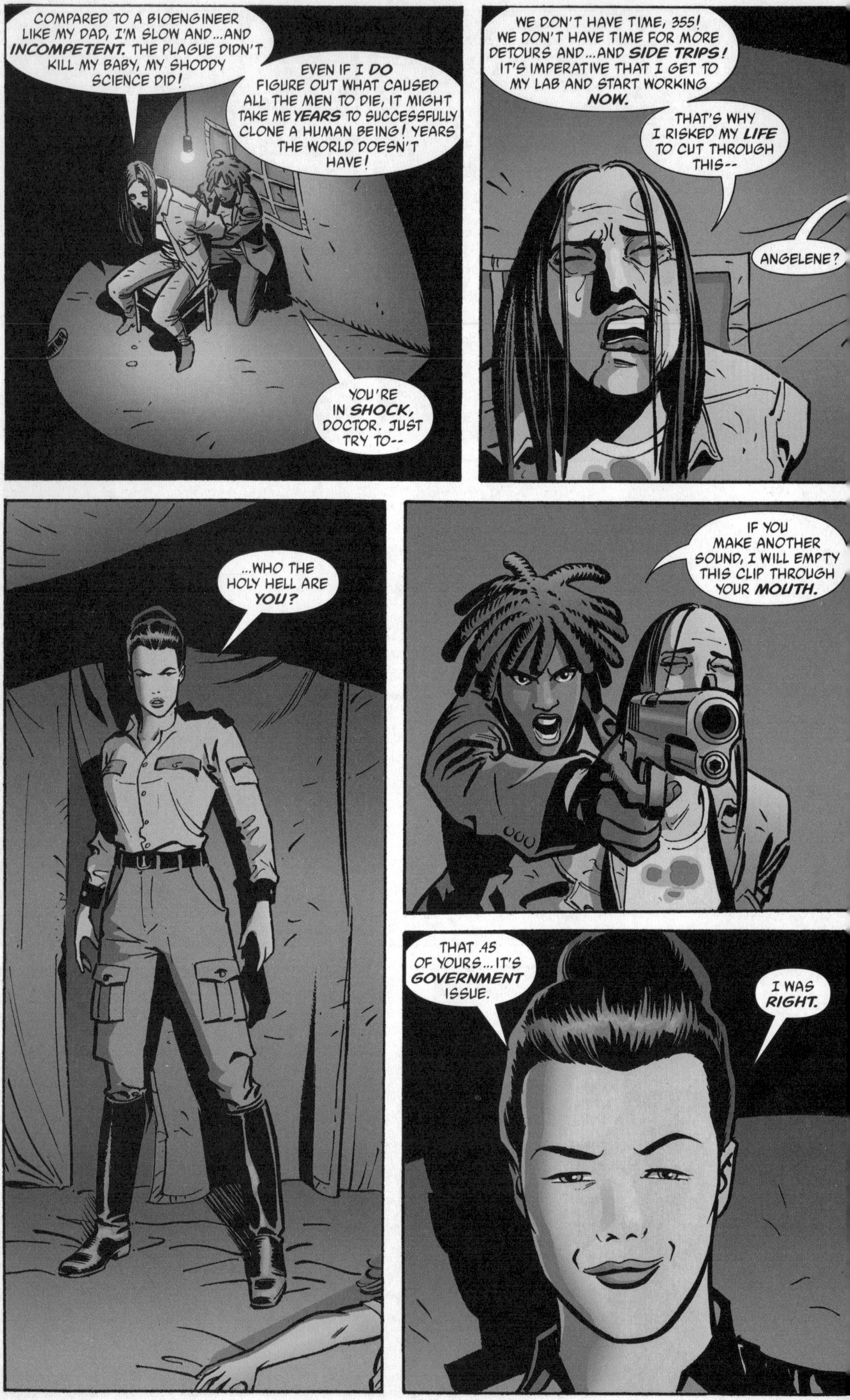

COMPARED TO A BIOENGINEER LIKE MY DAD, I'M SLOW AND...AND INCOMPETENT. THE PLAGUE DIDN'T KILL MY BABY, MY SHODDY SCIENCE DID!
EVEN IF I DO FIGURE OUT WHAT CAUSED ALL THE MEN TO DIE, IT MIGHT TAKE ME YEARS TO SUCCESSFULLY CLONE A HUMAN BEING! YEARS THE WORLD DOESN'T HAVE!
YOU'RE IN SHOCK, DOCTOR. JUST TRY TO--
WE DON'T HAVE TIME, 355! WE DON'T HAVE TIME FOR MORE DETOURS AND...AND SIDE TRIPS! IT'S IMPERATIVE THAT I GET TO MY LAB AND START WORKING NOW.
THAT'S WHY I RISKED MY LIFE TO CUT THROUGH THIS--
ANGELENE?
...WHO THE HOLY HELL ARE YOU?
IF YOU MAKE ANOTHER SOUND, I WILL EMPTY THIS CLIP THROUGH YOUR MOUTH.
THAT .45 OF YOURS...IT'S GOVERNMENT ISSUE.
I WAS RIGHT.

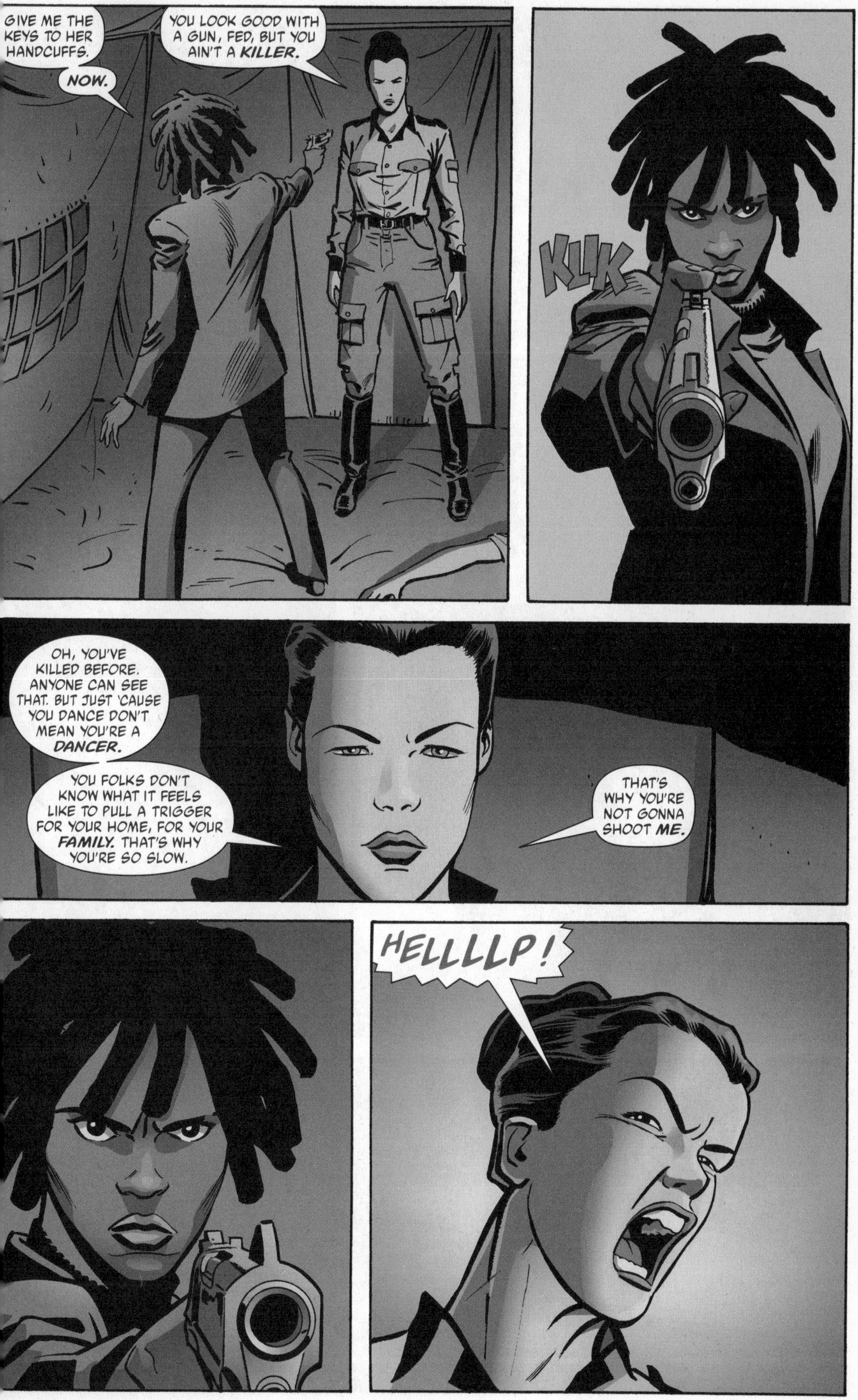
GIVE ME THE KEYS TO HER HANDCUFFS.
NOW.
YOU LOOK GOOD WITH A GUN, FED, BUT YOU AIN'T A KILLER.
KLIK
OH, YOU'VE KILLED BEFORE. ANYONE CAN SEE THAT. BUT JUST 'CAUSE YOU DANCE DON'T MEAN YOU'RE A DANCER.
YOU FOLKS DON'T KNOW WHAT IT FEELS LIKE TO PULL A TRIGGER FOR YOUR HOME, FOR YOUR FAMILY. THAT'S WHY YOU'RE SO SLOW.
THAT'S WHY YOU'RE NOT GONNA SHOOT ME.
HELLLLP!

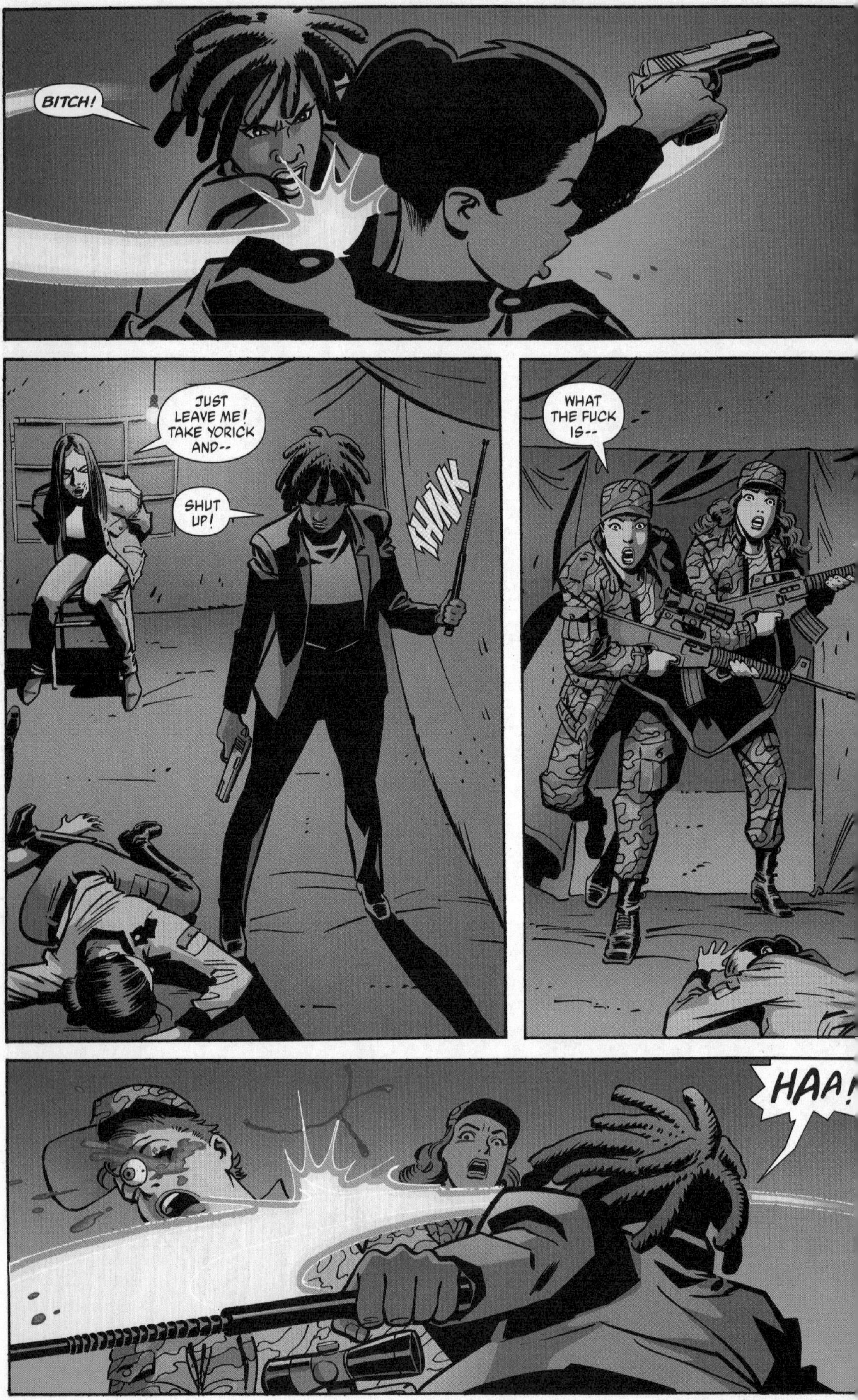
BITCH!
JUST LEAVE ME! TAKE YORICK AND--
SHUT UP!
THINK
WHAT THE FUCK IS--
HAA!

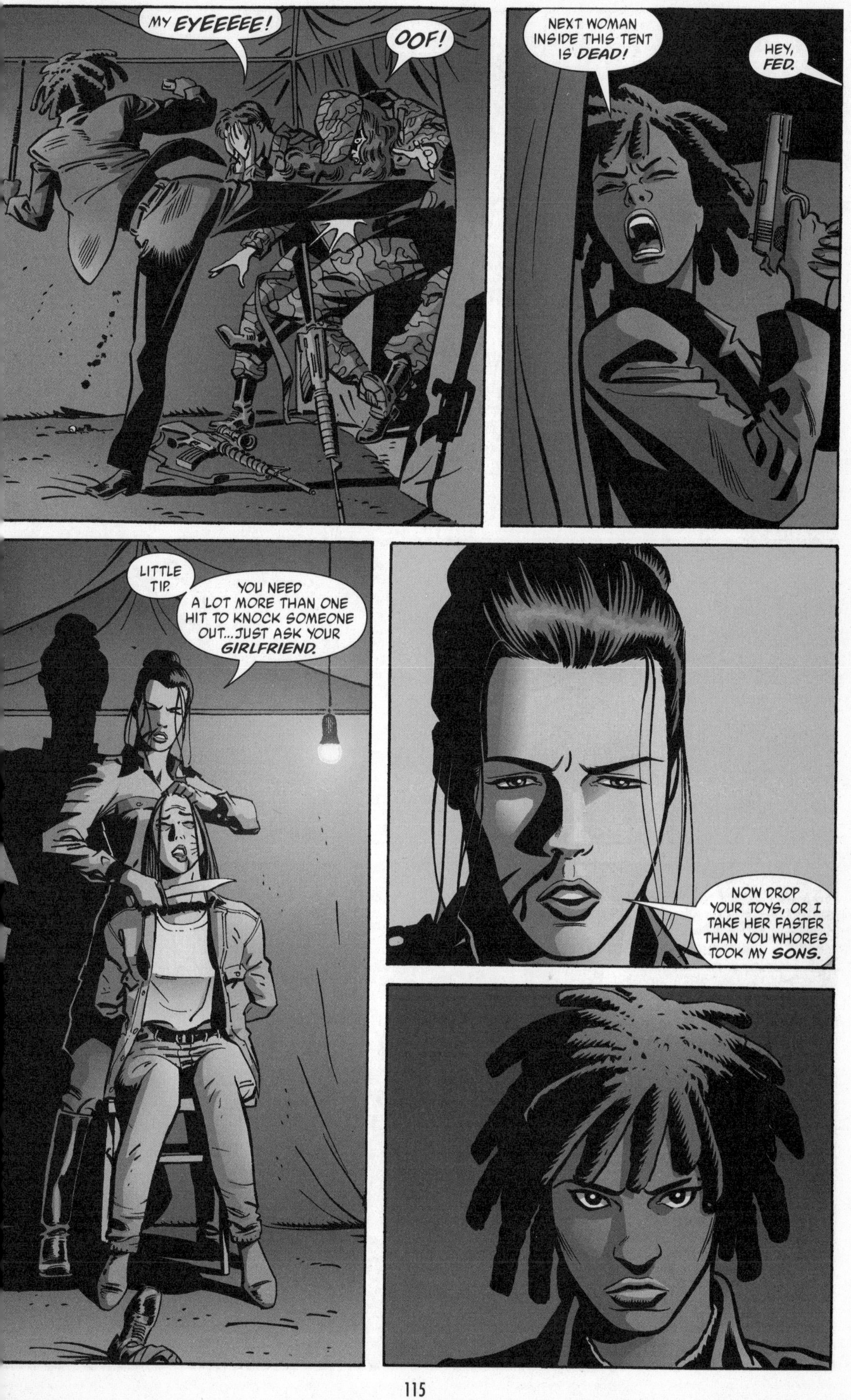
MY EYEEEEE!
OOF!
NEXT WOMAN INSIDE THIS TENT IS DEAD!
HEY, FED.
LITTLE TIP.
YOU NEED A LOT MORE THAN ONE HIT TO KNOCK SOMEONE OUT...JUST ASK YOUR GIRLFRIEND.
NOW DROP YOUR TOYS, OR I TAKE HER FASTER THAN YOU WHORES TOOK MY SONS.

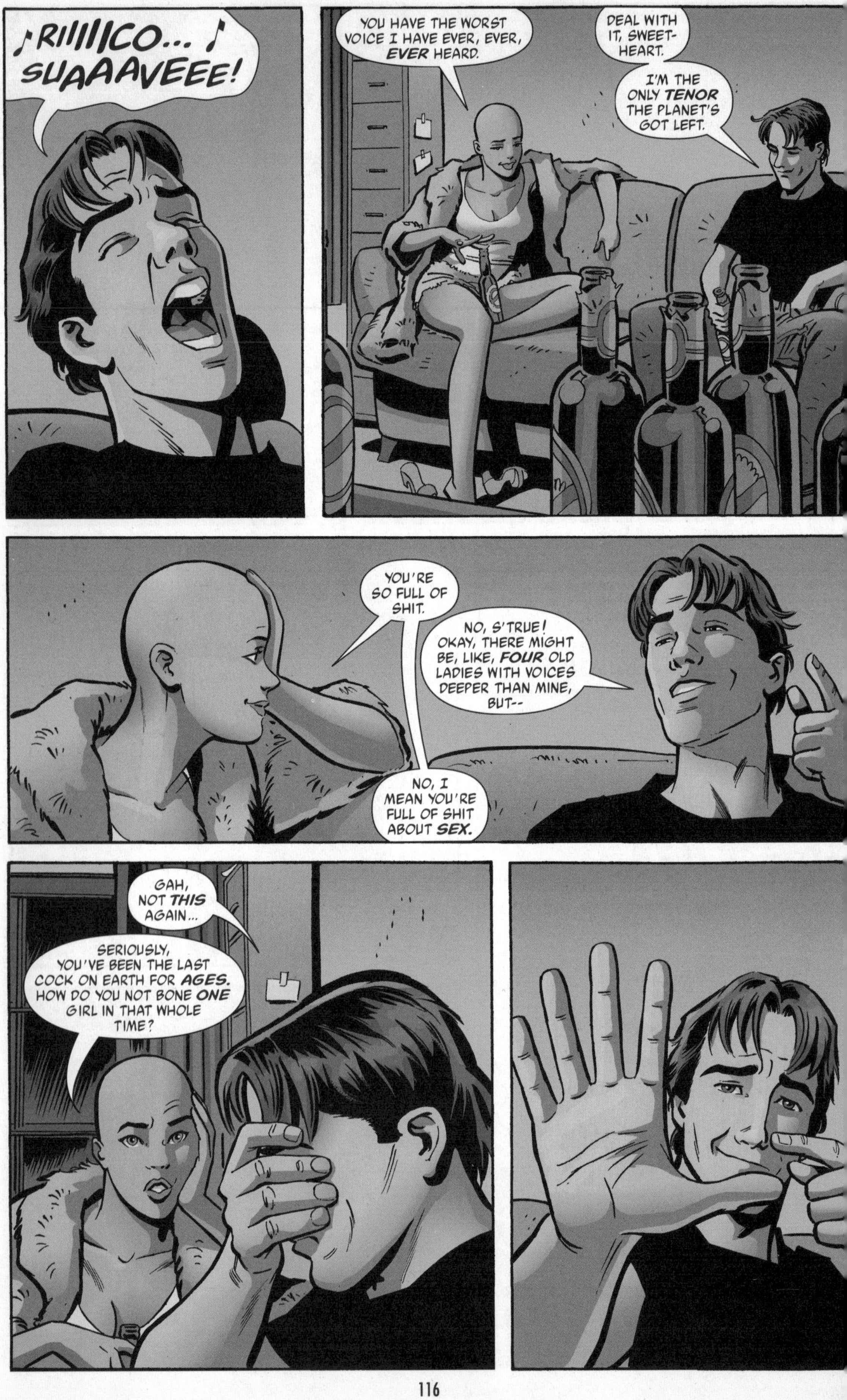
♪ RIIIIICO... ♪ SUAAAVEEE!
YOU HAVE THE WORST VOICE I HAVE EVER, EVER, EVER HEARD.
DEAL WITH IT, SWEET-HEART.
I'M THE ONLY TENOR THE PLANET'S GOT LEFT.
YOU'RE SO FULL OF SHIT.
NO, S'TRUE! OKAY, THERE MIGHT BE, LIKE, FOUR OLD LADIES WITH VOICES DEEPER THAN MINE, BUT--
NO, I MEAN YOU'RE FULL OF SHIT ABOUT SEX.
GAH, NOT THIS AGAIN...
SERIOUSLY, YOU'VE BEEN THE LAST COCK ON EARTH FOR AGES. HOW DO YOU NOT BONE ONE GIRL IN THAT WHOLE TIME?

AND SPANKING THE MONKEY'S **ENOUGH?**

THE WAY METHADONE IS ENOUGH FOR A HEROIN ADDICT, I GUESS.

AND **PLEASE** DON'T BRING MONKEYS INTO THIS...

HOW MANY TIMES?

IN A DAY? WELL, THERE WAS ONE PARTICULARLY TRYING INCIDENT DURING THE **CHICAGO** LEG OF OUR TRIP, AFTER WE STOPPED BY THESE OUTDOOR SHOWERS THE CITY HAD SET UP.

BY THE TIME I WAS DONE WITH THAT NIGHT'S SESSION, I WAS SO SPENT I THINK **BONE MARROW** STARTED COMING OUT.

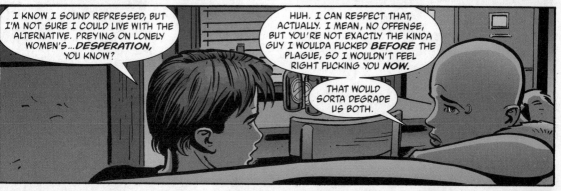

I KNOW I SOUND REPRESSED, BUT I'M NOT SURE I COULD LIVE WITH THE ALTERNATIVE. PREYING ON LONELY WOMEN'S...**DESPERATION,** YOU KNOW?

HUH. I CAN RESPECT THAT, ACTUALLY. I MEAN, NO OFFENSE, BUT YOU'RE NOT EXACTLY THE KINDA GUY I WOULDA FUCKED **BEFORE** THE PLAGUE, SO I WOULDN'T FEEL RIGHT FUCKING YOU **NOW.**

THAT WOULD SORTA DEGRADE US BOTH.

THAT IS THE NICEST THING ANYONE HAS EVER SAID TO ME.

CHEERS, BIG EARS.

DOWN THE HATCH, TIGHT--

RARF RARF RARF RARF RARF RARF

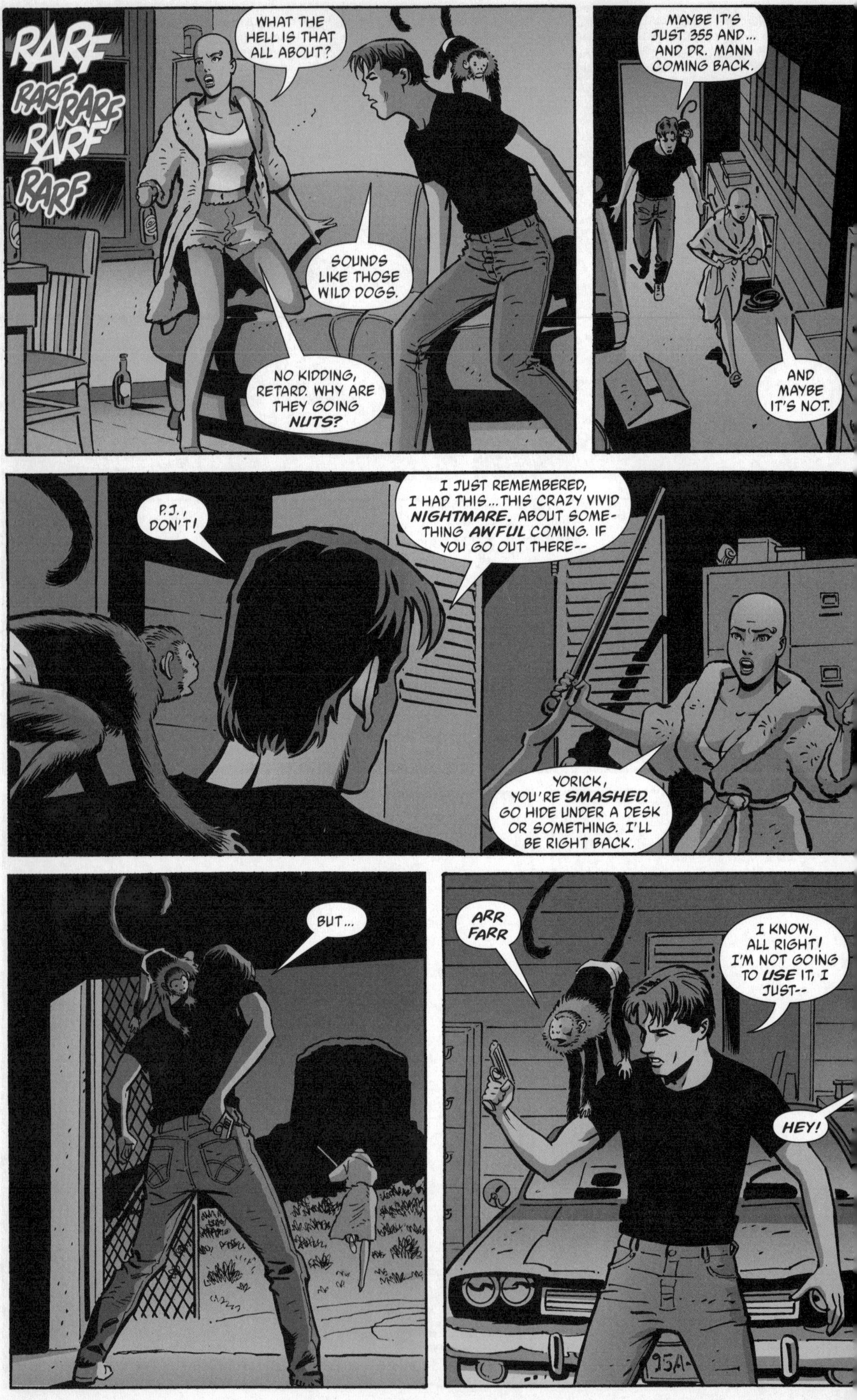
RARF
RARF RARF
RARF
RARF
WHAT THE HELL IS THAT ALL ABOUT?
SOUNDS LIKE THOSE WILD DOGS.
NO KIDDING, RETARD. WHY ARE THEY GOING NUTS?
MAYBE IT'S JUST 355 AND... AND DR. MANN COMING BACK.
AND MAYBE IT'S NOT.
P.J., DON'T!
I JUST REMEMBERED, I HAD THIS...THIS CRAZY VIVID NIGHTMARE. ABOUT SOMETHING AWFUL COMING. IF YOU GO OUT THERE--
YORICK, YOU'RE SMASHED. GO HIDE UNDER A DESK OR SOMETHING. I'LL BE RIGHT BACK.
BUT...
ARR FARR
I KNOW, ALL RIGHT! I'M NOT GOING TO USE IT, I JUST--
HEY!

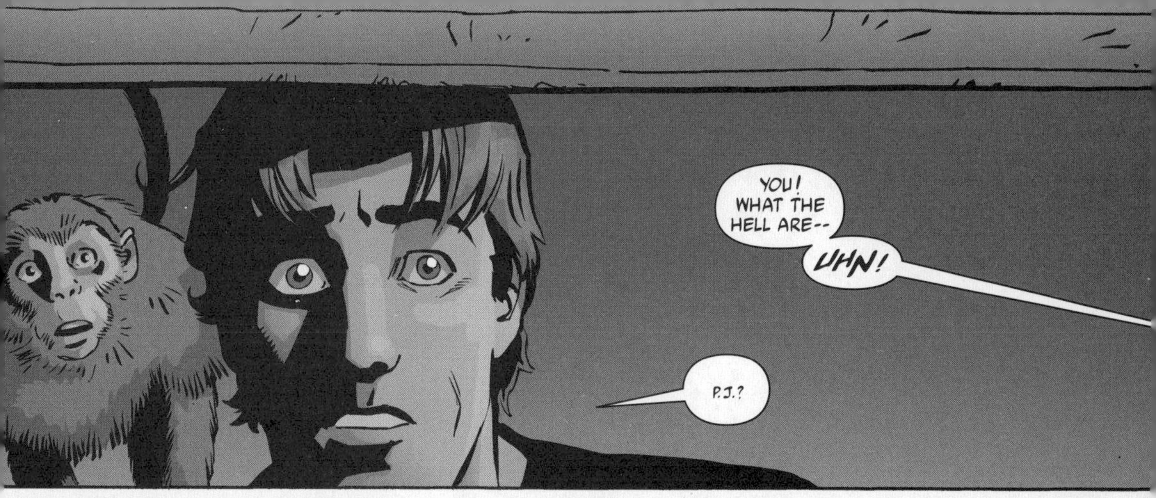
YOU! WHAT THE HELL ARE--
UHN!
P.J.?

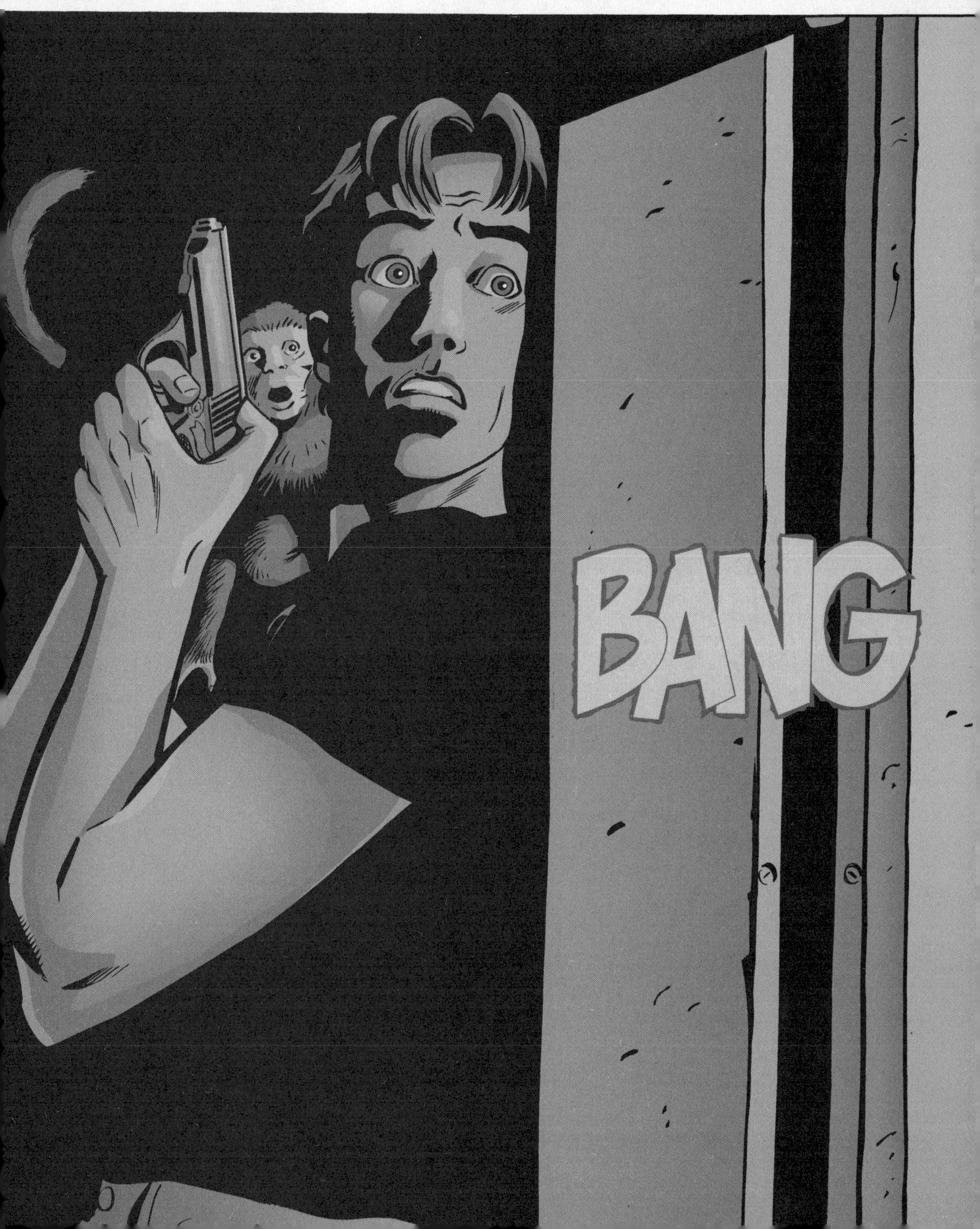
BANG

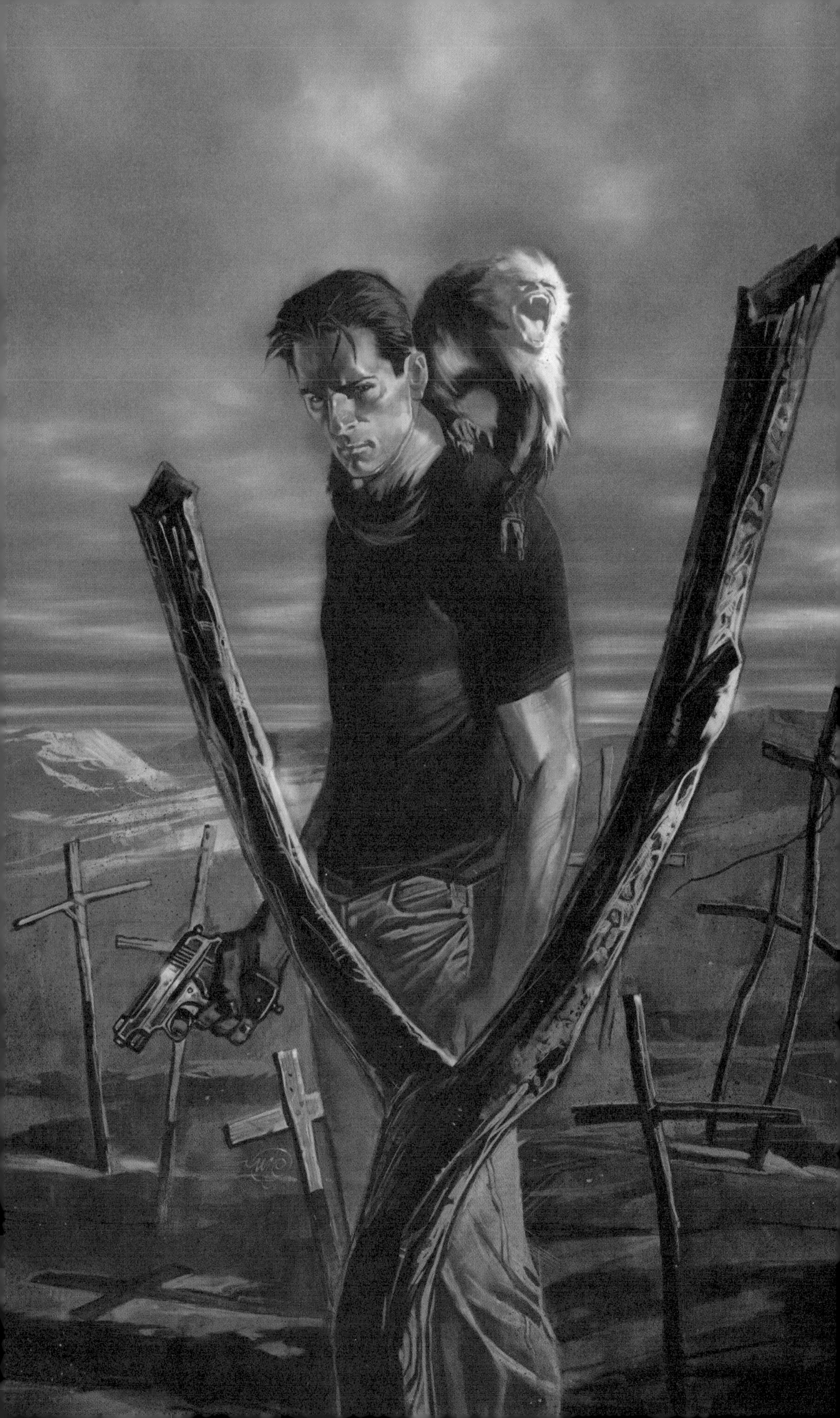

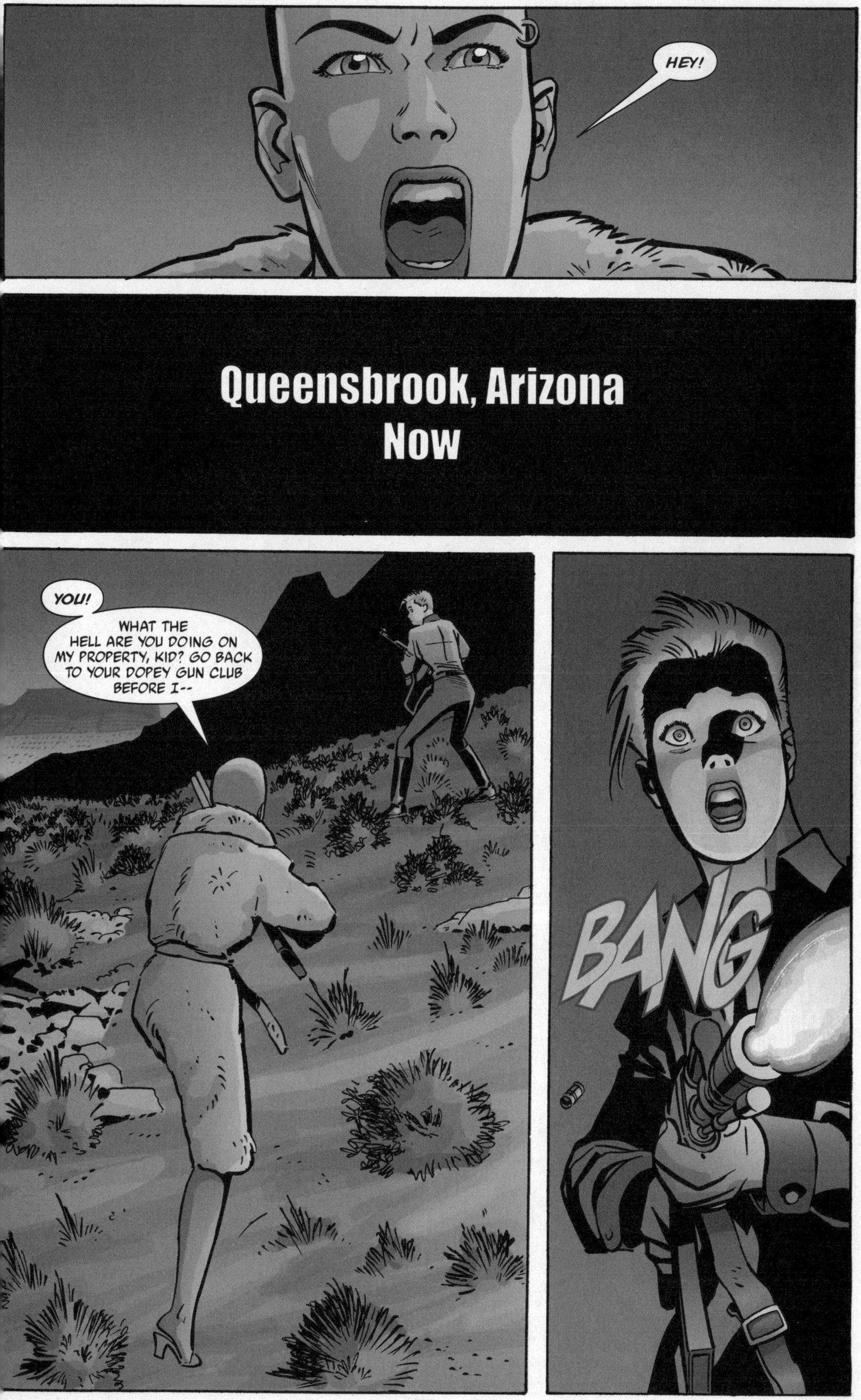
HEY!
Queensbrook, Arizona
Now
YOU!
WHAT THE HELL ARE YOU DOING ON MY PROPERTY, KID? GO BACK TO YOUR DOPEY GUN CLUB BEFORE I--
BANG

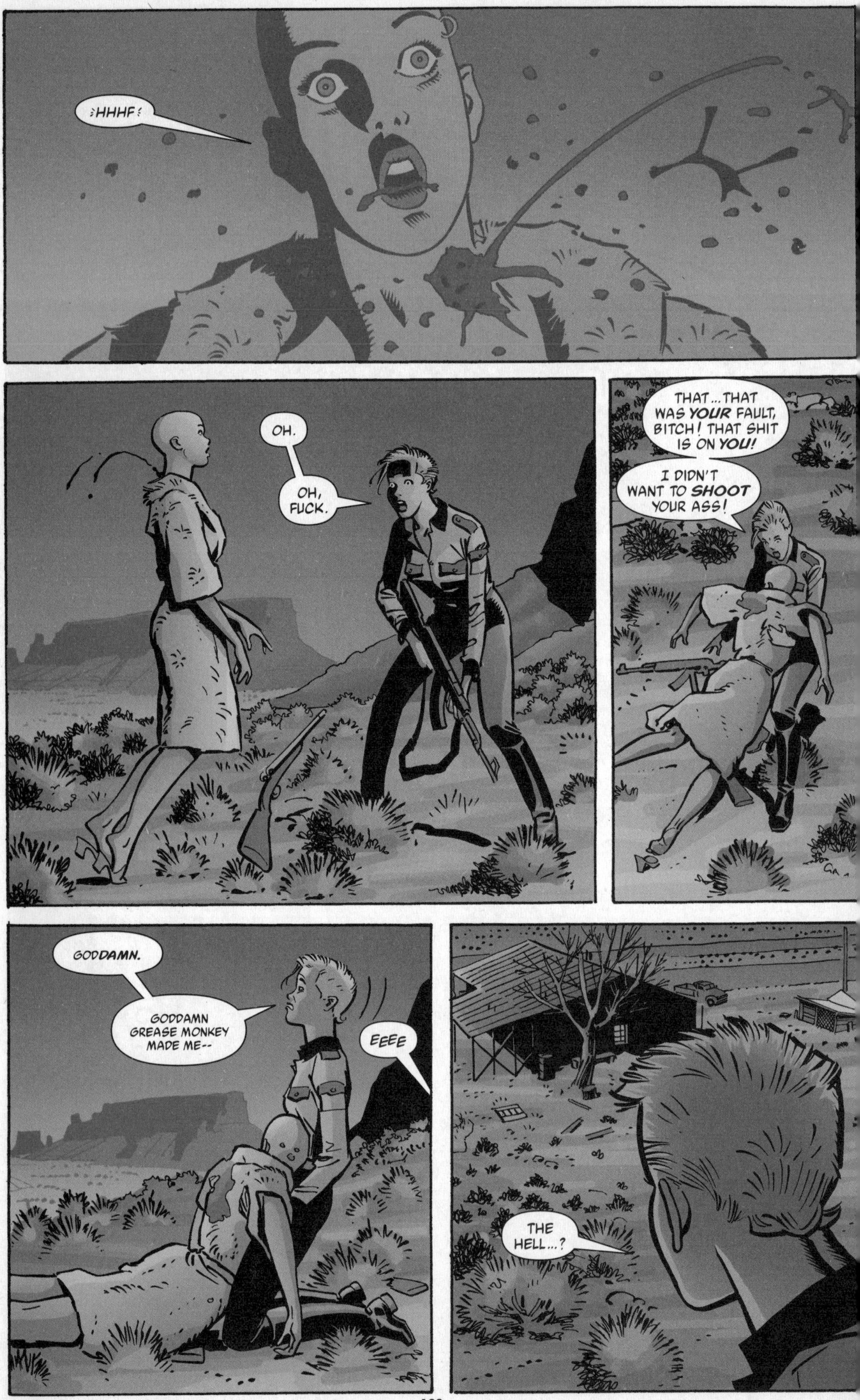

HHHF
OH.
OH, FUCK.
THAT...THAT WAS YOUR FAULT, BITCH! THAT SHIT IS ON YOU!
I DIDN'T WANT TO SHOOT YOUR ASS!
GODDAMN.
GODDAMN GREASE MONKEY MADE ME--
EEEE
THE HELL...?

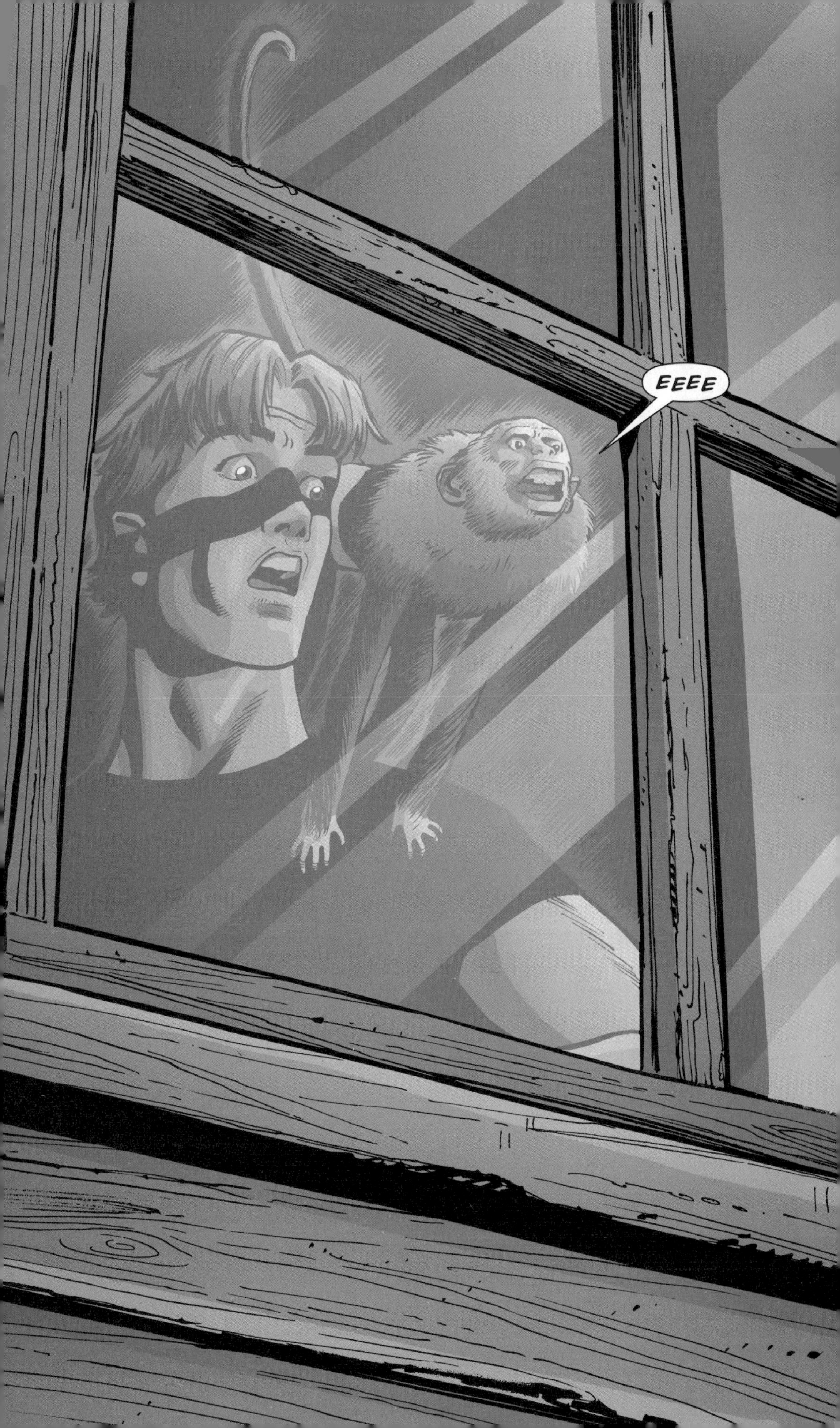
EEEE

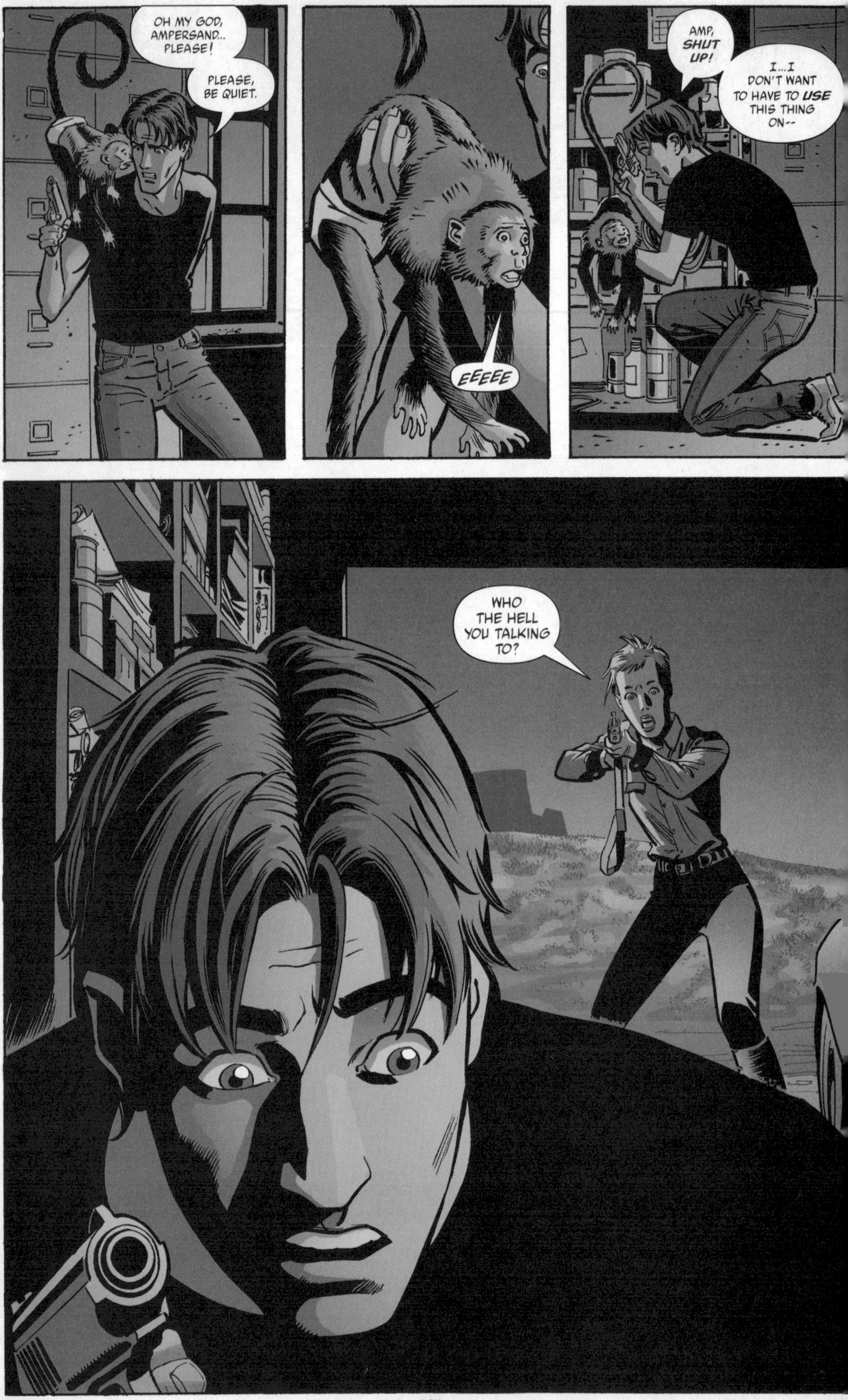

OH MY GOD, AMPERSAND... PLEASE!
PLEASE, BE QUIET.
EEEEE
AMP, SHUT UP!
I...I DON'T WANT TO HAVE TO USE THIS THING ON--
WHO THE HELL YOU TALKING TO?

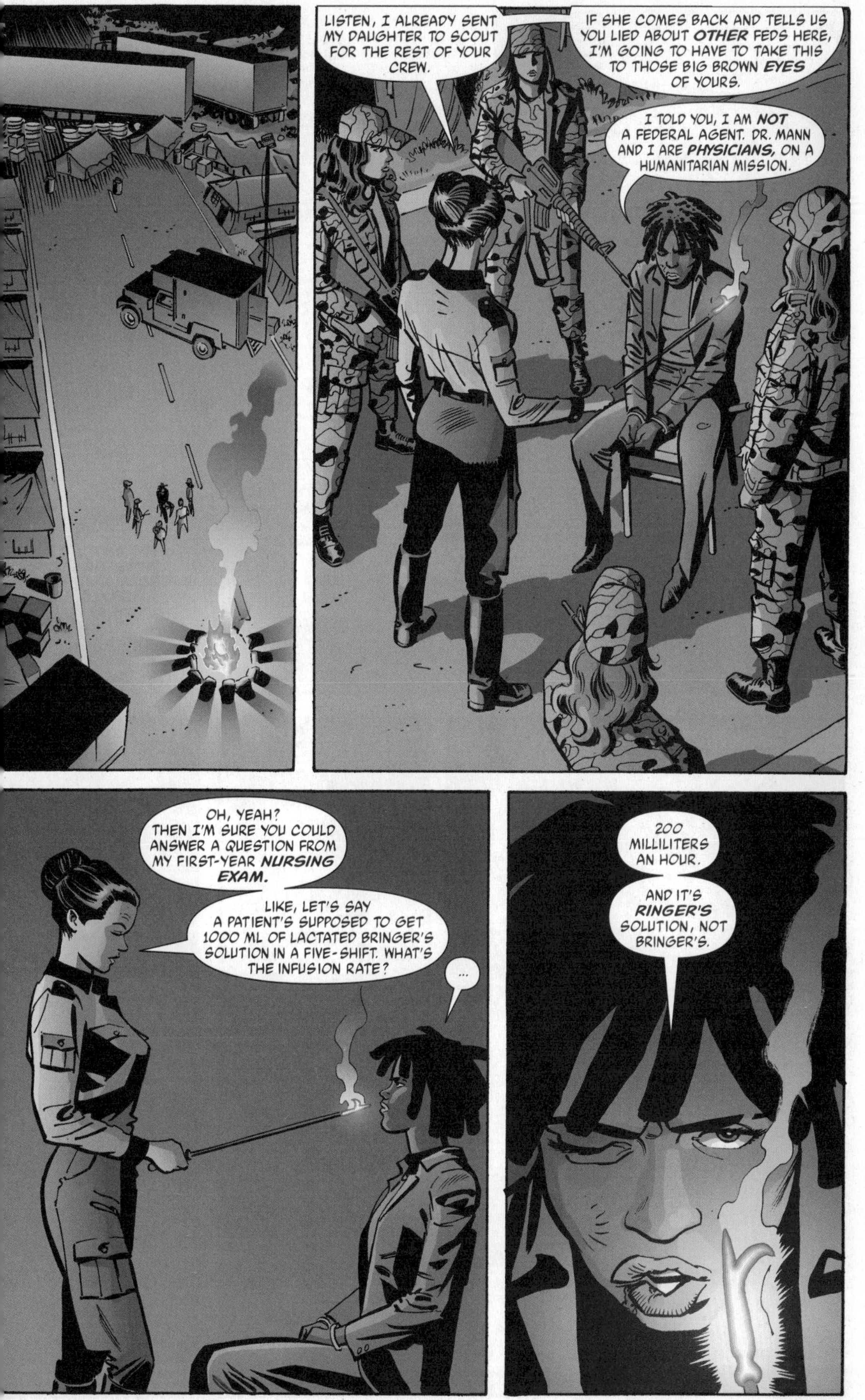
LISTEN, I ALREADY SENT MY DAUGHTER TO SCOUT FOR THE REST OF YOUR CREW.
IF SHE COMES BACK AND TELLS US YOU LIED ABOUT **OTHER** FEDS HERE, I'M GOING TO HAVE TO TAKE THIS TO THOSE BIG BROWN **EYES** OF YOURS.
I TOLD YOU, I AM **NOT** A FEDERAL AGENT. DR. MANN AND I ARE **PHYSICIANS,** ON A HUMANITARIAN MISSION.
OH, YEAH? THEN I'M SURE YOU COULD ANSWER A QUESTION FROM MY FIRST-YEAR **NURSING EXAM.**
LIKE, LET'S SAY A PATIENT'S SUPPOSED TO GET 1000 ML OF LACTATED BRINGER'S SOLUTION IN A FIVE-SHIFT. WHAT'S THE INFUSION RATE?
...
200 MILLILITERS AN HOUR.
AND IT'S **RINGER'S** SOLUTION, NOT BRINGER'S.

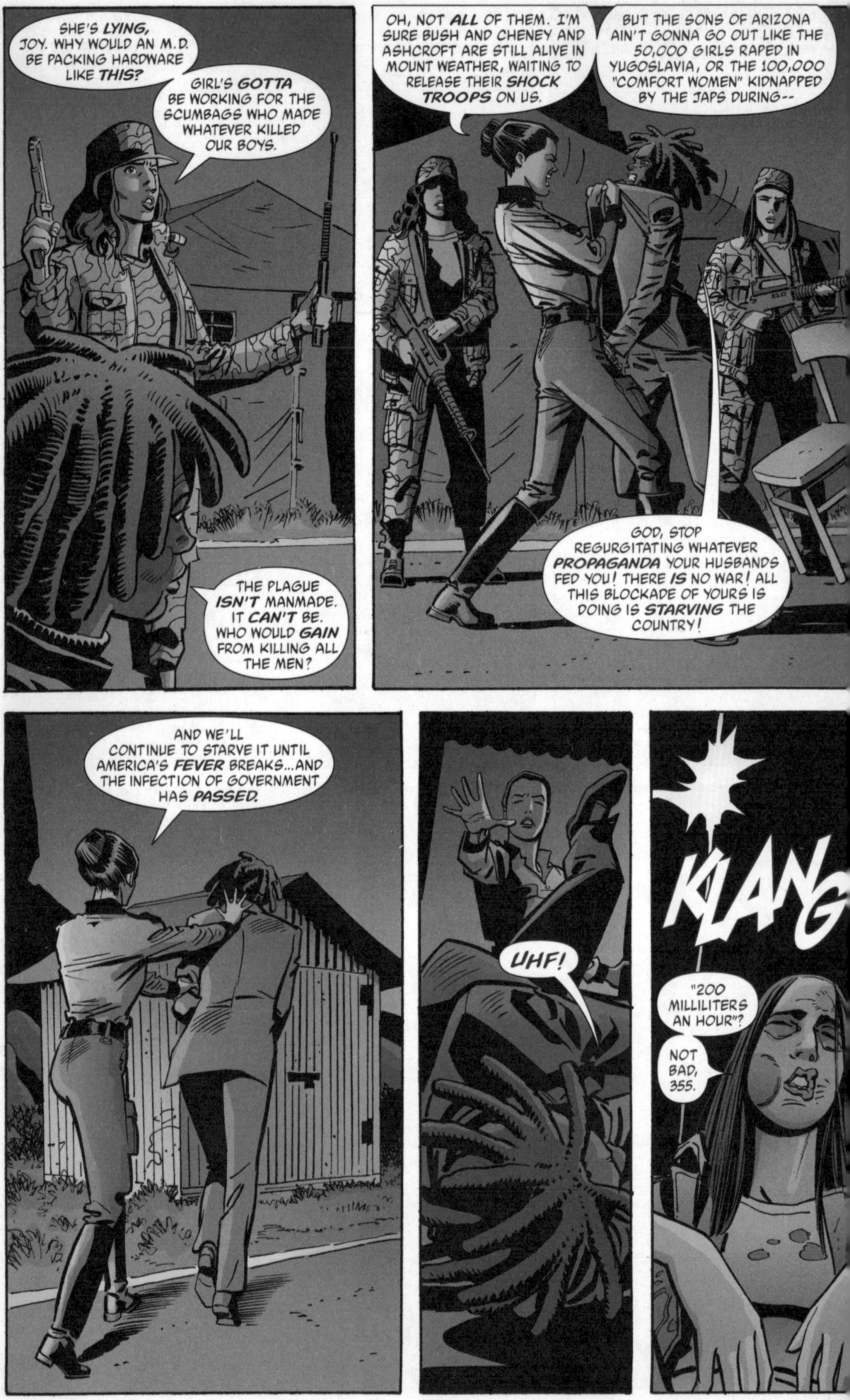
SHE'S LYING, JOY. WHY WOULD AN M.D. BE PACKING HARDWARE LIKE THIS?
GIRL'S GOTTA BE WORKING FOR THE SCUMBAGS WHO MADE WHATEVER KILLED OUR BOYS.
THE PLAGUE ISN'T MANMADE. IT CAN'T BE. WHO WOULD GAIN FROM KILLING ALL THE MEN?
OH, NOT ALL OF THEM. I'M SURE BUSH AND CHENEY AND ASHCROFT ARE STILL ALIVE IN MOUNT WEATHER, WAITING TO RELEASE THEIR SHOCK TROOPS ON US.
BUT THE SONS OF ARIZONA AIN'T GONNA GO OUT LIKE THE 50,000 GIRLS RAPED IN YUGOSLAVIA, OR THE 100,000 "COMFORT WOMEN" KIDNAPPED BY THE JAPS DURING--
GOD, STOP REGURGITATING WHATEVER PROPAGANDA YOUR HUSBANDS FED YOU! THERE IS NO WAR! ALL THIS BLOCKADE OF YOURS IS DOING IS STARVING THE COUNTRY!
AND WE'LL CONTINUE TO STARVE IT UNTIL AMERICA'S FEVER BREAKS...AND THE INFECTION OF GOVERNMENT HAS PASSED.
UHF!
KLANG
"200 MILLILITERS AN HOUR"?
NOT BAD, 355.

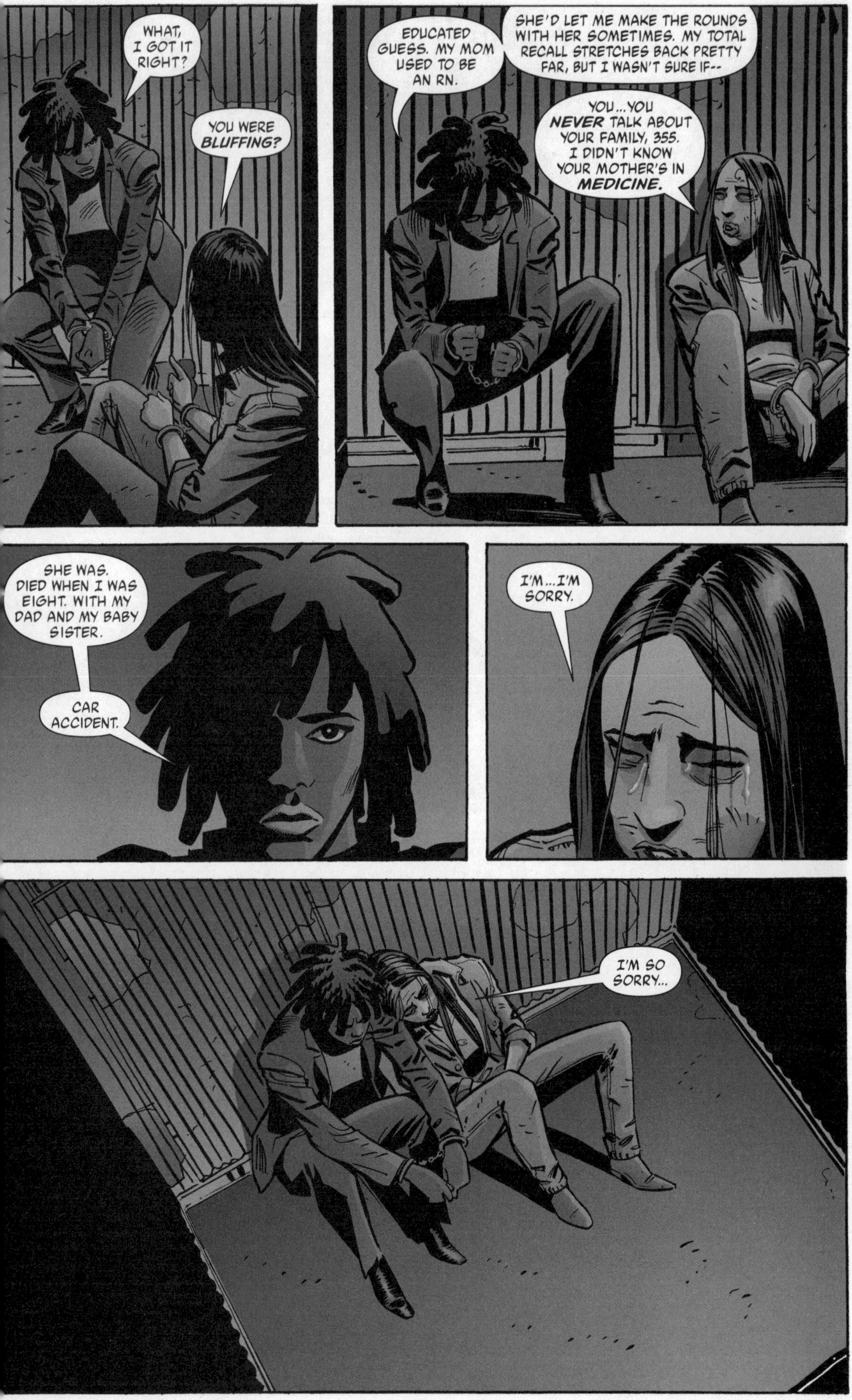
WHAT, I GOT IT RIGHT?
YOU WERE **BLUFFING?**
EDUCATED GUESS. MY MOM USED TO BE AN RN.
SHE'D LET ME MAKE THE ROUNDS WITH HER SOMETIMES. MY TOTAL RECALL STRETCHES BACK PRETTY FAR, BUT I WASN'T SURE IF--
YOU...YOU **NEVER** TALK ABOUT YOUR FAMILY, 355. I DIDN'T KNOW YOUR MOTHER'S IN **MEDICINE.**
SHE WAS. DIED WHEN I WAS EIGHT. WITH MY DAD AND MY BABY SISTER.
CAR ACCIDENT.
I'M...I'M SORRY.
I'M SO SORRY...

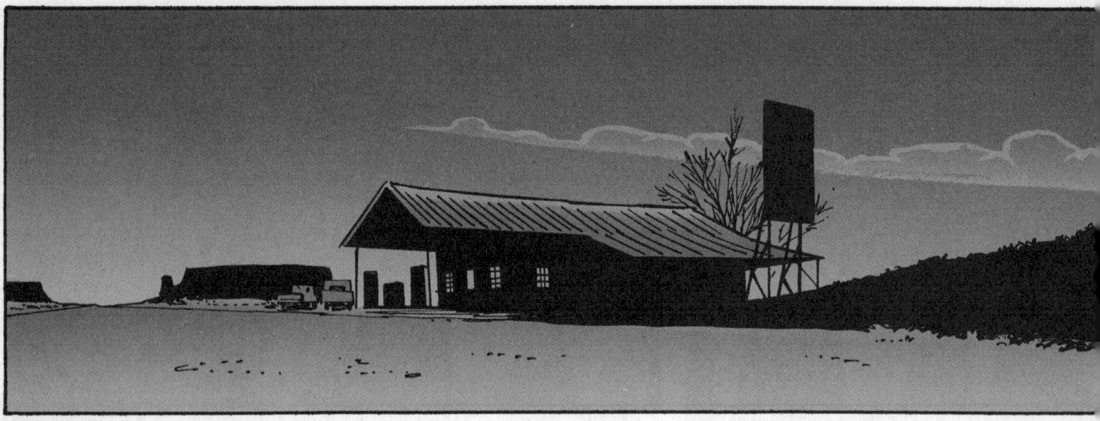

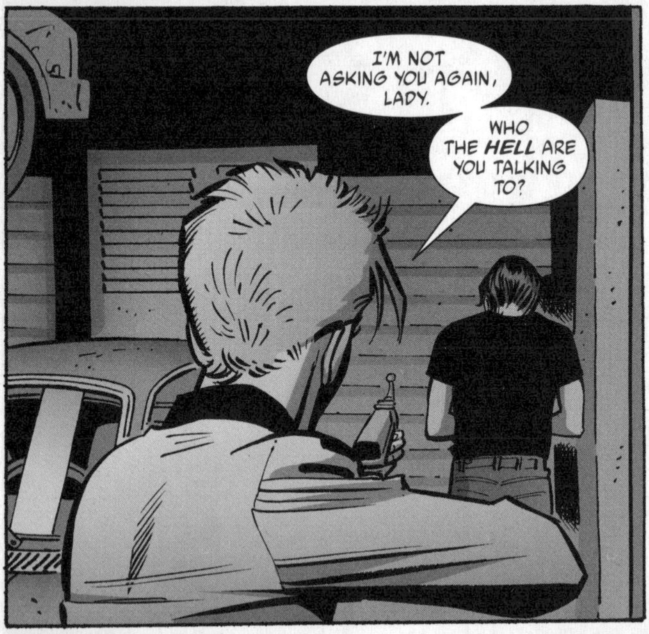
I'M NOT ASKING YOU AGAIN, LADY.
WHO THE HELL ARE YOU TALKING TO?

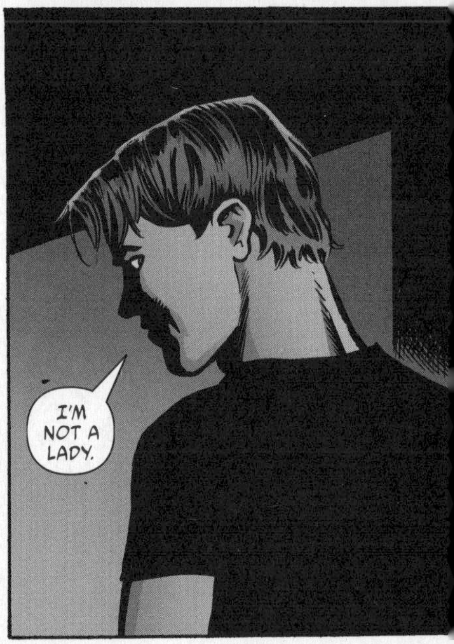
I'M NOT A LADY.

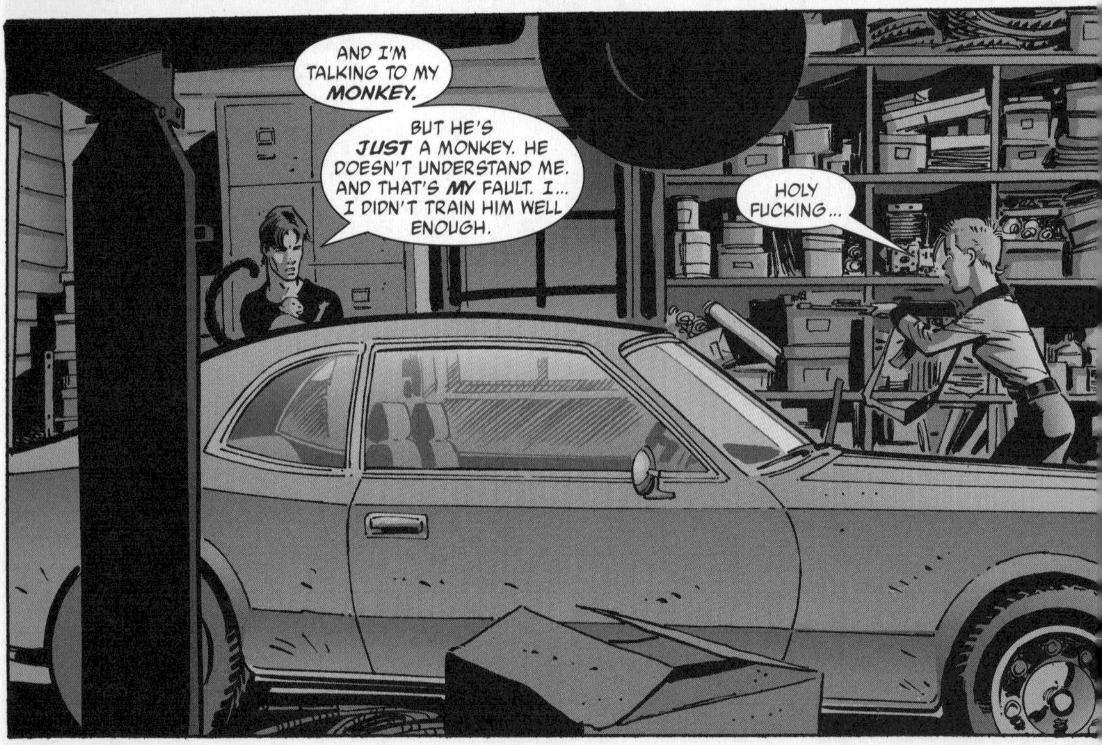
AND I'M TALKING TO MY MONKEY.
BUT HE'S JUST A MONKEY. HE DOESN'T UNDERSTAND ME. AND THAT'S MY FAULT. I... I DIDN'T TRAIN HIM WELL ENOUGH.
HOLY FUCKING...

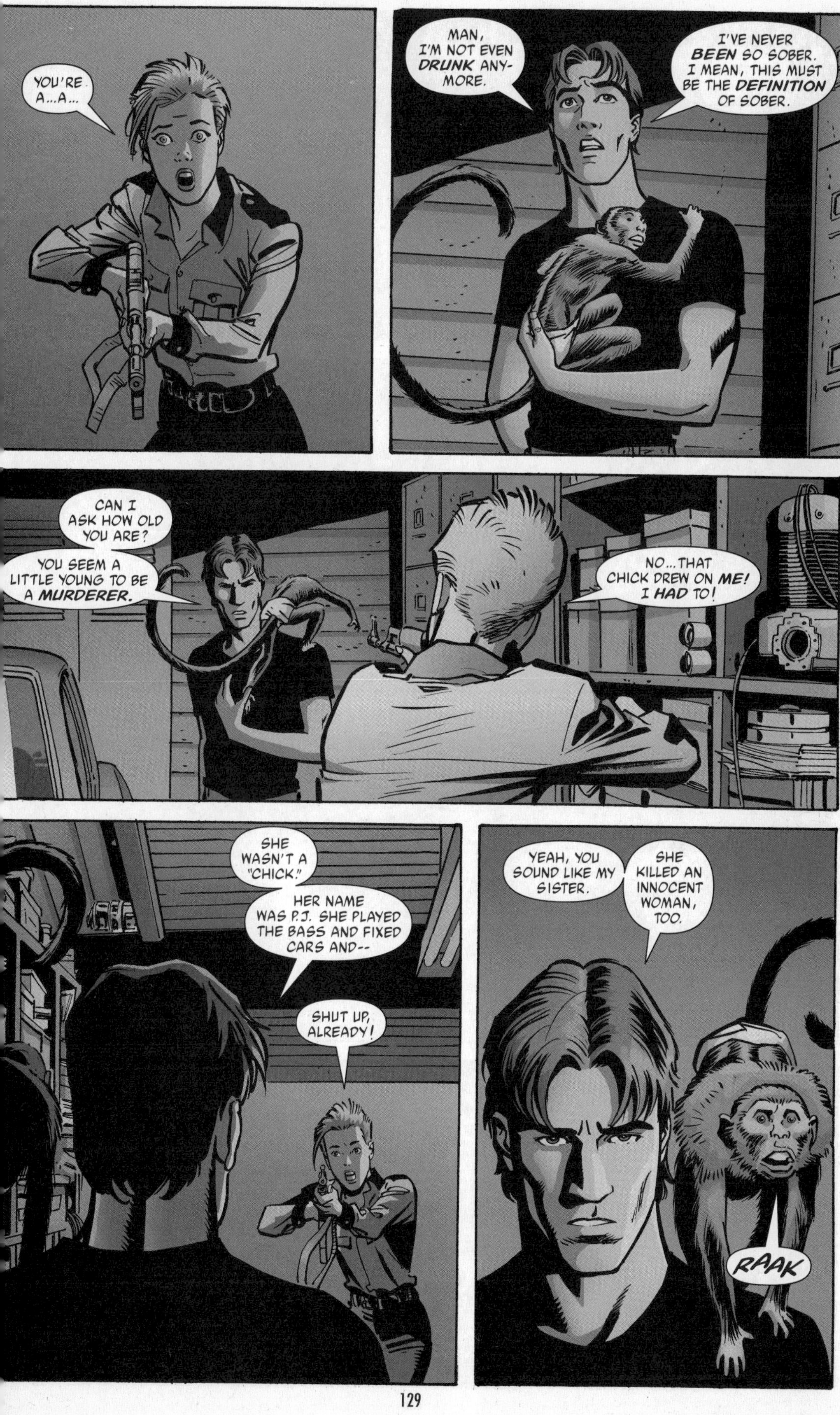
YOU'RE A...A...
MAN, I'M NOT EVEN DRUNK ANY-MORE.
I'VE NEVER BEEN SO SOBER. I MEAN, THIS MUST BE THE DEFINITION OF SOBER.
CAN I ASK HOW OLD YOU ARE?
YOU SEEM A LITTLE YOUNG TO BE A MURDERER.
NO...THAT CHICK DREW ON ME! I HAD TO!
SHE WASN'T A "CHICK."
HER NAME WAS P.J. SHE PLAYED THE BASS AND FIXED CARS AND--
SHUT UP, ALREADY!
YEAH, YOU SOUND LIKE MY SISTER.
SHE KILLED AN INNOCENT WOMAN, TOO.
RAAK

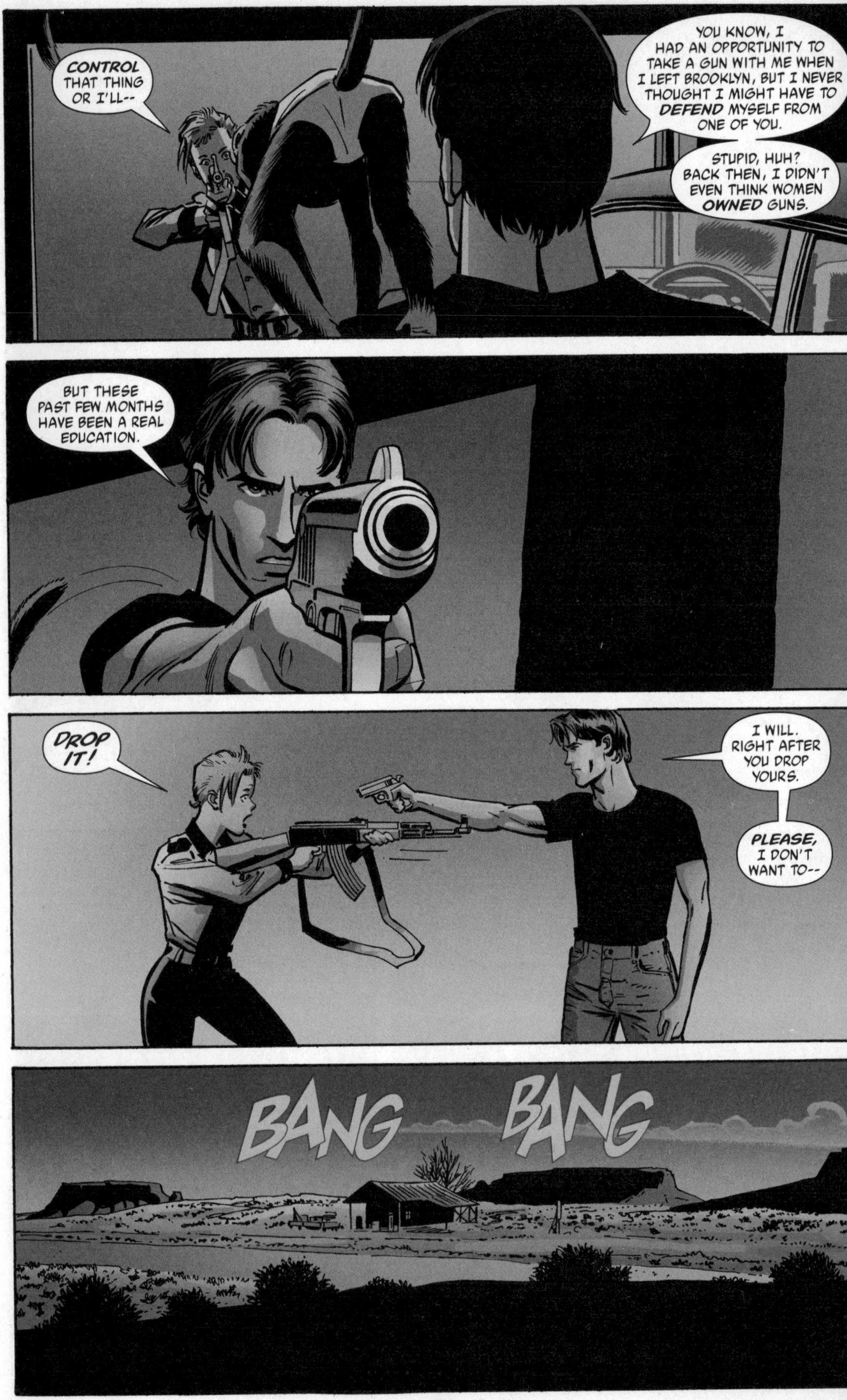
CONTROL THAT THING OR I'LL--
YOU KNOW, I HAD AN OPPORTUNITY TO TAKE A GUN WITH ME WHEN I LEFT BROOKLYN, BUT I NEVER THOUGHT I MIGHT HAVE TO DEFEND MYSELF FROM ONE OF YOU.
STUPID, HUH? BACK THEN, I DIDN'T EVEN THINK WOMEN OWNED GUNS.
BUT THESE PAST FEW MONTHS HAVE BEEN A REAL EDUCATION.
DROP IT!
I WILL. RIGHT AFTER YOU DROP YOURS.
PLEASE, I DON'T WANT TO--
BANG
BANG

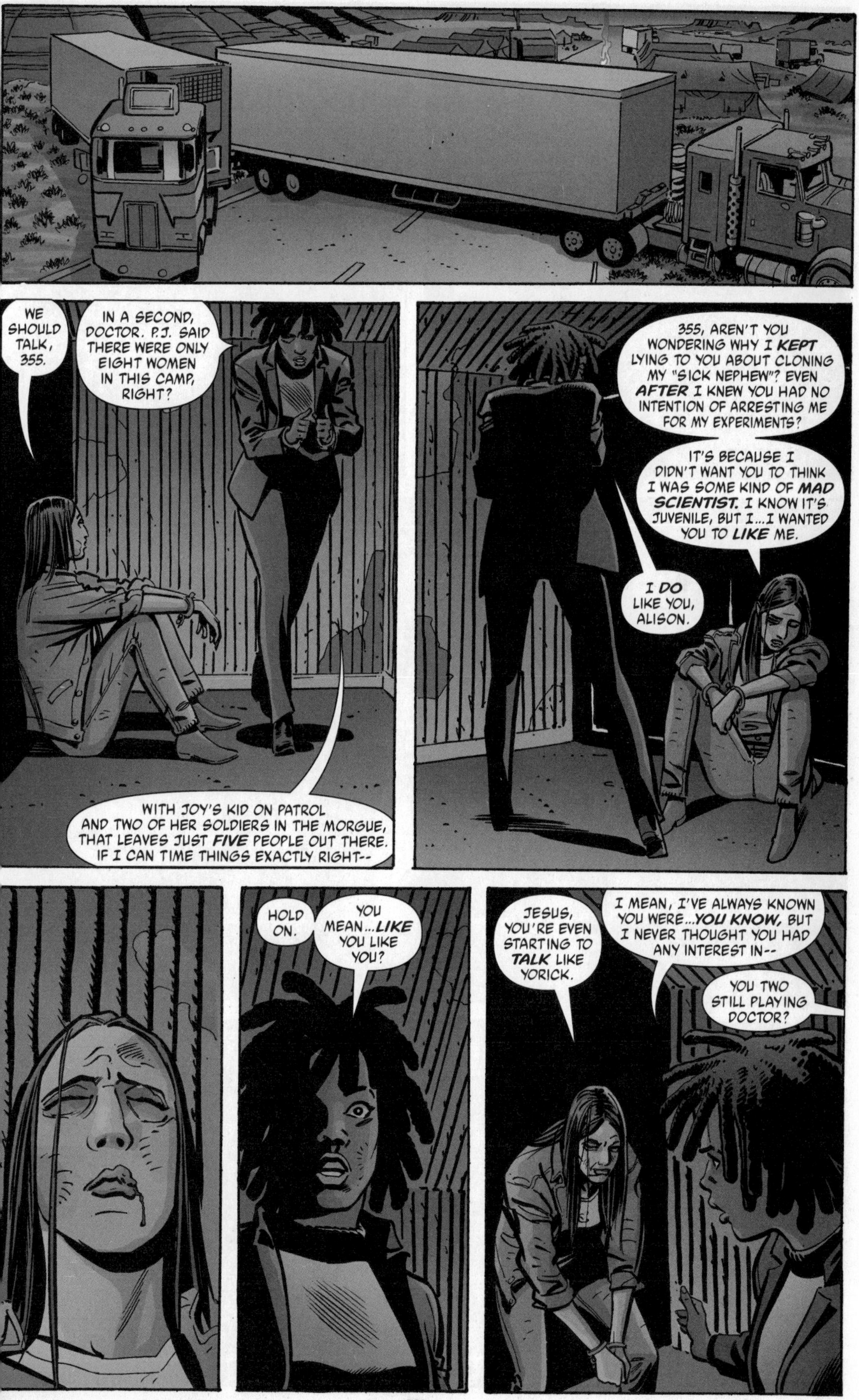
WE SHOULD TALK, 355.
IN A SECOND, DOCTOR. P.J. SAID THERE WERE ONLY EIGHT WOMEN IN THIS CAMP, RIGHT?
WITH JOY'S KID ON PATROL AND TWO OF HER SOLDIERS IN THE MORGUE, THAT LEAVES JUST FIVE PEOPLE OUT THERE. IF I CAN TIME THINGS EXACTLY RIGHT--
355, AREN'T YOU WONDERING WHY I KEPT LYING TO YOU ABOUT CLONING MY "SICK NEPHEW"? EVEN AFTER I KNEW YOU HAD NO INTENTION OF ARRESTING ME FOR MY EXPERIMENTS?
IT'S BECAUSE I DIDN'T WANT YOU TO THINK I WAS SOME KIND OF MAD SCIENTIST. I KNOW IT'S JUVENILE, BUT I...I WANTED YOU TO LIKE ME.
I DO LIKE YOU, ALISON.
HOLD ON.
YOU MEAN...LIKE YOU LIKE YOU?
JESUS, YOU'RE EVEN STARTING TO TALK LIKE YORICK.
I MEAN, I'VE ALWAYS KNOWN YOU WERE...YOU KNOW, BUT I NEVER THOUGHT YOU HAD ANY INTEREST IN--
YOU TWO STILL PLAYING DOCTOR?

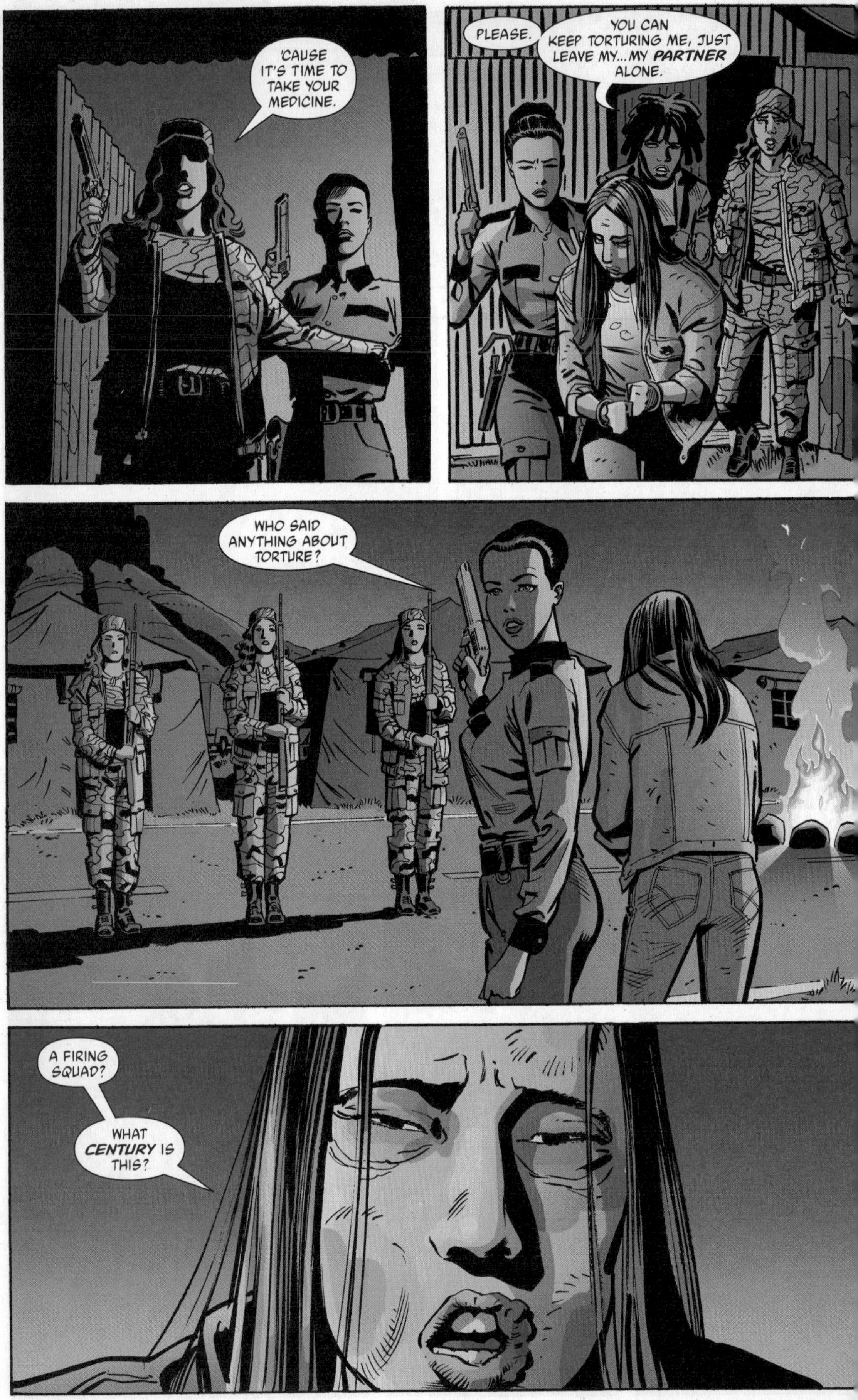

'CAUSE IT'S TIME TO TAKE YOUR MEDICINE.
PLEASE.
YOU CAN KEEP TORTURING ME, JUST LEAVE MY...MY PARTNER ALONE.
WHO SAID ANYTHING ABOUT TORTURE?
A FIRING SQUAD?
WHAT CENTURY IS THIS?

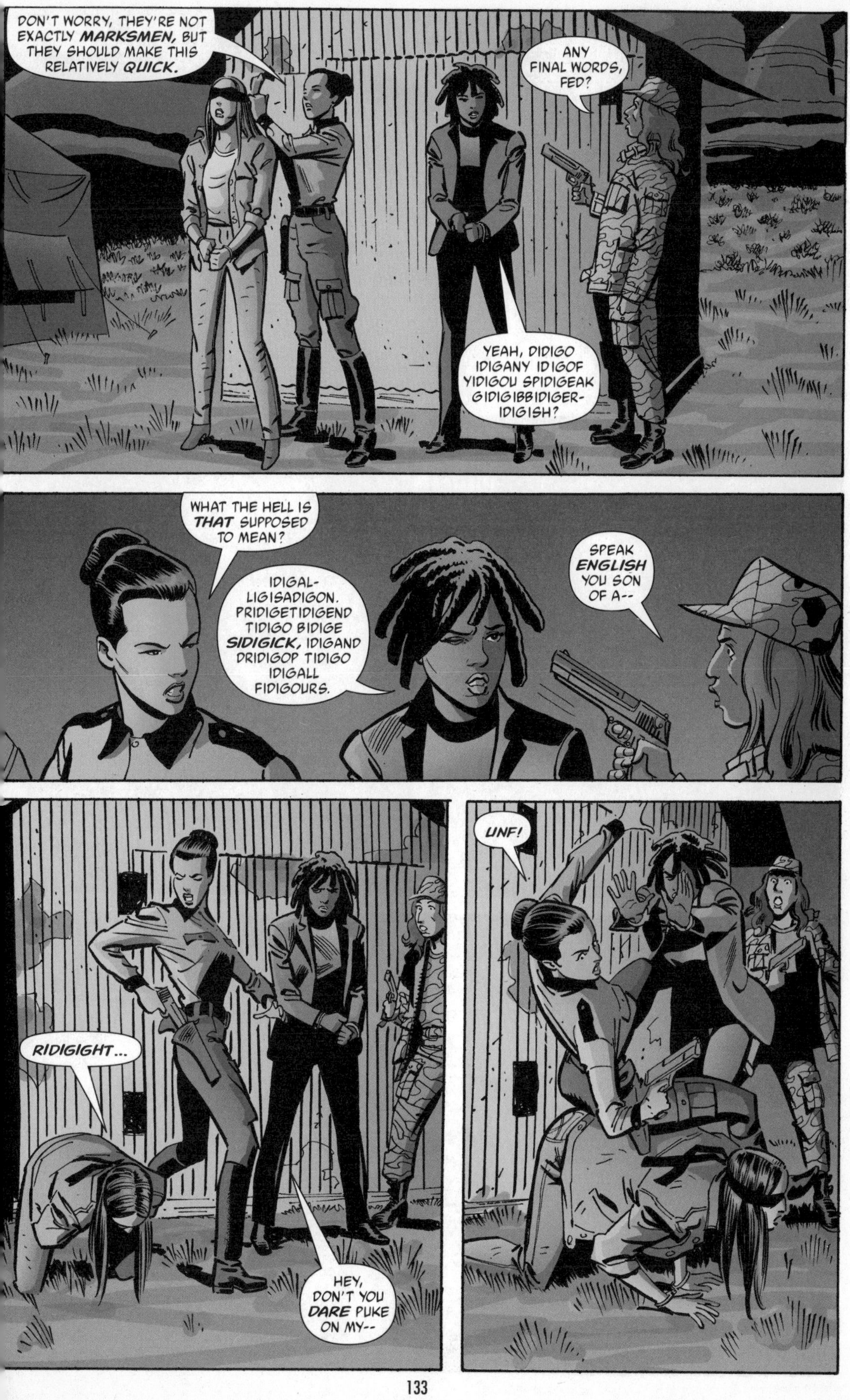
DON'T WORRY, THEY'RE NOT EXACTLY MARKSMEN, BUT THEY SHOULD MAKE THIS RELATIVELY QUICK.
ANY FINAL WORDS, FED?
YEAH, DIDIGO IDIGANY IDIGOF YIDIGOU SPIDIGEAK GIDIGIBBIDIGER-IDIGISH?
WHAT THE HELL IS THAT SUPPOSED TO MEAN?
IDIGAL-LIGISADIGON. PRIDIGETIDIGEND TIDIGO BIDIGE SIDIGICK, IDIGAND DRIDIGOP TIDIGO IDIGALL FIDIGOURS.
SPEAK ENGLISH YOU SON OF A--
RIDIGIGHT...
HEY, DON'T YOU DARE PUKE ON MY--
UNF!

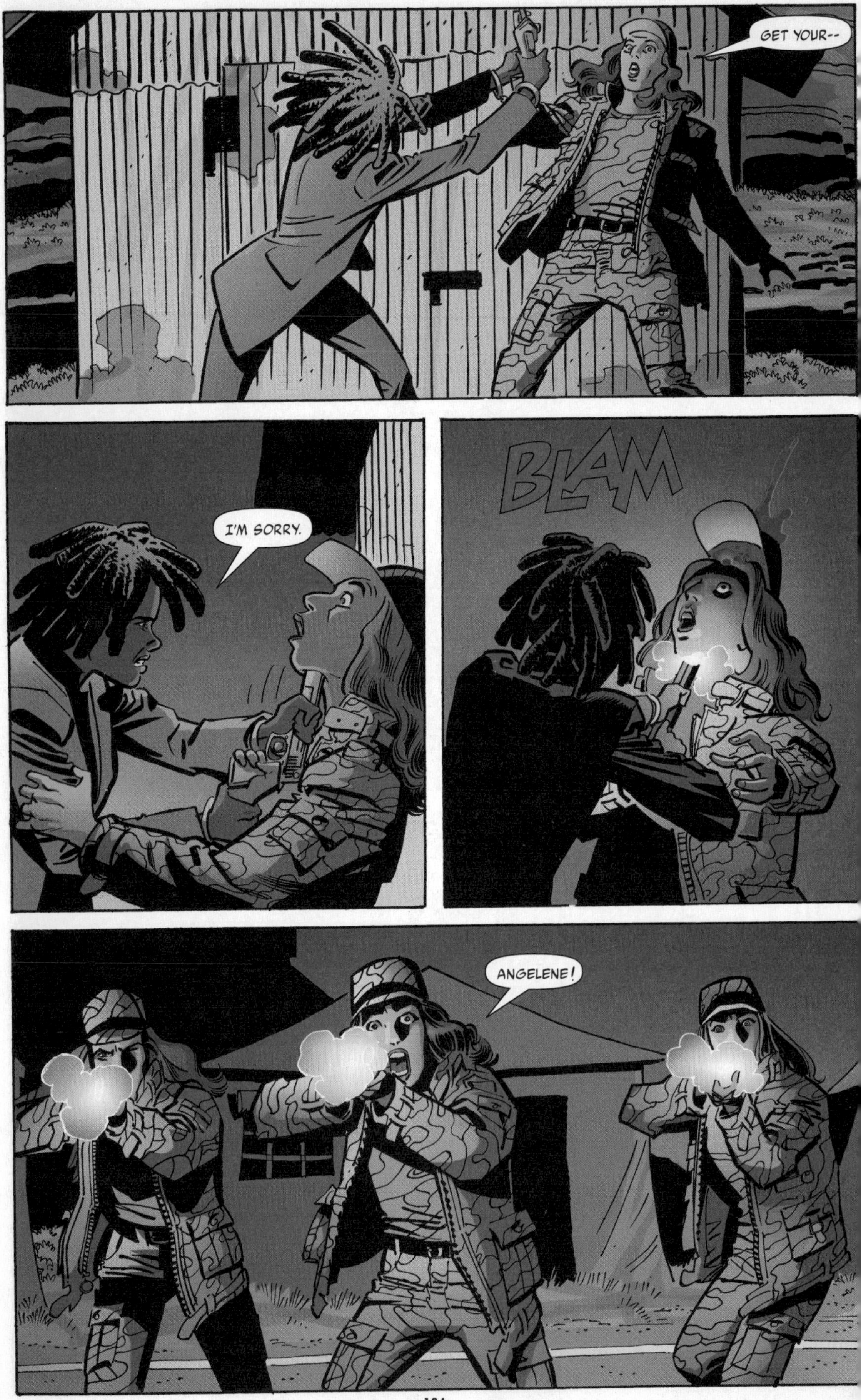
GET YOUR--
I'M SORRY.
BLAM
ANGELENE!

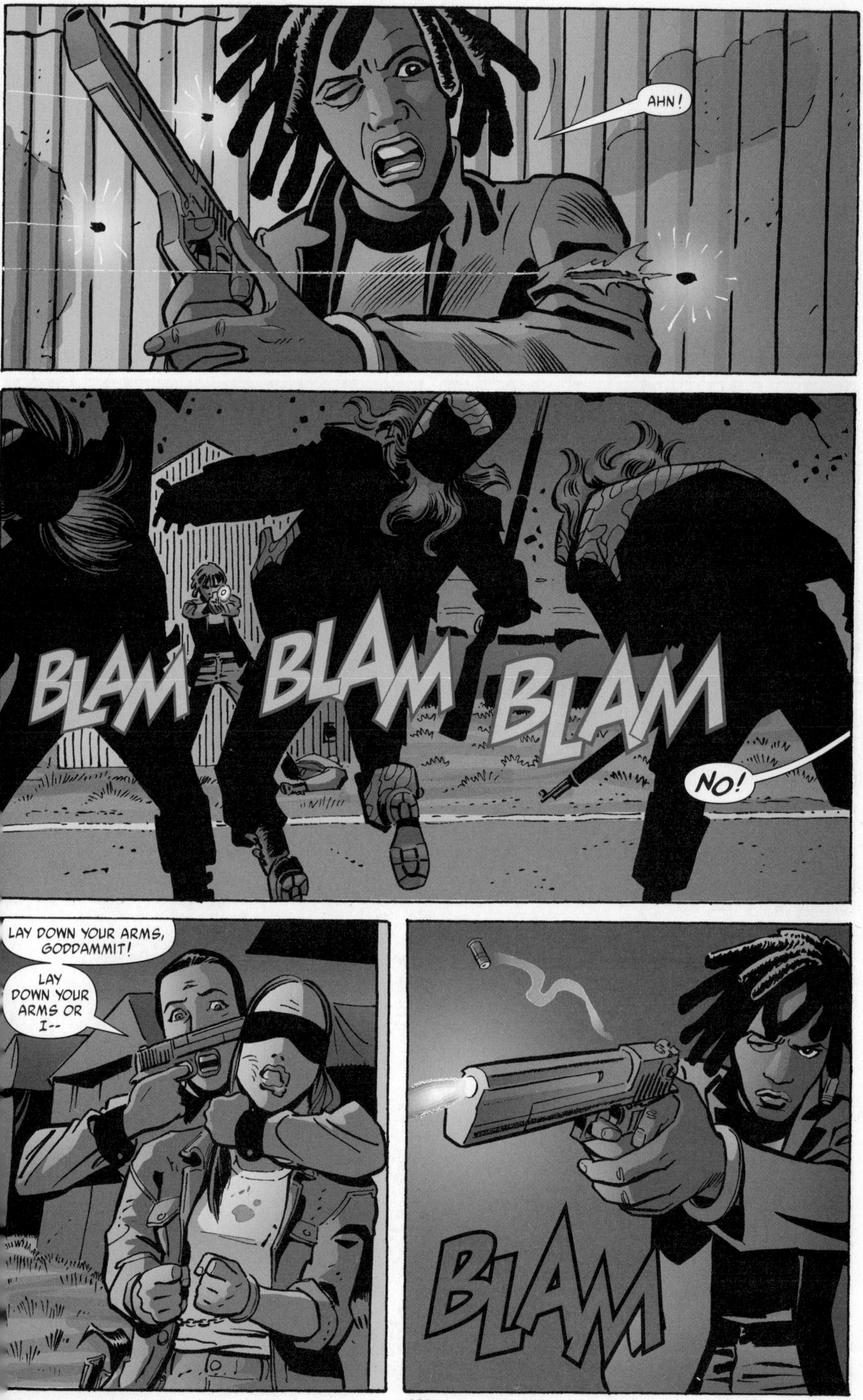
AHN!
BLAM BLAM BLAM
NO!
LAY DOWN YOUR ARMS, GODDAMMIT!
LAY DOWN YOUR ARMS OR I--
BLAM

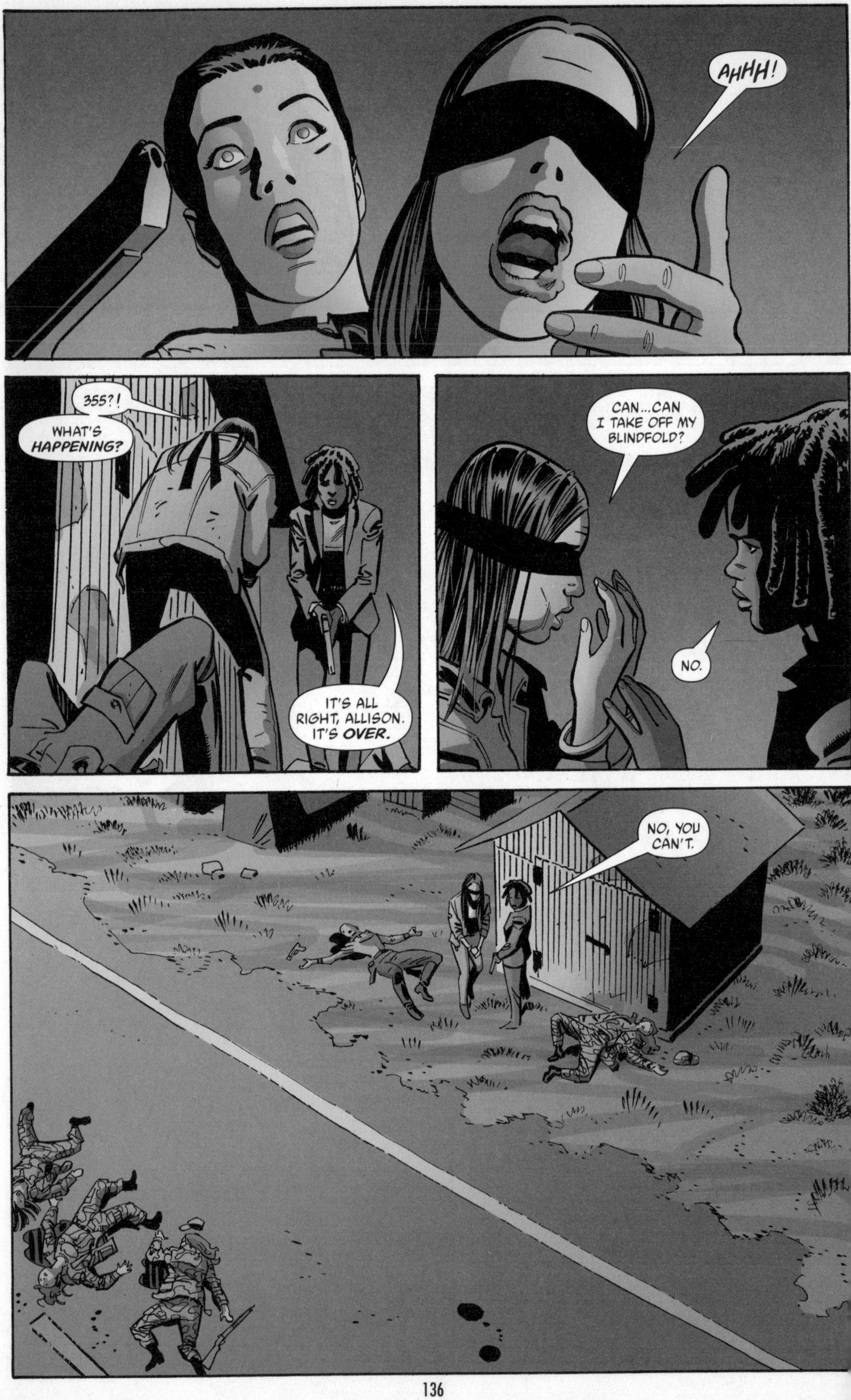
AHHH!
355?!
WHAT'S HAPPENING?
IT'S ALL RIGHT, ALLISON. IT'S OVER.
CAN...CAN I TAKE OFF MY BLINDFOLD?
NO.
NO, YOU CAN'T.

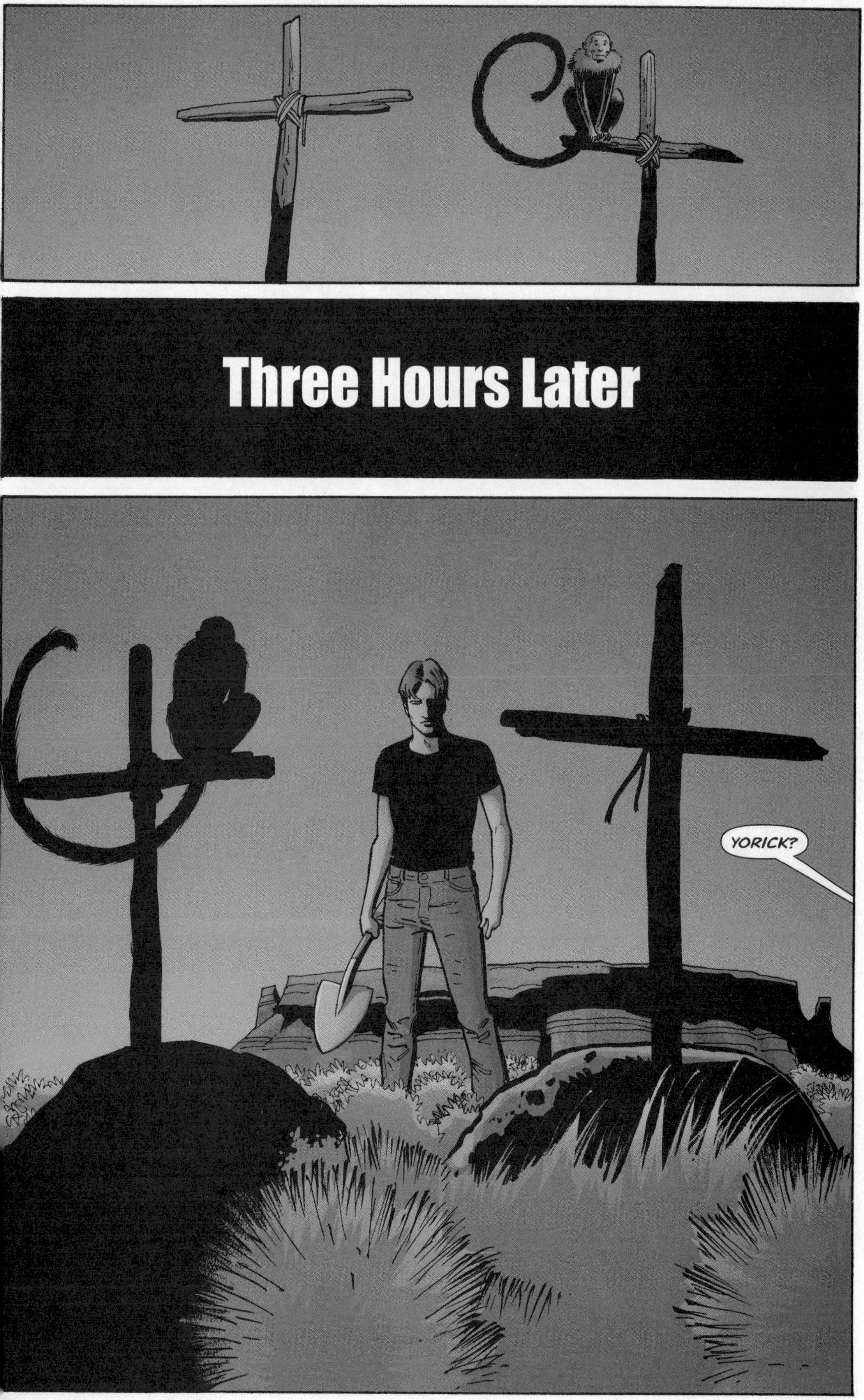
Three Hours Later
YORICK?

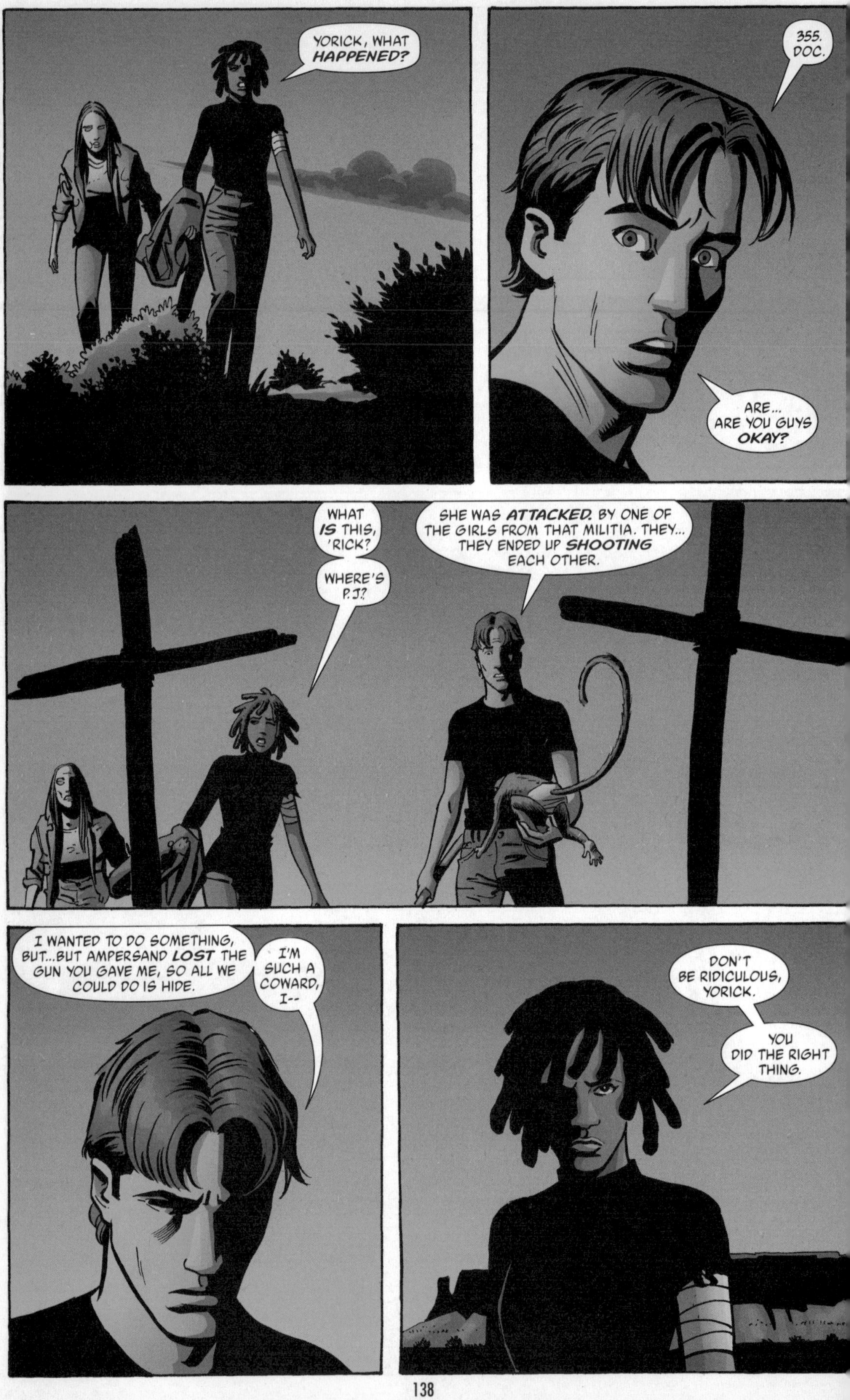
YORICK, WHAT HAPPENED?
355. DOC.
ARE... ARE YOU GUYS OKAY?
WHAT IS THIS, 'RICK?
WHERE'S P.J.?
SHE WAS ATTACKED. BY ONE OF THE GIRLS FROM THAT MILITIA. THEY... THEY ENDED UP SHOOTING EACH OTHER.
I WANTED TO DO SOMETHING, BUT...BUT AMPERSAND LOST THE GUN YOU GAVE ME, SO ALL WE COULD DO IS HIDE.
I'M SUCH A COWARD, I--
DON'T BE RIDICULOUS, YORICK.
YOU DID THE RIGHT THING.

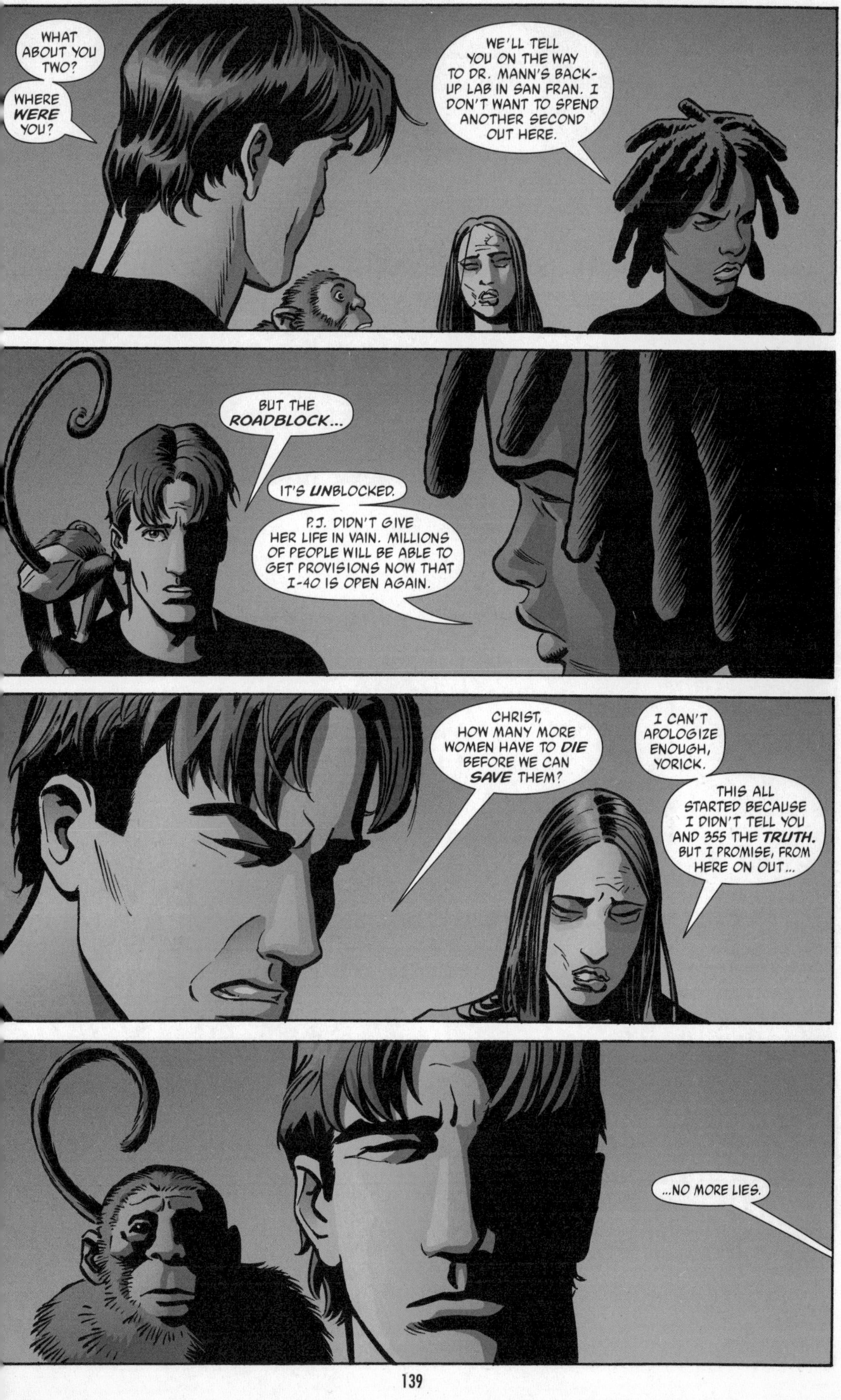
WHAT ABOUT YOU TWO?
WHERE **WERE** YOU?
WE'LL TELL YOU ON THE WAY TO DR. MANN'S BACK-UP LAB IN SAN FRAN. I DON'T WANT TO SPEND ANOTHER SECOND OUT HERE.
BUT THE **ROADBLOCK...**
IT'S **UN**BLOCKED.
P.J. DIDN'T GIVE HER LIFE IN VAIN. MILLIONS OF PEOPLE WILL BE ABLE TO GET PROVISIONS NOW THAT I-40 IS OPEN AGAIN.
CHRIST, HOW MANY MORE WOMEN HAVE TO **DIE** BEFORE WE CAN **SAVE** THEM?
I CAN'T APOLOGIZE ENOUGH, YORICK.
THIS ALL STARTED BECAUSE I DIDN'T TELL YOU AND 355 THE **TRUTH.** BUT I PROMISE, FROM HERE ON OUT...
...NO MORE LIES.

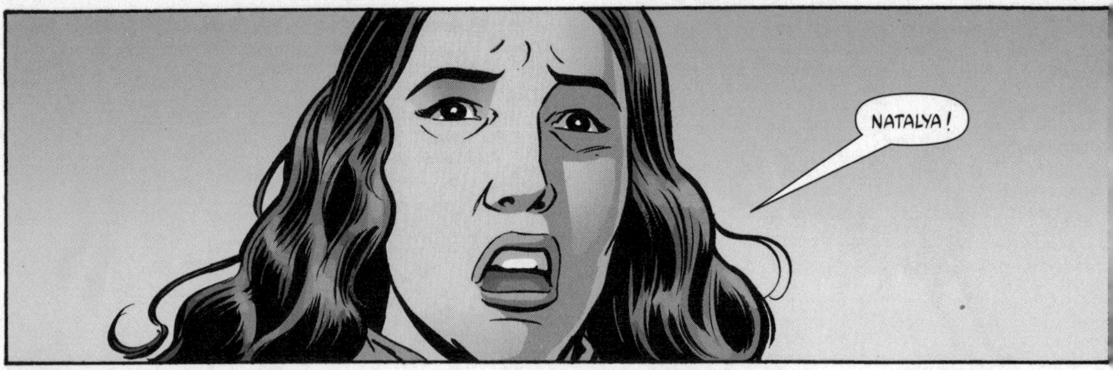
NATALYA!

Oldenbrook, Kansas
Now

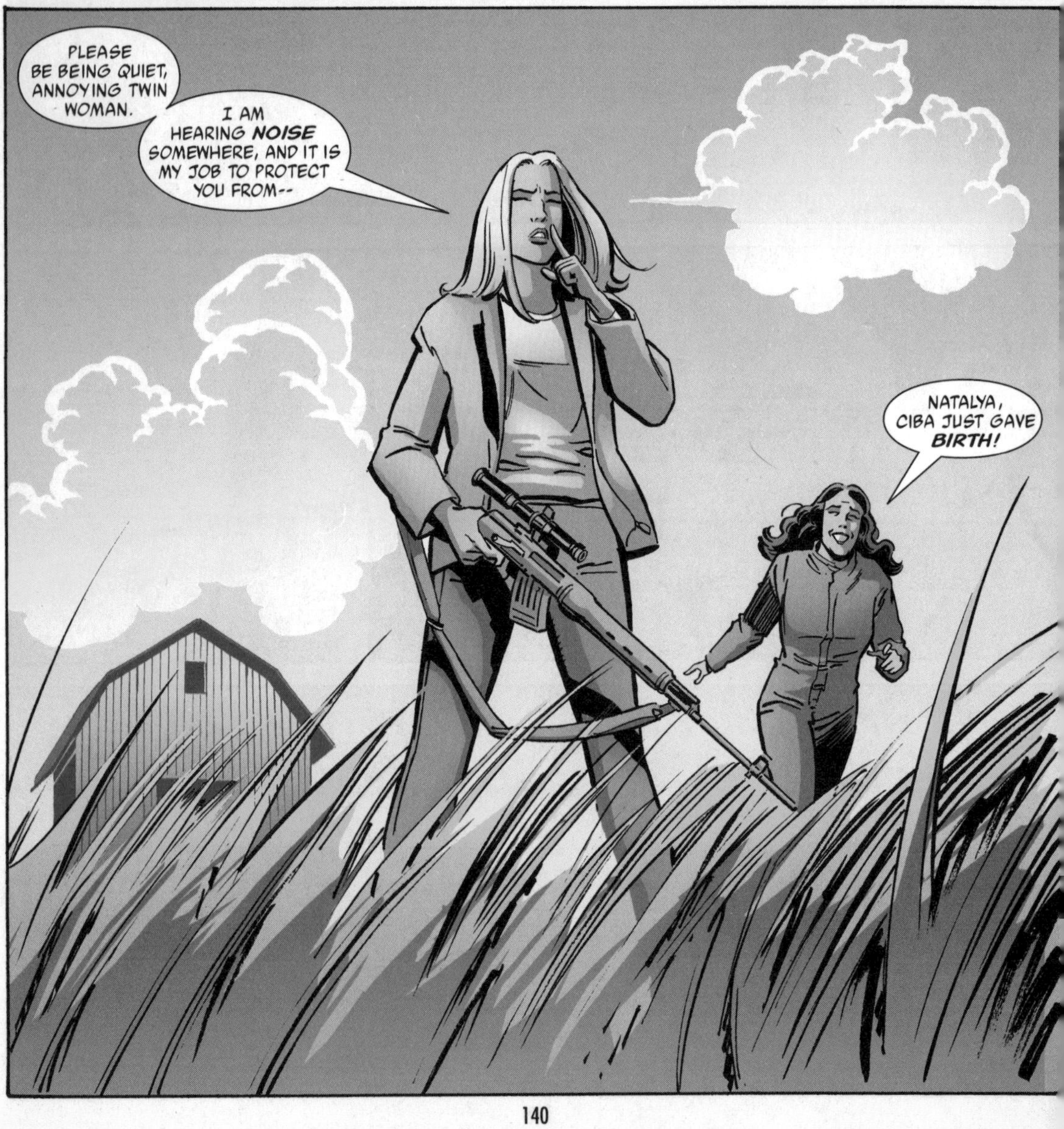
PLEASE BE BEING QUIET, ANNOYING TWIN WOMAN.
I AM HEARING NOISE SOMEWHERE, AND IT IS MY JOB TO PROTECT YOU FROM--
NATALYA, CIBA JUST GAVE BIRTH!

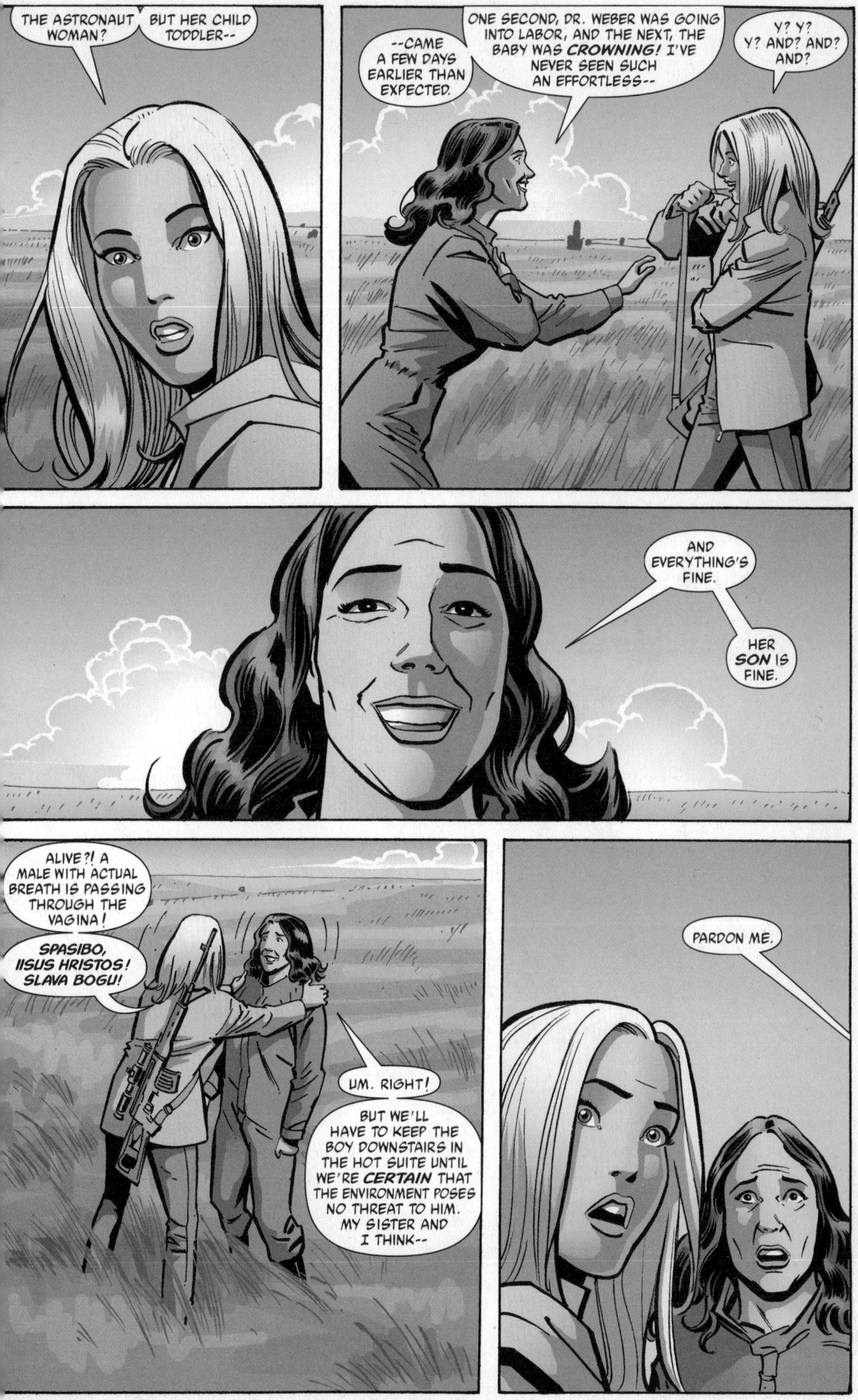
THE ASTRONAUT WOMAN?
BUT HER CHILD TODDLER--
--CAME A FEW DAYS EARLIER THAN EXPECTED.
ONE SECOND, DR. WEBER WAS GOING INTO LABOR, AND THE NEXT, THE BABY WAS CROWNING! I'VE NEVER SEEN SUCH AN EFFORTLESS--
Y? Y? Y? AND? AND? AND?
AND EVERYTHING'S FINE.
HER SON IS FINE.
ALIVE?! A MALE WITH ACTUAL BREATH IS PASSING THROUGH THE VAGINA!
SPASIBO, IISUS HRISTOS! SLAVA BOGU!
UM. RIGHT!
BUT WE'LL HAVE TO KEEP THE BOY DOWNSTAIRS IN THE HOT SUITE UNTIL WE'RE CERTAIN THAT THE ENVIRONMENT POSES NO THREAT TO HIM. MY SISTER AND I THINK--
PARDON ME.

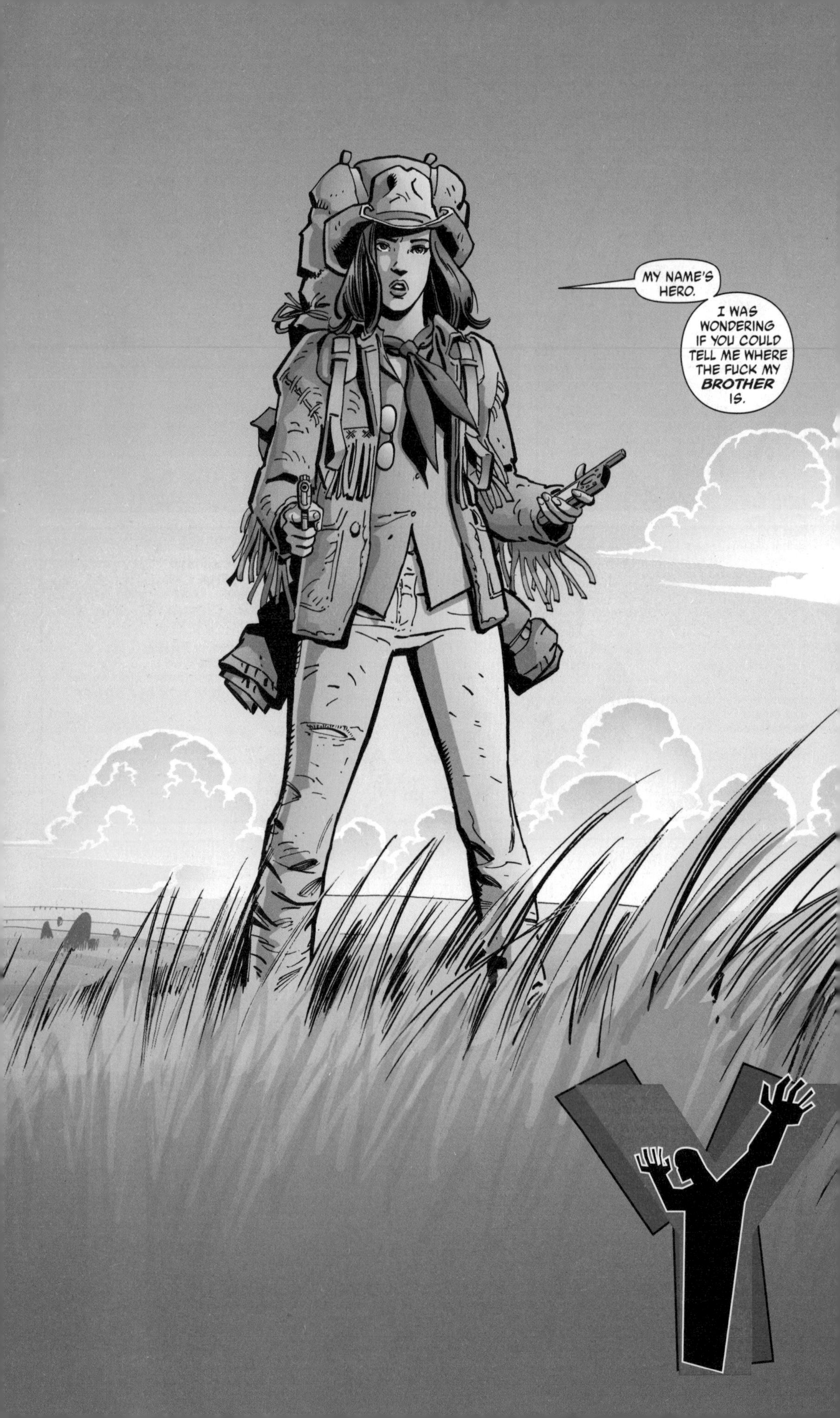
MY NAME'S HERO.
I WAS WONDERING IF YOU COULD TELL ME WHERE THE FUCK MY **BROTHER** IS.

100 BULLETS
Brian Azzarello/Eduardo Risso
With one special briefcase, Agent Graves gives you the chance to kill without retribution. But what is the real price for this chance — and who is setting it?

Vol 1: FIRST SHOT, LAST CALL
Vol 2: SPLIT SECOND CHANCE
Vol 3: HANG UP ON THE HANG LOW
Vol 4: A FOREGONE TOMORROW
Vol 5: THE COUNTERFIFTH DETECTIVE
Vol 6: SIX FEET UNDER THE GUN

AMERICAN CENTURY
Howard Chaykin/David Tischman/
Marc Laming/John Stokes
The 1950s were no picnic, but for a sharp operator like Harry Kraft opportunity still knocked all over the world — and usually brought trouble right through the door with it.

Vol 1: SCARS & STRIPES
Vol 2: HOLLYWOOD BABYLON

ANIMAL MAN
Grant Morrison/Chas Truog/
Doug Hazlewood/various
A minor super-hero's consciousness is raised higher and higher until he becomes aware of his own fictitious nature in this revolutionary and existential series.

Vol 1: ANIMAL MAN
Vol 2: ORIGIN OF THE SPECIES
Vol 3: DEUS EX MACHINA

THE BOOKS OF MAGIC
Neil Gaiman/various
A quartet of fallen mystics introduce the world of magic to young Tim Hunter, who is destined to become the world's most powerful magician.

THE BOOKS OF MAGIC
John Ney Rieber/Peter Gross/various
The continuing trials and adventures of Tim Hunter, whose magical talents bring extra trouble and confusion to his adolescence.

Vol 1: BINDINGS
Vol 2: SUMMONINGS
Vol 3: RECKONINGS
Vol 4: TRANSFORMATIONS
Vol 5: GIRL IN THE BOX
Vol 6: THE BURNING GIRL
Vol 7: DEATH AFTER DEATH

DEATH: AT DEATH'S DOOR
Jill Thompson
Part fanciful *manga* retelling of the acclaimed THE SANDMAN: SEASON OF MISTS and part original story of the party from Hell.

DEATH: THE HIGH COST OF LIVING
Neil Gaiman/Chris Bachalo/
Mark Buckingham
One day every century, Death assumes mortal form to learn more about the lives she must take.

DEATH: THE TIME OF YOUR LIFE
Neil Gaiman/Chris Bachalo/
Mark Buckingham/Mark Pennington
A young lesbian mother strikes a deal with Death for the life of her son in a story about fame, relationships, and rock and roll.

FABLES
Bill Willingham/Mark Buckingham/
Lan Medina/Steve Leialoha/Craig Hamilton
The immortal characters of popular fairy tales have been driven from their homelands and now live hidden among us, trying to cope with life in 21st-century Manhattan.

Vol 1: LEGENDS IN EXILE
Vol 2: ANIMAL FARM
Vol 3: STORYBOOK LOVE

HELLBLAZER
Jamie Delano/Garth Ennis/Warren Ellis/
Brian Azzarello/Steve Dillon/
Marcelo Frusin/various
Where horror, dark magic, and bad luck meet, John Constantine is never far away.

ORIGINAL SINS
DANGEROUS HABITS
FEAR AND LOATHING
TAINTED LOVE
DAMNATION'S FLAME
RAKE AT THE GATES OF HELL
SON OF MAN
HAUNTED
HARD TIME
GOOD INTENTIONS
FREEZES OVER
HIGHWATER

THE INVISIBLES
Grant Morrison/various
The saga of a terrifying conspiracy and the resistance movement combating it — a secret underground of ultra-cool guerrilla cells trained in ontological and physical anarchy.

Vol 1: SAY YOU WANT A REVOLUTION
Vol 2: APOCALIPSTICK
Vol 3: ENTROPY IN THE U.K.
Vol 4: BLOODY HELL IN AMERICA
Vol 5: COUNTING TO NONE
Vol 6: KISSING MR. QUIMPER
Vol 7: THE INVISIBLE KINGDOM

LUCIFER
Mike Carey/Peter Gross/Scott Hampton/
Chris Weston/Dean Ormston/various
Walking out of Hell (and out of the pages of THE SANDMAN), an ambitious Lucifer Morningstar creates a new cosmos modeled after his own image.

Vol 1: DEVIL IN THE GATEWAY
Vol 2: CHILDREN AND MONSTERS
Vol 3: A DALLIANCE WITH THE DAMNED
Vol 4: THE DIVINE COMEDY
Vol 5: INFERNO

PREACHER
Garth Ennis/Steve Dillon/various
A modern American epic of life, death, God, love, and redemption — filled with sex, booze, and blood.

Vol 1: GONE TO TEXAS
Vol 2: UNTIL THE END OF THE WORLD
Vol 3: PROUD AMERICANS
Vol 4: ANCIENT HISTORY
Vol 5: DIXIE FRIED
Vol 6: WAR IN THE SUN
Vol 7: SALVATION
Vol 8: ALL HELL'S A-COMING
Vol 9: ALAMO

THE SANDMAN
Neil Gaiman/various
One of the most acclaimed and celebrated comics titles ever published.

Vol 1: PRELUDES & NOCTURNES
Vol 2: THE DOLL'S HOUSE
Vol 3: DREAM COUNTRY
Vol 4: SEASON OF MISTS
Vol 5: A GAME OF YOU

Vol 6: FABLES & REFLECTIONS
Vol 7: BRIEF LIVES
Vol 8: WORLDS' END
Vol 9: THE KINDLY ONES
Vol 10: THE WAKE
Vol 11: ENDLESS NIGHTS

THE SANDMAN: THE DREAM HUNTERS
Neil Gaiman/Yoshitaka Amano
Set in Japan and told in illustrated prose, this adult fairy tale featuring the Lord of Dreams is beautifully painted by legendary artist Yoshitaka Amano.

THE SANDMAN: DUST COVERS —
THE COLLECTED SANDMAN COVERS
1989–1997
Dave McKean/Neil Gaiman
A complete portfolio of Dave McKean's celebrated SANDMAN cover art, together with commentary by McKean and Gaiman.

THE SANDMAN COMPANION
Hy Bender
A dreamer's guide to THE SANDMAN, featuring artwork, essays, analysis, and interviews with Neil Gaiman and many of his collaborators.

THE QUOTABLE SANDMAN
Neil Gaiman/various
A mini-hardcover of memorable quotes from THE SANDMAN accompanied by a host of renditions of Morpheus and the Endless.

SWAMP THING: DARK GENESIS
Len Wein/Berni Wrightson
A gothic nightmare is brought to life with this horrifying yet poignant story of a man transformed into a monster.

SWAMP THING
Alan Moore/Stephen Bissette/John Totleben/
Rick Veitch/various
The writer and the series that revolutionized comics — a masterpiece of lyrical fantasy.

Vol 1: SAGA OF THE SWAMP THING
Vol 2: LOVE & DEATH
Vol 3: THE CURSE
Vol 4: A MURDER OF CROWS
Vol 5: EARTH TO EARTH
Vol 6: REUNION

TRANSMETROPOLITAN
Warren Ellis/Darick Robertson/various
An exuberant trip into a frenetic future, where outlaw journalist Spider Jerusalem battles hypocrisy, corruption, and sobriety.

Vol 1: BACK ON THE STREET
Vol 2: LUST FOR LIFE
Vol 3: YEAR OF THE BASTARD
Vol 4: THE NEW SCUM
Vol 5: LONELY CITY
Vol 6: GOUGE AWAY
Vol 7: SPIDER'S THRASH
Vol 8: DIRGE
Vol 9: THE CURE
Vol 10: ONE MORE TIME

Y: THE LAST MAN
Brian K. Vaughan/Pia Guerra/
José Marzán, Jr.
An unexplained plague kills every male mammal on Earth — all except Yorick Brown and his pet monkey. Will he survive this new, emasculated world to discover what killed his fellow men?

Vol 1: UNMANNED
Vol 2: CYCLES
Vol 3: ONE SMALL STEP